Dear Dr. Elrishi

Thank you for all your
help and support.

Here's to your appearance
in the sequel!

Jodie

About The Author

This is the bit where the author gets to prove their credibility
and expertise in their chosen subject, right? Hmmm. I am not sure
I am that much of a credible mother. I hog all the Lego,
I eat from the kids' snack box when they are out and I tell them that the
police will put them in jail if they don't sit still in the car.
I am no expert, either. More of an anti-expert, making it up as I go along.
I wrote this book because, quite frankly, the whole pregnancy and new
mother thing was utterly shocking, bewildering and ridiculous
and I had to write it down to really believe I was experiencing it.
And it was a whole lot cheaper than therapy.
And because I just bloody well can't shut up, I also blog at
www.motheringfrights.wordpress.com

About the illustrator

I'm Laura Slinn, a London-based illustrator,
godmother and auntie twice over and Playdoh aficionado.
I think this gives me enough experience to visually
document the wonder of parenthood without getting sick in my hair.
If you'd like to see more of my work please go to
www.lauraslinn.com

WOMB WITH A VIEW

JODIE NEWMAN

Womb with a View

ISBN 978 - 0 - 9574417 - 0 - 5

Published by: Blue Elephant Publishing
Tel: 0844 800 9143

Designed and typeset by: Sparkle for You
www.sparkleforyou.co.uk

It is hard to know where to start on the thanks front.
Perhaps alphabetically? Maybe not, I would hate to come across as
anally retentive. Geographically? Hmmm. Geography is not my strong
suit. I am of an age where traditional geography, like learning where one
country is in relation to another, was replaced with much more useful
nuggets like how oxbow lakes were created. Damn them. Whilst I have
had frequent need to know whereabouts on the globe a country is
(and failed miserably), I have never, ever been asked to explain the
intricacies of erosion and soil deposits. So instead, in no particular order:

Ben, my international man of frog's legs and intelligence. He dem-
onstrated unwavering dedication to the book and gave me copious
feedback, erudite editing and much thought-provoking critique (some
of which I actually understood). The pay was shit (by which I mean
non-existent) but his reward will be in garlic. He made an indescribable
difference. As the man does himself. Thank you.

Caroline, the ever-patient editor, sorter-outer and designer. Without her,
this book would still be just some bits of A4, stapled at the corner and
sporting baby food stains. Thank you.

Laura, the illustrator extraordinaire. So talented, you might not
want to bother with the words, just look at the fabulous, funny pictures.
Thank you.

My family. A source of unwavering support and love, always waving
their pom-poms for me (whilst probably thinking 'for fuck's sake, stop
it now') and being generally quite amazing. If I can be a parent to my
offspring as mum and dad are to me, it will be job bloody well done. It
will be a fucking miracle, but a job well done nonetheless. Mum. Dad.
If only you knew how bloody fantastic you really are and how much you
have made me... well, me. Thank you.

And so to my boys. Our new edition, Blake, who has taken
dribbling to a whole new level. You never know, he might just provide
the material for the second book. Scarcely anything would be possible
without Mike. He is less my rock, more my entire landscape.
And biologically speaking, Ellis certainly would not have been possible
without him. Ellis, who has the incredible ability to make you grind your
teeth to enamel stumps one moment, and then take your breath away
in the next. He is part me, part Mike and wholly himself.
I cannot wait to see him be who he will be.
To you both: thank you. And I'll get this in early: no, Ellis, you can't
borrow the bloody car and yes, you have to tidy your room because
I sodding well say so.

DISCLAIMER

This is not a medical book. You may have guessed that already. It is also not a book packed with foetus facts, such as 'at this stage, your baby will be the size of a walnut', which sends you scuttling off to Tesco as you haven't seen a walnut since you went round your gran's last Christmas. Nor is it a book that gives you tips on baby-rearing through aligning your chakras or knitting a baby hat from your placenta in order to achieve an inordinate sense of wellbeing.

It is a book full of the random, often nonsensical – or perhaps more often than not – pointless ramblings of someone who got pregnant and happened to find the funny side of it (well, most of it). When I told a friend that I was writing such a book, he suggested the subtitle be 'The cynics guide to pregnancy and motherhood.' I thought that fairly accurate, but didn't put it on the front cover for fear he would want paying.

Any advice or useful information that has found its way into these pages is entirely accidental and bears no resemblance to proper advice, either practical or otherwise. You should take it with a pinch of salt (just make sure it is low sodium salt, I would hate to be blamed for aggravating your high blood pressure).

When trying to glean information from my female friends about being pregnant and giving birth (I did try the male ones – they mainly rolled their eyes, grimaced and went a little pale) I got the sense that they were holding back on me. There was a liberal use of euphemism and obfuscation, interspersed with 'oh, I don't really remember' and 'well, you know...'

But that was the trouble. I didn't know. And now I bloody well do.

ON PREGNANCY TESTING KITS

I saw an advert on television promoting a new type of pregnancy testing kit - one that did not rely on a display of lines to tell you if you had conceived, but instead spelt it out in black and white: Pregnant, or Not Pregnant. What sort of a moron do you have to be, I mused, not to be able to comprehend the difference between a single line and a plus sign? Surely, if that small task was beyond the intellect of the tester, there should be alarm bells ringing at the local social services office as to whether such a woman could possibly be responsible for raising a child in nine month's time. So it was with confidence that I purchased a twin pack of pregnancy testing kits (who does just one test? No one believes the first one, it's the rules) that used the single line / crossed line indicator. Back at home, perched on the bath, I read the instructions. Twice. Then I read them again, just to be sure. Right. A minus sign: not pregnant. A plus sign: pregnant. Easy. I unwrap the test and assume the position. Why did I only buy two? What if I miss with the first wee? Does it matter if I've had lots of water to drink today? What if I drop it? What if the copious amounts of beetroot that I ate at lunch affect it?

Manoeuvring the test into position, I start to pee and waggle the tester unceremoniously under me, managing to cover from wrist to fingertip with wee as I attempt to ensure I hit the target. I am just thankful that I took my watch off before I started. Then the wait begins. Seconds creep by, slower and slower. I won't look at the test until the time is up, I promise myself, then peer anxiously at the display. Okay, that's the last time I look until it's ready. I peek again, not sure how to decipher the faint lines that are appearing. Finally, I can look. A horizontal line. Crossed with a vertical one. Suddenly, my mind empties of every useful morsel of information, including the instructions on how to decipher the pregnancy test. What did a cross mean, for fuck's sake? Is that pregnant, or not? Why did they have to make these things so difficult to understand? Why did I not spend the extra few pounds on the test that spells it out in plain English? I rifle around in the bin for the screwed up instructions, peeling off an errant cotton bud to re-read the relevant paragraph. Okay, so a cross means I am pregnant. I look again at the test. A cross. We have been trying for nearly two years, waiting for this moment. My first thought? "Oh shit."

THE INITIAL GP APPOINTMENT

There was once a concept called Continuity of Care in the medical profession; a patient sees the same medical practitioner over a period of time or course of treatment in order to foster greater understanding of patient needs and imbue the relationship with trust and empathy. I too, have regular pregnancy check-ups with my GP. She follows a somewhat revised version of this concept: Continuity of Scare.

My very first appointment to let her know that I am *with child* is a litany of 'don'ts' and not many 'do's', delivered so fast that I am still reeling from the shock of contemplating a diet without a single egg, hard-boiled or otherwise, whilst the GP has already moved on to the cheery news that I am considered high risk due to the double whammy of having a high BMI and being old. An 'aged carrier', or some such phrase, is used at some point. Nice. As part of the GP's pep talk she mentions that I would have to have two GTT tests, which detect gestational diabetes. I nod dumbly, trusting that the Internet will fill in the gaps in my knowledge of this particular affliction. I say fill in the gaps –

there is actually not one iota of knowledge in my head pertaining to this topic to create a gap between, but this is exactly what the internet was invented for, wasn't it?

She then runs through the litany of other tests that I will undergo, all designed to possibly (but with no guarantees) pick up the huge raft of abnormalities, anomalies and generally horrible stuff that could befall the foetus in the first twenty weeks. I entered the appointment with a certain amount of joy and optimism. I leave with the burden of being both high risk and having the sneaking suspicion and a hard kernel of fear that everything, given half a chance, will go spectacularly and irrevocably wrong.

Back at home, I nonchalantly Google 'gestational diabetes', only to be confronted with an almost infinite number of websites jostling for position, eager to deliver the bad news. It transpires fairly quickly that, whilst gestational diabetes is bad for the mother, boy oh boy, is it ever bad news for the baby. It seems that the baby would not contract an outbreak of pustules, nor arthritis, nor develop a stutter, but pretty much every other fatal or semi-fatal side effect is up for grabs. Having read the good news on a number of sites, progressively getting more and more anxious, I come to the cheerily named *www.diabetesthesilentkiller.com,* at which point I close down Google: ignorance is definitely bliss. It is with an irony that is not lost on me or my suddenly alcohol-free kidneys, that pregnancy evokes more of those 'Christ, I need a drink' moments per day than any other situation that I have encountered, at precisely the time when alcohol is strictly out of bounds. The GP was at great pains to emphasize that no drinking is safe during pregnancy. This is akin to advising that crossing the road is not safe and should never be attempted.

Theoretically, I can see the point, but such didactic, lowest-common-denominator advice does not distinguish between cartwheeling back and forth across the M1 with gay abandon and a blindfold, and using the pedestrian crossing to reach the other side of the High Street to get some chocolate. Metaphorically speaking, of course. I would never sully my pregnant temple with something so nutritionally deficient as chocolate. I stick to Fruit Pastilles, on the reckoning that a packet must constitute at least one of the required five fruit and veg a day it is claimed we need. Throw in an Orange Maid ice-lolly and a Cherry Coke, and I've surely consumed over half the required nutritional intake before I've even left the High Street.

A HEALTHY START IS ALL-IMPORTANT

It is at about this point in proceedings that I am struck with an awful, guilt-inducing thought. A few weekends before I knew I was pregnant, Mike and I had been to Paris to see a very dear friend of mine. It was a rather momentous occasion purely as, after many years of empty threats about visiting, I had actually got there. So we made the most of the trip, eschewing all cultural highlights that the city had to offer and instead, eating and drinking like our lives depended on it. One particular evening-to-early-hours-of-the-morning affair involved a fair drop of the red stuff followed by a guided tour of the finest rums our euros could buy. Our excursion into the blurred world of rum-drinking was fascinating indeed, particularly the interesting after-effect whereby my brain seemed to be functioning perfectly, allowing lucidity of thought and speech, whilst my legs had temporarily ceased functioning completely (in hindsight, the bit about being lucid was probably just a rum-induced hallucination). The following morning I felt like I had never felt before. I felt sicker than a sick thing in sick land having a sick day and my stomach, well, all my insides, felt absolutely terrible. This wasn't just a hangover. This was a sick-to-your-toes, don't know where to put yourself, want to curl up and die

hangover. I mentioned that this wasn't like any hangover I had ever had, and made some derisory comment about perhaps the food being off, but we were in the culinary capital of the world and my protestations fell on French ears.

And so now I am pregnant, and realise that I had marinated my precious little foetus in copious amounts of rum for 48 hours. Granted, it was the best quality rum that money could buy, but still. I am imagining that there are better ways to kick-start a bunch of cells into life than to put them in a warm bath of very strong rum, add some runny French cheese and buckets of red wine, stir and leave to simmer.

BOOKING IN WITH THE MIDWIFE

The first checking-in appointment with the midwife is a new, never-to-be-repeated-if-I can-help-it experience. In essence, it is a tick-box, form-filling, information-gathering exercise, where we plough through a terminally long and detailed form: name, address, next of kin, genetic defects and the like.

"Are you related to the father?" the midwife asks, pen hovering over an empty box. Now, here is a curious question. Having already established about a hundred and fifteen pages ago that I was married, surely the answer to this is already known. Maybe it is one of those cunning ruses employed by questionnaires to ask you the same question three times in a slightly different format, in order to identify the pathological liars and downright forgetful amongst us.

"Errr...yes, he's my husband..." I offer tentatively.

"No, I mean, is he your brother, or your cousin?" I check my knuckles. No, there is definitely no gravel-rash, proving that they had not been dragging on the ground of late. Then I laugh at the sheer ridiculousness of the question. The look on the midwife's face tells me that this is not an appropriate response, and I demurely deny any blood relations with my husband to allow her to emphatically tick her box and move on.

What seems like three days later, the midwife turns over to the final page, telling me that she now has to run me through the benefits of breastfeeding. Just in case the fourteen posters on the walls around us, depicting a variety of ethnically diverse mothers and their gurning babies suckling contentedly at the breast, with fifty point type proclaiming Breast is Best and a subtext that any woman who denies their child breast milk is clearly EVIL, have passed me by.

She starts innocuously enough; breast-fed babies have better immune systems, have less allergies and the like – so far, so predictable. But it seems that the list she is reading from is designed as a sliding scale of outlandish claims. At some point, a while after stating that breastfeeding helps language development (and I have finished mentally running through the food that I need to pick up from Tesco that afternoon), the midwife proclaims that breastfeeding your baby gives him or her a higher IQ and I call a halt to proceedings.

"I'm sorry," I begin, "but *that* I just cannot believe. My husband and his three brothers went nowhere near a breast until they hit puberty and they are all highly intelligent people, degree educated at some of the most prestigious universities." Okay, it may be a little smug as a response, but I had really had my fill of the seemingly inexhaustible list of medical and societal woes that would befall your child if you deny them the right of the breast.

She looks up from her list, wide-eyed and slightly stunned, obviously never having encountered such breast-based negativity (or is that breast-beating?).

"Well," she finally replies, "there are new studies out all the time about the benefits of breastfeeding...most of them should probably be taken with a pinch of salt..."

I am not sure if I should be heartened by such flagrant and instantaneous capitulation in the face of challenge, or be depressed by it. Either way, I am relieved to see that she feels it would be imprudent to carry on with her list, although I must admit, I am now slightly intrigued as to the final claims she would have made about breastfeeding. A better sense of humour, perhaps? More likely to become a lawyer? An inherent understanding of the off-side rule? An increased ability to sustain an orgasm?

ON THE DISAPPEARANCE OF THE DEFINITIVE ARTICLE

Call the grammar police, someone has made off with the definitive article. As a consequence, neither the GP nor the gaggle of midwives can describe my foetus as 'the baby'.

"How's baby?" asks the midwife. "THE baby is fine, thanks," I reply.

"Have you felt baby kick?" enquires the GP. "No, THE baby has yet to kick, though if you insist on dropping 'the' again when you refer to THE baby, I fear I will be kicking you up THE arse," I nearly reply.

They don't drop the 'the' in any other sentence. They don't say "pop up on couch for me please." They don't ask "When did you last see consultant?" I don't say "Please, shut fuck up."

KEEPING IT UNDER YOUR HAT

We don't actually believe that I am pregnant, despite the two pregnancy tests insisting otherwise, until I return from the first GP appointment. At which point, we really have to accept the diagnosis of a medical professional (an approach that we revise as the pregnancy progresses in order to save what is left of our sanity). And so disbelief is usurped by a general fear of Something Going Wrong. This syndrome, coupled with its twin, Is That Normal? is a two-pronged attack on rationality, level-headedness and an ability to take everything in your stride.

Every twinge, every ache and every unnamed sensation is, obviously, an early symptom of miscarriage. We talk very little about having a baby in these early weeks, primarily because it is too surreal to actually be happening, and secondly, because so much could go wrong, it is unlikely we'll ever make it past the first scan. That scan, at twelve or thirteen weeks, becomes the only thing we focus on. We are both adamant that we don't want to tell anyone else about the baby until after the scan, apart from my family. This only becomes tricky when we socialise. There is nothing more indicative of a pregnancy when a confirmed, hardened drinker asks for a lime and soda in a quiet and slightly embarrassed voice. I brazen it out with talk of antibiotics to cure a severe dose of cystitis, threatening to share all the gory details until we change the topic.

"Oh, but you can drink on the antibiotics you get for cystitis," a friend proclaims confidently.

"Not these ones," I reply quickly, "I distinctly remember the doctor telling me not to drink." I cast desperately around for a change of conversation, but the effort of lying has diminished my power of small talk.

"Let's see the bottle, I know which ones you can drink on." No one likes to discover that a friend turns out to have a diploma in the use of antibiotics, so I wave away her offer of medical advice, promising I will have a glass or two later but that I actually have quite a thirst so want to stick to the soft drinks for now, all delivered as nonchalantly as possible without actually being able to look her in the eyes.

WAITING FOR THE SCAN (WEEK 7)

These early weeks pass interminably slowly. Every day I wake with the sensation of impending doom, waiting to be struck down with morning sickness. Morning sickness. Now there is a misnomer if ever there was one. When I do succumb to it, around week seven, I soon realise that to describe it as morning sickness is like describing flu as *lunchtime sniffles*. The feeling of nausea may, I concede, start in the morning, but it carries on all bloody day and well into the evening. The waves of nausea mean that I don't even want to open my mouth for fear of encouraging a torrent of sick to spurt forth, although for the week that the morning sickness lasts, I am not actually sick. Eat ginger, the books say. Eight ginger nuts in, I feel just as sick, but now am not sure if it is due to the pregnancy or gorging on biscuits. Bizarrely, a lot of the time, eating is the only time that I don't feel sick; the moment I stop, the nausea returns. But I have to get over the hurdle of that first mouthful and the thought of food is enough to bring on a fresh wave of sickness, so it is a real ordeal to actually get started on the whole eating thing. Something, it has to be said, that had never been problematic before.

The nausea arrives with its old stable mate, pregnancy fatigue. I had read a description of a pregnant woman who was so tired, she actually got in from work and went to sleep at the bottom of the stairs, lacking the energy to reach the bedroom. Pah, I scoffed, what a girl. You wouldn't catch me doing that. And indeed, I never did, but only because we have a spare bedroom downstairs. Working from home, I have to say, does make these early days of pregnancy easy. It means that, whenever the fancy takes me, I can pull up my tee shirt to inspect my belly, poke it randomly and ponder what is going on inside without any colleagues being there to witness such unbecoming behaviour. It means I can shove ginger nuts into my mouth with gay abandon without being judged harshly by the office anorexic. And it means that at about two o clock every afternoon, when my head suddenly weighs roughly the same as a large anvil and I actually don't have the strength to keep it off the desk, I can crawl to the spare bedroom for a couple of hours constitutional. I would have felt guilty about sleeping in the middle of the afternoon, but quite frankly, I am too fucking tired to care.

THE FIRST SCAN (WEEK 12)

Days plod by, the date of that nuchal fold scan creeping ever closer. Our local health authority don't offer a nuchal fold scan as part of the deal – but are very generous with the leaflets from our local private clinics that will provide the service for a fee. I still don't actually know what a nuchal fold is, so I have decided that it is probably an advanced way of folding napkins into wine glasses for pretentious dinner parties. ("For god's sake, Manuella, swans are so last decade. Do the nuchal fold, and make sure the label isn't showing.") The midwife convinced me that there was no point having a dating scan (the free one) as well the nuchal fold scan (the one that costs about the same as a weekend break), as they may throw up conflicting answers about the due date. It is slightly unnerving to know that something that seems so medically precise and technologically advanced as a scan does, in fact boil down to a bit of finger-in-the-air (well, I suppose it could be put somewhere a lot worse) guess work.

The only trouble with this strategy is that you get lulled into a false sense of luxury and patient care at a private clinic. Cheery receptionists point you to comfortable seats and offer you a drink whilst you peruse the selection of newspapers. Caring nurses operate the scanning machine, explaining the process in detail and making sure you are happy. Laid out on the bed, my stomach basted with clear jelly (I was half expecting a lemon and a sprig of thyme to be shoved up my bum) the scan finally begins. Our foetus, it turns out, is a tad camera shy and turns resolutely away from the scanner, so that no useful measurements can be taken. So, wiping off the jelly and pulling up my trousers, we go for a brisk walk down the High Road for twenty minutes to try and get it to turn over and face the music, only to find on our return that it hasn't moved a muscle and we have to repeat the whole brisk walk thing again. Already it is demonstrating the genetic tendency of its mother toward slothfulness. Another attempt, another twenty minute walk. No one told me to wear tracksuit and trainers, for crying out loud.

Finally, s/he deigns to show us their best side and measurements are hurriedly recorded, a quick snapshot taken and all is confirmed as well. We leave clutching a couple of photos of a prawn-like creature and an enormous sense of relief. And henceforth, our baby is known as Prawn.

LETTING THE CAT (OR PRAWN) OUT THE BAG (WEEK 13)

So, having had an all clear from the first scan - well, as all clear as the medical profession will ever give you, quoting risk scales and percentages rather than actually stating something equivocally and covering themselves in case they are wrong and you have a lawyer in the family – we now feel we can tell our friends and the rest of our family.

As a childless couple, we have been regaled with tales from our friends with children about the wondrous experience of child rearing, of how amazing it is and what we are missing out on. The moment that we tell them we are having a baby, that halcyon description curiously metamorphasises into unnerving schadenfreude that we will soon be enduring the unremitting hell that is having a young baby to look after. There is nothing more sinister than that smile that parents give you when you tell them you are expecting. It is a smile like no other: there is a smidge of happiness in there, but mainly, it comprises a knowing smugness that we have no idea what we are letting ourselves in for.

On the whole, it has to be said that our friends are far more excited by the news than we ever were. I begin to feel a tad mean toward Prawn that we have gone straight from the 'oh shit' moment of finding out I was pregnant, directly to the worry of everything going to plan, completely bypassing the dancing round the kitchen and whooping with delight phase, nor collecting £200 for passing go, (even more of a shame given the price of prams these days).

It is only now that friends start to leak the truth about parenthood. The previously gloating tales of their baby sleeping through from the first week, of being able to take the new arrival in their stride, quickly become stories of sleepless, desperation-filled nights and all-round baby chaos, delivered with a barely disguised undercurrent of glee that we, too, will soon be experiencing the same misery.

NO ONE TOLD ME YOU COULD DO THAT

It is such a relief to have had the first scan. Twelve weeks of waiting. Three whole months of anxiety. I am discussing this with a friend, along with laughing about the fact that I had bought two pregnancy tests. 'Oh', she says breezily, 'I bought eight. I just didn't trust the first seven.' Four months ago

I would have scoffed at such lunacy. Now I nod, thinking what a jolly good idea that was. I am also bemoaning the fact that the first scan takes such a long time to arrive, during which time you are constantly worrying about what is going on in there – if indeed, anything is. "Oh god, I know," she agrees. "So I went for a private scan. Well, two, in fact. Just to put my mind at rest."

No one told me you could do that. It didn't even cross my mind that I could go outside of the NHS for some peace of mind. If only I had known, I would have had it for my birthday. Difficult to wrap, but what a gift. And beats bloody toiletries hands down.

I'LL NAME THAT BABY IN THREE...

Naming your baby. My god, there's a minefield if ever I tiptoed across one. What a bloody palaver. I sort of thought it should be meaningful, the name you choose for your precious offspring. A name steeped in history, familial or otherwise, or a name that resonates with meaning and poetry. I look back at my family and am struck by my grandmother's name: Stella. I think it will make a great name if we are having a girl, so I run it past Mike. "I am not naming a child of mine after a beer, even if it is premium strength." Hmmm, this is not good. I canvas opinions and it is pretty clear that all the men immediately think of beer, and most of the girls think it a great name. Perhaps we should go for it, and then name the next child Kronenbourg. I tell Mike I will 'put it on the back burner' (i.e. I will let this slide until I have thought of a strategy to make him change his mind) and we get down to the task of creating a shortlist of names.

We start by just sitting with a pad and paper in front of us and trying to conjure names up out of thin air, but end up just drawing silly faces and highly mature cartoons of men's genitalia, so resort to the tried and tested path of Googling to give us a bit of inspiration. There are plenty of charts of popular names, which obviously must be avoided unless you want your offspring to be in class, have her name called, and be one of eight that turn round to respond. We trawl through list upon list until our eyes go googly (a medical term meaning you've been searching for too long) and we rustle up a list of our own. Mike is more for the traditional names, I want something a little bit more... well, less like a name you might find in an Enid Blyton book.

It's a tricky thing, finding a name. I want something slightly unusual, but not so unusual that it becomes a social stigma. It's fine being Apple, FiFi Trixibelle, or MoonUnit when you are the product of a celebrity - most people wouldn't have the nerve to take the piss, and those that do you can afford to have killed, but for mere mortals, being named after space hardware or a fruit might be a tad more problematic. "So, Kumquat, what makes you think you have the qualities that would make you a great Customer Services Manager?" "Err...if I told you I have a sour centre but a sweet rind, would that swing it?"

In the end, all the list making is slightly in vain, as one day I am reading a newspaper article and there is a boy featured called Ellis. What a bloody great name, I think, and luckily, Mike agrees. I should have then gone back to check that the article wasn't about a mass murderer or a boy with no brain, but by that time, the paper was gone.

And so comes the next naming dilemma: to tell or not to tell? I think most parents-to-be err on the side of keeping their own counsel as to the contents of their name shortlist. I can see their point. It is a little socially awkward to excitedly pronounce the names of your impending bundle, only to be met with stifled giggles or barely concealed retching. Particularly if it's from your own mother.

LEAKY PANTS

I am with a midwife for a routine check up. She is a friendly lady, with a nice line in hair bobbles and a boss eye.

I pluck up the courage to ask her about a slightly embarrassing condition I have developed: a leaky vagina. Nothing alarming or enough to make my shoes squelch, but enough to make its presence felt and my gusset to be just slightly damper than it should be.

She tips her head to one side, looking both at me and the poster on the wall to my left. "Ahhh," she says, with a little smile. "Bless you. It's totally normal. Didn't you know?" No, I bloody didn't know, you patronising bobble-headed twit. It hasn't been mentioned in any of the pregnancy books I have read, it wasn't written as a warning on the pregnancy testing kit: 'WARNING: pregnancy may cause slight seepage' ...so what am I supposed to do? Google 'leaky minge'? I'd have a screen full of hard-core porn before I could say "pass the Tena Lady please".

THE GGT TEST

I am at the hospital, waiting with a roomful of people all clutching little numbered tickets and staring at the display, watching numbers slowly flash up indicating that the next person can shuffle off to get their blood test done. For once, I don't need one of those tickets as I am here for my GGT test – to test for gestational diabetes.

I have an initial blood test on arrival. I, like most of the population, would prefer not to have a needle stuck in my arm, but I am not phobic about it. I get a bit sweaty, perhaps, and always think it will be much more painful than it actually is. On reflection, I think the sweating and trepidation is more to do with the hilarious print outs that the blood test girls have pinned up in their cubicles – a variety of scrappy pieces of paper, printed out on a printer which I would guess has seen better days (all of which occurred in the last decade), each with different poems and quotes on but all along the lines of 'you don't have to be mad to work here, but it helps'. Having a pointy metal stick puncturing your skin is one thing, but there is no need for that sort of pain to be inflicted on innocent people.

The lady mixes up a cloudy looking concoction into a plastic cup and hands it to me. I am not sure if I am supposed to soak dentures in it or use it to clean the sink, but she makes me drink it. I do so reluctantly, humming loudly in my head to try and block out the taste and stop myself gagging.

I am told not to eat and not to leave hospital premises, so I depart the cubicle and settle down for a fascinating two-hour wait. I do as much of the crossword as I can (not much) and read the paper from front to back, even reading the international news and weighty opinion pieces, which I usually skim over on the way to the reviews and TV listings. I had slightly under-estimated the quantity of reading matter required for a two hour wait and so comb the paper again to make sure a couple more pages have not materialised since I last looked, then doodle all over the cryptic crossword.

Finally, the two hours are up and with glee I return to the cubicle to have another load of blood sucked from me.

THE TWENTY-WEEK SCAN

As soon as the first hurdle of the twelve-week scan is over, there is a brief, if short-lived respite from the litany of worries. The Prawn has been given the rubber stamp of medical approval, and we rejoice. For about a week. Then we start to look toward the twenty-week scan. This is the one that really matters now. The first one? Pah, a walk in the park. Well, two brisk walks down the High Street. The next one? This is where the name says it all: the anomaly scan. If the baby has any anomalies, this is where you get to find out and possibly be faced with the most heart-rending decisions of your life.

The scan is offered on the NHS, so we duly turn up at the local hospital at our allotted time. Some time way past our allotted appointment, we are taken to the scanning room. A large, jolly woman in a white coat greets us. She has a very over-enthusiastic perm that puts me somewhat in mind of Brian May. With me up on the couch, Brian applies the jelly and starts to skid the monitor about on my stomach, casting around for the best angle. To no great surprise, Prawn turns out to have his arse to camera, which is no use to man nor beast but puts me in mind of his dad first thing in the morning. Brian perseveres for a while, but eventually tells me to leave, drink a litre of water,

go for a brisk walk for twenty minutes and... as if my ears deceive me... eat a bar of chocolate. Now that, it has to be said, is probably the best piece of medical advice that I have ever heard and the only one that I gladly follow with gusto. Perm or no perm, Brian knows how to give the best instructions.

We leave the hospital grounds, as there is only so long you can lap the same car park, and only so much entertainment to be had from watching people driving round and round, believing that a free car parking space will spontaneously appear just so long as they keep moving. We trundle into the wood opposite, coming across a large group (a cluck?) of chickens. Or hens. Or some other flavour of strutty, feathery type birds. Note to self: must swot up on wildlife before Prawn arrives, so as not to repeat a rather embarrassing incident with a nephew a few years back. Me to nephew: "Oh, look at those birds flying." Nephew to me, with a slightly more supercilious tone than I felt was strictly necessary: "I think you'll find they are geese." We walk through the wood, me chomping on chocolate and glugging water purchased at no small cost from the hospital shop, before returning, only to be told by Brian that we have to repeat the process again: go for a walk and drink another litre of water.

"And eat more chocolate?" I ask, optimistically.

"No, no more chocolate required."

"Sure? I mean, if it will help, I could always force some more down..."

But chocolate seems off the menu, so I go back to the shop, buy more water, much to the consternation of the two white haired ladies behind the till (one to press the buttons, one to primp her curls and exclaim "well, I never did, you must be thirsty") and off we go again. By this time, the novelty of the wildlife is wearing a little thin, and as we contemplate the possibility that we could actually be spending our entire day walking round the wood whilst waiting for Prawn to turn over, I decide that there is a more proactive approach I could be taking. So as we head back, I spin, jump and hop, trying to encourage Prawn to, quite literally, move his bloody arse. An image of an ice cube in a glass springs to mind, where however much you spin the glass round, the cube stays where it is; and I wonder whether a foetus would be subject to the same law of physics, and indeed, if so, what is that law called? Maybe the law of inertia? Perhaps if it has no name up to this point, it shall henceforth be known as Prawn's law.

As we approach the hospital, I suddenly need to wee like I have never needed to before. There are almost two litres of water vying for space against the Prawn, and as I tiptoe into the waiting room, hunched over from the pain of a bladder creaking at the seams, I just pray that I don't sneeze, cough or laugh. No one wants to have to paddle through the contents of a pregnant woman's bladder just to get to the magazines on the waiting room table.

And so to the third time lucky. Finally, Prawn has rolled over, no doubt delirious with joy at tasting chocolate, and is striking a pose. We both stare at the black and white image on the screen, trying to comprehend that the living thing in front of us actually inhabits my stomach.

Brian rattles off all the prerequisite measurements with alarming speed, and all is in order, with the right number of limbs in the right places, all organs present and correct. The relief is immense and instantaneous.

Brian enquires if we want to know the sex. Now, we have discussed this, and both immediately came to the conclusion that we would find out. Quite frankly, neither of us could actually think of one reason why we wouldn't want to know in advance. It's all very well being blasé about plunging your hand into a bag of Revels and popping one in your mouth without knowing the flavour (although for some, even this is too much of a high risk strategy, in case they end up with the coffee one), but not knowing the sex of your baby? I had canvassed some views from friends. During these conversations, it transpired that some had lied to us, knowing the sex of their baby but not telling anyone, saying instead that they didn't know. This is too much for my brain to compute, quite frankly. Some had decided to not find out, saying that there was little enough surprise left in childbirth these days. Personally, I think childbirth has way *too* many surprises in it, like the level of pain, the time it can drag on for, the numerous bodily functions that will sabotage your futile attempts to cling onto any shred of dignity you may have left, the fact that a large baby is trying to squeeze through a ridiculously small hole like some kind of side-show contortionist freak, so any surprises that we can take out of the equation beforehand seem sensible to me.

"It's a boy," Brian confirms. We both smile at each other, simultaneously realising that either flavour is just fine and dandy by us. My only relief is that having a boy will mean that I will not be surrounded by pink, a colour that brings on waves of nausea and an outbreak of hives just thinking about it. Frilly things, twinkly bits, sparkles – none of these will be part of the deal with a boy. Well, not until he is old enough to make his own sartorial and decoration-based decisions. In which case I can just play the Parenting Top Trump winning hand of: "Not whilst you live under my roof, thank you."

Just in case she seems a tad emphatic, Brian goes on to explain that they can only ever be 97% certain that they are correct when it comes to telling what sex the baby is. So there is a 3% chance we are having a girl. Maybe we'll paint the skirting boards pink; that would be about the right proportional representation.

The final task for Brian is to get us a souvenir photo. The scan is turning out to be just like a trip to Alton Towers; a long wait for the main attraction, over-priced confectionery, a roller-coaster of excitement, and a photo to take home and pin on the fridge. Many freeze frames later, she tuts and tells us that, because the baby is at a bit of a strange angle, the only photo she can get is one in which he looks, and I quote directly, "like an alien". Now, she may be a guitar virtuoso with an impressive back catalogue of hits, but there is no need for Brian to be quite so insulting about our son. Everyone gets a photo: ergo, I want a bloody photo. I look at the screen, and staring back at me is the pale, surreally elongated face of an alien with black, sunken eye sockets. Mike and I exchange a glance. Maybe we'll skip the photo after all.

THE NAME GAME 2

Now we know that Prawn is a boy, we luckily avert Stella-gate, which is just as well, as although I still love the name, Mike did have a point. I would not have liked to be named after a beer (although Cobra has a certain 'don't-fuck-with-me' ring about it).

Some people had said to me that they would only choose their baby's name once they had seen the baby to make sure that the name suited them. I am still a little curious about this approach. "Well, we were all for calling him James, but as soon as we saw him pop out, we decided that Mucky-Blob-Boy was much more him."

Mike and I decide that we are fine to let people know the name we have chosen – we had settled on it and no amount of sniggering would sway us. We get a pretty good reaction all round, bar one friend who I tell. "Oh," she says, with a very weak smile, "that's....." Eventually, I go off, have a pee, come back and she is still casting round for an adjective. "....nice." Nice. Oh the horror of mundane horrors: nice. However, we stick with it. Just as Prawn will have to.

BACK AT THE GPS

The very next day after the twenty-week scan, I am back in the GP's surgery waiting room, flicking through a seven month old copy of Chit Chat, Tittle Tattle, Nitter Natter or some such woman's periodical. Eventually, the doctor appears and calls my name. I approach her, but am stopped in my tracks by her shocked expression.

"Where's baby?" she asks.

Now, there is a question. What do they teach doctors at medical college these days? Maybe she was away when they did the pregnancy module. Or is it another trick question?

I point tentatively to my stomach. "In here..?"

She stares at my stomach with consternation, before I heard the metallic echo of a penny dropping somewhere in the depths of her brain.

"Oh, sorry, I thought you were someone else - another patient." I follow her into her room, slightly concerned at how this check up is already panning out and hoping that the *other patient* wasn't scheduled for some minor surgery or an internal examination due to suspected haemorrhoids.

"Have you got indigestion have you got swollen ankles have you got con-stipation?" she rattles off, not waiting for a reply as, being as I'm pregnant, she knows that I will be answering in the affirmative.

She flicks through my notes, scattering loose pages from her desk onto the floor and dropping her pen a couple of times. I notice her briefcase, open on the floor, contents spilling out, though it is difficult to distinguish between the rubbish that belongs in her case and the other pieces of doctor-related detritus that are scattered round her floor. Now I am not particularly an advocate of the 'tidy desk, tidy mind' philosophy; I tend more toward the 'tidy desk, *tiny* mind' school of thought. I like a bit of working mess as much as the next desk monkey, but her room really is taking it all a bit far. Towers of small cardboard boxes flank a tottering pile of papers, flaccid fingers of surgical gloves are escaping from a creased box and more books snake under the desk. A small mouse is using the ladder in Dr. Scatty's tights as a means of escape. Okay, there is no mouse. But she does have a ladder in her tights and from that point on I do call her Dr Scatty. But not to her face. I'm not that stupid. Don't ever insult a woman who has the medical right to stick her hand in places that would make your eyes water.

"Have you felt baby kick?" Dr Scatty enquires.

"No," I reply, unconcerned. I have previously read that it can take up to week twenty three to feel the baby, particularly if it is the first baby, and even more so if you are carrying, let's say, a little extra padding.

The doctor's face drops. "What, nothing?" she asks, incredulously.

"No."

"Well, this is concerning."

I shrug. I am still feeling the joy of the twenty-week scan, where I witnessed Prawn jiggling around with my own eyes. What could possibly have happened in the following twenty-four hours? I point this out to Dr Scatty, but she is still frowning profusely.

"I'm not happy about this." And suddenly, nor am I. In the face of the untrammelled concern of a qualified medical practitioner, my confidence in Prawn's health quickly withers.

Dr Scatty thinks long and hard, staring into space. Correction, there is no space to stare into - instead she gazes at a pile of books. I don't know if she has been watching too many TV talent shows, but she has got that 'overly-long-and-drawn-out-suspenseful pause' down to a fine art.

Many seconds tick by, giving my brain plenty of time to pre-empt what she is about to say. I am just pondering the likelihood of being whisked to A&E in an ambulance for some unknown but Prawn-threatening condition when she snaps out of her reverie. "Right, I want you to really concentrate on feeling baby kick this weekend. Plenty of sitting still, focusing on baby, and if you haven't felt him move by Monday, then ring me up and I will get you back in on an emergency appointment."

Advice to sit down for two days, which I would normally have greeted with glee, is significantly tempered by the mention of the word 'emergency' and I feel very miserable indeed. How can Prawn, not twenty-four hours ago, have been womb-dancing to his heart's content but now be totally still? The trouble is, there are just too many possible answers to that question - none of which I want to contemplate.

"Any other questions?" Dr Scatty asks.

It seems somewhat futile to voice the concern that I had wanted to ask about in the face of such bad news, but I plough on anyway.

"Err, yes. I have really painful nipples. I mean really painful." I am a tad embarrassed with all this nipple talk, but the pain I am experiencing really needs to be stopped. It sometimes feels that someone has set light to them, and the sensation is so strong that more than once I have actually peered into my bra half expecting to see a small conflagration.

"Oh, poor you," she says. "You might have your milk coming down." I have no idea what this means and it certainly doesn't sound evil enough to be causing such pain, but I am not that concerned. All I want is the miracle of modern medicine to provide me with the appropriate cream, pill or lotion to soothe my burning bosoms and I will be on my way.

"Cabbage leaves."

"I'm sorry?"

"Cabbage leaves. That will help the pain. Put one down each bra cup."

There is silence as I take this piece of advice on board. We have machines that can see inside your head, we have technology that allows us to perform operations through a hole the size of a pea and yet I am being told to shove pieces of vegetation down my bra? And can I get them on prescription?

I am sure I had other queries for Dr Scatty, but quite frankly, after the whole cabbage leaf revelation, I can no longer remember what they were, - or, indeed, care.

I drive home, imagining popping into Tesco and approaching a young assistant with a cabbage in my hands. "Excuse me," I would ask. "Do you have this in an E cup?"

NATURAL BIRTH IS BOLLOCKS (IT'S OFFICIAL)

I am at the midwife's for a check up. I see a lovely midwife, let's call her Frenchie, who is somewhat unsurprisingly, French. As we bring the check-up to a close, she asks me what I think about pain relief drugs during childbirth. "As much as I can and as frequently as possible," is my response. Now, I am not against a drug-free birth. Just so long as it is not mine. I have taken a wide variety of drugs in my time, most legal, a few not. And I have come to the conclusion that, apart from the one that made my skin look like an uncooked chicken and made me feel lousy (and that was one of the legal ones) drugs are a jolly good idea. I have suffered with very bad period pain for as long as I have had periods and wishing the pain away with simply the power of my mind, or playing my ovaries soothing music, has never really cut it in terms of pain eradication. Two max-strength Nurofen Plus, on the other hand, usually makes it a lot more bearable. I have had several bouts of tonsillitis in my time, and fervently believe in the power of antibiotics to help me feel better. A GP who, for some reason, was trying not to prescribe them to me, told me that the antibiotics would only speed up the recovery – the tonsillitis would eventually go of its own accord. Fine. I believed her. But when you have a sadist sawing its way through your tonsils with a rusty saw and you'd rather spit your saliva into your hand rather than swallow it, give me speedy relief in the form of two little pills three times a day any time.

So I had decided early on in my pregnancy that I would sign up for every chemical, pill, injection or inhalant that was on the drugs trolley. Is there really a drugs trolley? Please let it be manned by an elderly lady with a frilly white apron who lets you choose the drug of your choice in much the same way as you might choose a cup of tea and a Jammy Dodger.

And, it has to be said, I am not good with pain. This may sound a ludicrous thing to say, given that I imagine there are very few people walking the earth who love nothing more than a good bout of excruciating agony to make their day go with a swing, but I have come to the conclusion that some people are just much more...stoical. Maybe it's a pain threshold thing. Perhaps some people simply have a much higher pain threshold than me. A bit like being able to sit through a musical.

I admire those with the talent to endure pain without a murmur. My mum once fell down a flight of stairs, fracturing both wrists and a cheekbone, but sat at home for two days maintaining it was just a sprain and a bit of chafing and that everyone should stop fussing. I wish I could be like that, I think it is so noble. I have tried to be stoical in the face of pain, but I just can't manage it. I seriously consider calling an ambulance if I stub my toe on the leg of the bed.

Having been so adamant about wanting lots of drugs during the birth, I prepare myself for a lecture from Frenchie about the joys of experiencing a drug-free birth and how I should really reconsider. Instead, she replies, "Good, trying to give birth without drugs is such a load of bollocks." Christ, I could have kissed her. In fact, I may well have done just that.

WEEK 22. SPONSORED BY RENNIE.

Before I got pregnant, I would never leave the home without my keys, mobile and purse. Now, I can quite happily forget all of those items, just so long as I have a bumper pack of Rennies in my pocket. Everything I eat gives me indigestion. Even when I don't eat, I seem to get indigestion. My indigestion gives me indigestion. So those little silver cubes of soothing putty-like gunk become my best friends. They are the solver of all my problems and every room in the house is punctuated with little screwed-up Rennie wrappers, like a little breadcrumb trail of bilious burping and wince-inducing heartburn. In bed is the worst, and laying on my back is the nadir of all positions. I can almost feel the indigestion creeping up my throat, a slow wave of acid. More than once I get catapulted out of sleep by a gush of acidic, disgusting – and for want of a better description – *stomach contents*, hitting the roof of my mouth. I didn't realise that a pregnant woman could move that fast, as I leap to the bathroom sink in almost a single bound to spit it out before it dissolves all my teeth. A vigorous teeth clean and one Rennie later, however, I am back in bed and content. Ahh, Rennie, my little square of stomach sanity. I love you.

PRAWN DANCING

Needless to say, just over tenty-four hours after Dr Scatty frightened the life out of me with talk of dead, lifeless babies (okay, they weren't her exact words, but at four o clock in the morning as I am waiting for the latest Rennie to kick in, I swear that is exactly what she said to me) I feel Prawn kick. Hurrah! He's alive. And kicking. I immediately share the news with Mike over the phone and we are relief incarnate.

And so Prawn dancing begins. Every evening, as Mike and I sit down to watch whatever rubbish we can't get enough of, I balance the Sky remote on my stomach. Soon enough, Prawn starts his evening workout and the remote control starts to wobble, sway and, during those particular high kicks that Prawn is mastering, bounce onto the sofa. It means that Mike is as aware as I am of what Prawn is up to, and we take great delight in watching the remote jolting about atop my tummy. It rivals the TV as entertainment any night of the week.

DECORATING THE NURSERY

The time has come to turn our thoughts to decorating. I start to scour the Internet for furniture, accessories and ideas. My word, there is a lot of crap out there. Is there such as thing as a set of drawers that are not plastered in pictures of teddies or trains? Apparently not. Can I find a wardrobe without novelty knobs featuring kites or clouds? Scarcely. How about a blind that does not roll down to reveal a cornucopia of badly drawn animals or chugging multi-coloured tractors? Not really. And trying to avoid items with Disney characters emblazoned all over them is like trying to get though a day being pregnant without thinking something bad has happened to your baby. It's almost a physical impossibility. Luckily for our bank balance and my sanity, my sister has very kindly emptied her loft of a cot, changing unit and variety of other items, leaving me to find the remaining yet crucial elements such as wall murals. I decide upon a very funky looking moose sporting a stripy scarf and with a dragonfly companion for one wall (who knew that a large mammal from North America and an insect with a bulbous bottom could be such good friends?) and a rather cool-looking tower block, with flames coming from the windows, which are being extinguished by a small herd of elephants and a giraffe with an exceedingly long neck carrying a large bucket of water. Prawn may grow up with a warped sense of the function and relationships of various animals, but at least he won't be surrounded by nauseatingly cute crap at every waking moment.

We paint the nursery 'Ocean White' or some such misnomer for a paint that describes itself as 'white with a strong hint of blue' and which turns out to be, well... white. I did try to eschew the 'blue for a boy' tradition and start with a notion that Prawn's nursery should be green, but it was squashed under the weight of three million websites that all sold items for a boy's bedroom in blue, blue or blue. True, I did find outlets that broke the mould and sold gorgeous looking kids furniture, designed in Italy, in a range of fabulous colours and with a design flair that would have put Charles Eames to shame. But once I had wiped the mist from the PC screen, the result of too much heavy breathing as I lusted after these items, I saw the price. And that was the end of that. Back to Ikea, Mothercare et al.

HOLIDAY

Ah, the pure, unadulterated bliss. We are on holiday in Portugal with my parents. Mike and I have strict agendas, to do stuff that we know we won't get time for once Prawn arrives. So Mike plays copious amounts of golf and I do copious amounts of lounging around.

As with any holiday, all rules can be abandoned, as they don't count once you leave the country. So I break my alcohol ban and allow myself the odd ice-cold beer (in this heat, it's practically medicinal) and the odd glass of wine. These forbidden elixirs are like angels dancing on my tongue, and worth the cost of the flight alone. Delicious.

Given that I had read you shouldn't go overboard on the sunbathing when pregnant (apparently, simmering womb juice doesn't do the baby any favours) I don't go out of my way to catch the rays, but it seems they go out of the way to catch me. Despite high factor sun cream, I brown faster than a Delia turkey on December the 25th, which is a little disconcerting. The shade becomes my friend, which is fine by me, as it means there is always a lounger free by the pool and it keeps my beer cooler (may the guardian of over-stringent pregnancy guidelines strike me down).

USELESS ADVICE #1

One of the most unwanted side effects of being pregnant is the unsolicited, uninvited and basically bloody useless pieces of advice that people feel duty bound to burden you with. One of the earliest I receive is to get as much sleep as I can before the birth as I won't be getting much afterwards. This is wrong, wrong, wrong on so many levels. Firstly, as far as I know, sleep is not like baked beans or frozen peas; if you know of an impending shortage of these food items, you can rush down the shops, load up a trolley and fill your cupboards, safe in the knowledge that when the rest of the world runs out, you can still eat your peas and beans until they are oozing out of every orifice. You can't stock up on sleep in quite the same way, I am sure. I can't

sleep solidly for a week and then not need so much as a nap for the next month - it just doesn't work like that.

And the advice overlooks one important factor: sleeping when pregnant is not as easy as it should be. My body is knackered from dealing with my new visitor, who has made himself very comfortable in his amenity-laden accommodation and has booked in for a nine-month stay. I foolishly assumed that Mother Nature would therefore make sleep easy, to restore my energy and give my body and brain time to recover. But oh no. She's a bitch, that Mother Nature. If it's not the indigestion keeping you awake, it's the nipple pain. Or the incessant thoughts racing round your head involving anything and everything, from thinking about the birth, to trying to ignore the fact that you need the toilet. Again. And if that doesn't ensure a sleepless night, the endless and futile pursuit of finding a comfortable position can keep you entertained for a full four hours straight. If the holy grail of comfort is eventually discovered, usually involving a position found only in hardcore porn movies or a reconstruction of a fall from a twenty-story tower block, it will be at that precise moment that Prawn wakes up and decides he had better do fifty laps of the womb to keep himself in trim. The person who imparted this 'sleep now, stay awake later' pearl of wisdom repeated it to me a few weeks later, just in case I wasn't irritated enough the first time round. I would have punched his bloody lights out, but quite frankly, I was just too damn tired.

USELESS ADVICE #2

Many people who offer me advice start with the immortal phrase: "Everyone gave me loads of advice when I was pregnant, and it was so annoying, so I won't do the same to you." This is usually followed by a small pause (I resist the temptation to call it a pregnant one) before they continue with "But..." and then go on to give me loads of advice that is highly annoying. And in some kind of post-modern ironic way, one person then actually says, "But my best advice to you is to ignore all the advice that you are given."

"So," I say, "Let's re-cap on that conversation shall we? First, you tell me that you won't give me advice as you yourself recognise that it is highly irritating. Then you go on to give me advice, about something that I have already forgotten as it was so crap, and then you conclude by telling me to ignore all advice anyway?"

Okay, I admit, I didn't say that. I just smiled and nodded, as if I was carefully assimilating all those precious gems of enlightenment (whilst secretly wishing they would just fuck off).

THE DURACELL BUNNY DOESN'T LIVE HERE ANY MORE

I am back at the hospital, waiting to see the consultant. It is a general check-up, but not one entrusted to the midwives to carry out, as I am old, or overweight, or they don't like the cut of my jib, or they can't find my jib, or something. I don't know why I am surprised not to see the same consultant as I had for my last check up, as having two consecutive appointments with the same specialist is seemingly against the laws of the Hipprocratic oath, but nevertheless there is not a slightly hunched man in a crumpled shirt with a spectacular gravity-defying comb-over sitting at the desk, but a much younger lady instead, with a warm smile and a friendly welcome. Perhaps it is a good thing after all.

I lie on the bed, now used to the pre-scan basting of my stomach. Smiley scans my tummy with the Doppler, staring intently at the wall to aid her listening. The Doppler is a fairly unprepossessing bit of kit, but its name does conjure up a certain amount of expectation. The first time I was Doppled - this, I fear, is not an accepted medical term but it should be - I was hoping that the heartbeat (ba boom, ba boom) would be in one pitch at first, but, like a speeding ambulance, would then change pitch as it went past (bo bim, bo bim). Alas, either Prawn wasn't moving fast enough or they should change the Doppler's name.

"Hmmm," she says, skidding about some more on the glistening mound of flesh. We both listen for the heartbeat. There is silence.

"Hmmm," Smiley repeats. I was hoping for a more medical-based commentary at this point to allay my fears that suddenly, Prawn's heart is nowhere to be heard.

"Hmmm," she reiterates for the third time. I realise that I am now holding my breath, praying for that slightly squelchy heartbeat that puts a smile on my face every time I hear it.

I look at the consultant and she looks at me, still roaming the Doppler back and forth across my stomach like she is idly ironing her tea towels. Suddenly, there is a very quiet snippet of what could be a heartbeat. She whips the Doppler back to where it was a moment ago. Nothing. She moves it incrementally one way, then back again. I am getting impatient with this metal-detector-like hunt and have to clench my fists to stop myself snatching the bloody thing from her hands and having a go myself. Wait, there it is again. A faint heart beat.

"It is very far away," she pronounces in her thick Spanish accent. Okay, I think, so how far away? Physically, there is only so far away it can be, let's face it. We're not talking three feet. Prawn is not hiding in the next room. He has not taken advantage of a very cheap flight to Amsterdam to get a change of scenery and a bit of sun on his face. He is in my tummy, and whilst that is bigger than it ever has been, relatively speaking, he still has to be pretty close. So what the hell does she mean: far away? I begin, of course, to worry. Maybe her English is not great. Maybe she says 'far away' but really means something else. Like 'nearly dead' for instance. I am beginning to wish for Comb-Over to be here instead. He may lack charm and the ability to face up to his bald spot, but possibly makes up for it by being able to find a baby's heartbeat.

Smiley, not so smiley now, starts to move the Doppler around, pressing very hard indeed. I wince with discomfort and wonder if she is going to keep on pressing until she makes contact with my spine. She finds the faraway heartbeat again for a moment, and then it is gone.

"Something is wrong," she says. No shit, Sherlock.

"Hmmm." Oh Christ, don't start with the 'hmmms' again, please.

"Ahh!" Smiley proclaims. I await an explanation with trepidation.

"The batteries are dead," she says, holding up the scanner and rolling her eyes. She disappears from the room, presumably heading for the battery cupboard. Ten minutes of heartbeat failure turns out to be because the bloody Duracell Bunny has stopped his incessant drumming. Meanwhile I have aged another five years.

THE WORLD OF PRAMS (SORRY, BABY TRAVEL SYSTEMS)

The time comes that we must buy a pram for Prawn. Being novice parents-to-be, we thought this would be a fairly simple task. Hah. How wrong can two people be? We canvas opinions from friends. Top of the list is the Bugaboo, the pram of choice for Yummy Mummies. Except they are not called prams anymore. They are travel systems. Which, as far as I can tell, means that for the several hundred pounds for which it is advertised, you get four wheels and a frame, with everything else as an optional, expensive extra. "Oh, you want handles, madam? That will be another £150. But you really don't want the basic handles. *These* are the latest handles, with ergo-grip technology and tri-positionable wrist supports. It's not worth *not* spending the extra £60 to have these." Friends bemoan the fact that theirs did not come with a cup holder, and that they had to fork out another chunk of cash for this essential piece of pram ware. No cup holder? Good god, that's practically child abuse.

I start to get irrationally irritated (irrational? Irritated? Whilst pregnant? Who'd have thought?) by that smug little circular logo that appears on the hood of seemingly every other pram, sorry, travel system, on the High Street. It really is the pram *du jour*. We do a little calculation to see what it would cost to get the travel system but give up when it creeps past £700, and flick to cheap-prams.com or some such site, to pick ourselves a functional, highly untrendy pushchair that will see Prawn through from birth to the moment we turf him out and make him walk. It isn't fashionable, it isn't stylish, and (oh, the ignominy, may the god of over-priced products strike me down with his spear, no doubt designed by Phillippe Starck) I will have to (I can hardly say it) hold my cup in my own hand (sob). But it saves us a fortune.

THE SOCIAL LIFE OF A PREGNANT WOMAN

This can basically be summed up in one word: boring. Or maybe two: boring and tiring. Or maybe another two: horrifically sober.

I know people can be sniffy about the inability to enjoy yourself without alcohol – it is a damning indictment on the shallowness and emptiness of someone's life when they can't have a good night out without imbibing some of the hard stuff. But hey ho, so be it. Shallow and empty as charged, Your Honour. It's not that every time I went out before becoming pregnant I got roaring and utterly drunk. I just enjoyed having a few glasses of the red stuff, and enjoyed being in the company of people who were also enjoying the same. So going out whilst pregnant seems...a little pointless.

One night we are out to dinner with a friend and her new boyfriend. I start the evening with high hopes, only a fraction of that optimism being dented when I realise that anything on the menu I actually want to order is out of bounds due to some unspecified risk to your unborn baby (I didn't know Baby Death by Brie is a medical condition but apparently so). The wine is flowing, just not into my glass. I am rapidly running out of interesting non-alcoholic drinks to imbibe, and even a lovely waiter who takes it upon himself to make me an alcohol-free cocktail can't make me feel that I am not missing out. I am also getting tired. Of course, carrying Prawn around, feeding him, knitting him eyebrows and cooking up bones for him is tiring in itself. Add to this the fact that I am out and about at a time of the evening when I am usually considering getting into my jimjams and bed with my bumper pack of Rennies, and the fact that I am not shovelling alcoholic stimulants down my throat makes for an extremely tiring night. Plus the new boyfriend is turning out to be a right bore, further adding to my fatigue and eroding my patience. Boring and tiring. And horrifically sober.

We also attend a wedding of some dear friends. It is a lovely day. For them. For me? Boring and sober...and...well, I think I've made my point.

CAN I BORROW YOUR BASKET, MOSES?

We discover that apparently it is the law that your newborn child has to sleep in a Moses basket. Having an aversion to wicker, particularly when coupled with pastel coloured frills and diminutive blankets sporting oh-so-cute animals, I look for the alternative. There is none.

Well okay, I think, at least we won't actually have to spend any money on one, because the second clause of that same law is that you never *buy* a Moses basket - as someone you know will lend you one. So we put out a few calls to friends and family, enquiring as to the whereabouts and possible loanability of their basket.

"Oh, sorry, Jim and Ang have it I think."

"My sister borrowed it a while back – I think she passed it on to friends."

"We borrowed ours from a friend at work so can't help, sorry."

"We have one, but it's in Hull as my brother-in-law has just been using it."

"Why are you asking me, you idiots? I don't have any bloody kids."

We are starting to get a little desperate. Where are all these sodding Moses baskets then? We continue to rely on Moses law – that before too long, one would come floating along – but to no avail. Eventually, we have to actually go into a shop, pretend to have an avid interest in wicker products and part with our hard-earned cash for a glorified shopping basket, complete with foldaway stand. It isn't until we get it home and assemble it that I realise a washing-up bowl on the coffee table would do much the same thing, but by then it is too late.

So this entire thing about never buying a Moses basket is a complete foetal myth. However, in our vain and arduous attempts to find the aforementioned sleeping vessel we do uncover the real truth about them: there appears to be only one other Moses basket in the entire country. And it's in fucking Hull.

HILARIOUS PARENTS

We have a slightly unnerving reaction from some friends who we tell we are having a baby. "Oh my God, you will make hilarious parents." Hilarious parents? Hilarious? I can't even begin to decipher how much of an insult this is, or indeed, if it even *is* an insult, although I am pretty sure that it is. I don't ask for clarification at the time, I think I am too busy smiling through gritted teeth, but later wish I had as the phrase keeps coming back to me, much like indigestion – frequent and unwelcome. Hilarious in what way? As in fun and laughter-filled, or so utterly crap it will be laughable? Which all starts me thinking about a test for parents. Perhaps we are going to be rubbish at being a mum and dad. Who knows? Whilst I am not advocating a test whose results determine who should have the right to procreate, for fear of treading ground already stamped threadbare by Daily Mail readers, at least it would give you some indicator of your likely success. Just to prepare you, perhaps.

It could be a multiple choice, so that you have a one in four chance of getting it right – which in itself might be indicative of life as a parent – and cover a wide variety of scenarios. Such as:

What or who do you consider an appropriate baby-sitter?
a) Grandparents
b) CBeebies
c) The dog
d) A box of matches and yesterday's paper

What would you never do as a parent?
a) Slap my child
b) Call it Britney, Chardonnay or Merlot
d) Dress your child in smaller versions of the clothes you wear
e) Have a pram without a cup holder

What sleeping arrangements have you organised for your newborn?
a) A Moses basket from Hull
b) A dog basket
(having given the blanket a quick once-over with the Hoover)
c) Your sock drawer
d) Your Bag for Life from Sainsburys lined with a tea towel

Perhaps then, depending on your score, you could be made to wear graded (think McDonalds' gold stars) Learner Plates, so that everyone knows what to expect. Those with five star plates can hang them off their fucking cup holders and make the rest of us feel rightfully inadequate.

BLOOD PRESSURE RISING (WEEK 27)

At a routine appointment with the midwife, it appears my blood pressure is slightly raised. Not surprising, given how much we have so far spent on baby paraphernalia, but the midwife says she will keep it monitored, and have I considered yoga? Even if I didn't have a huge belly, I wouldn't consider yoga, what with all that tying your legs in knots and trying to sit still. And apparently, they don't even have a television to watch while you are doing it. But with a huge belly? I have visions of a Weeble, except this one would fail the quality checks and definitely fall down – and stay down.

However, I am not impervious to the suggestions of people in medical uniforms, so I duly trot (I mean waddle) to the car and head home to check out any local classes on the Internet. The only one local to me is something called Bikram Hot Yoga. Already being a sweaty pregnant woman in summer, I am grimacing at everything that name implies, and indeed, further investigation reveals that it is basically all the fun of yoga, in a really hot room. Could they make it any more appealing? Maybe Bikram Hot Shit Yoga, where you are doing yoga in a really hot room, surrounded by steaming cowpats. However, I am let off the hot yoga hook with the website's warning that it is not suitable for pregnant women. No, really?

So I rifle through the leaflets that the midwife had given me (after I have fished them out from underneath the passenger seat of the car, which in itself counts as my daily exercise given the effort that I expend in doing it) and come up with Hypnobirthing. I have vaguely heard of this, from my sister, who knows someone who raved about it, and so I do a bit of reading on the subject. One site claims that with hypnobirthing, you do not have to endure the severe pain of labour. Already I am liking the sound of this and push all thoughts of pasta-knitting, hemp-wearing weirdos from my mind. The site is at pains (probably not that appropriate a phrase to be honest) to allay any fears - you are completely awake and in control during your birth with your self-hypnosis - which quite frankly, I find a little disappointing. But no pain? Really? Where do I sign up?

HYPNOBIRTHING (WEEK 29)

Which is why Mike and I, along with five other couples, find ourselves at the first of four evening classes for Hypnobirthing. When I asked Mike to come with me, to his credit he agreed with only mild derision of the concept.

Our teacher (I use the term loosely) has obviously worked hard on her appearance. A bright green tee shirt stretches across her formidable bosoms, emblazoned with the slogan 'Hypnobirthing Rocks!' in large, white capital letters. I am surprised that she has enough self-control to only use the one exclamation mark, as she strikes me as the sort of person that is exceedingly liberal with her application of chirpy punctuation. A pair of black leggings do a valiant job of trying to contain her thighs and a pair of bright green socks finish off the ensemble, tucked into a pair of pumps. Now, you don't just roll out of bed and accidentally create a look that good. It takes effort to match a tee shirt and socks with such tonal accuracy. But hey, I am sitting here in a cotton version of a two-man tent and not a matching accessory in sight, so perhaps I should pipe down.

It has to be said, the session gets off to a fairly inauspicious start. I paraphrase and summarise for the sake of brevity and my own sanity, but there is an early description by Bosoms of some experiments done with water crystals. Apparently, some were told loving, warm messages of encouragement and support such as "you are beautiful" and "well done, you, what a great job", whilst other water crystals were told nasty, hateful things like "I hate you" and "by Jove, you're an ugly buggar." Let me reiterate; I am paraphrasing. But only just. I am on the edge of my seat at this point, partially from the suspense of how this incredible experiment will turn out, but mainly to stop me wetting myself from the strain of holding in the laughter. Bosoms explains that those water crystals that were showered with love formed into beautiful, symmetrical structures whilst those that were roundly abused... well, didn't. They formed asymmetrical structures so ugly that people would scratch out their own eyeballs rather than look at them (okay, I admit, I did make that very last bit up).

The group is stunned into silence and whatever link Bosoms makes between that and Hypnobirthing is lost as I try really, really hard to make the look on my face resemble thoughtfulness rather than the incredularity and slightly panicked 'can I get my money back' look that I fear it is actually displaying. There is a lot of toe-gazing as I concentrate intently on not even glancing in Mike's direction. No one wants to be barred from a Hypnobirthing class for uncontrollable hysteria. And just when I think it can't get any better, Bosoms then goes on to explain a further experiment (someone obviously had way too much time on their hands) whereby when heavy metal was played to water crystals, boy oh boy, did they turn ugly. Personally, Ace of Spades would make it into my Desert Island Discs list any day of the week, so I think it a little harsh to single out that particular genre of music.

Once the Introduction to Utterly Bonkers Experiments is over, we then start the session in earnest. We pair up with someone else in the group and have to discuss what we want from our impending childbirth. I tell the bloke I am paired with that I want as many drugs as I can get my hands on. We then reconvene and are asked to 'share' our thoughts, at which point my partner totally shops me to the group about my horribly anti-hypnobirthing wish for pain-relieving narcotics. I feel slapping him would not be appropriate at this juncture, so I just laugh feebly. Bosoms gives me a steely glare and I just stare at her green socks for a while until she moves on to the next couple.

We learn some great relaxation techniques that night though, although every time I am getting close to total calm, I remember those bloody water crystals being force fed insults and heavy metal and start giggling again. We leave armed with an instruction to practise every night, and for the women to listen to the hypobirthing CD we felt obliged to purchase. I can't wait.

THE HOSPITAL TOUR

On Saturday morning, when there are a thousand other things we could be doing – buying more random baby paraphernalia, going to Tesco, sleeping – we arrive at the local hospital for our tour. We join a group of parents in the waiting area, which is silent. There is the occasional whisper, the odd smile, but the men are mainly thinking about where they would rather be (anywhere) and the women are all trying to decide whether this is really a good idea. I am not sure. On the up side, you get to see what it's like. On the down side, you get to see what it's like.

Finally a midwife appears and in we all file, past the secure door, the obligatory ignored hand wash and into one of the wards. An image immediately pops into my head: battery chickens. Rows of beds and rows of women, lying beached and swollen. I'm sure they were all having the time of their lives, but it makes me feel miserable.

Then we get to see the labour rooms. They have, the midwife explains, had them decorated to make them feel like home, so that the medical equipment isn't too obvious or threatening. As I walk in, I spot a wall of instruments that I swear wouldn't have looked out of place in Guantanamo Bay. Clipped to the wall around the bed are all manner of bits of kit that I really don't want to think about. I don't know what it was like before they decorated – perhaps all that kit was in a huge, rusty steel box marked PAIN in big red letters. But painting the room lemon yellow does not constitute making it look more like home, that's for sure. We all stand around the walls, trying not to imagine ourselves on that bed, having various bits of that equipment put into places we didn't want. The midwife chats on for a while but I, for one, have no idea what she says. Her mouth is moving but all I can think about is that wall of torture.

It is spotlessly clean, however, which is a relief. My only other medical intervention within the last five years had been a tiny bit of surgery to remove a small, benign lump on my shoulder. As it was so minor, the GP carried out the surgery with the help of a Practice Nurse at his surgery. All was going well until the very end, when I had been stitched up and nurse told me to slowly get up from the bed upon which I was lying face down. As I raised myself onto my elbows, I came face-to-face with a lump of me near the edge of the bed. A small but unmistakable bit of what the GP had cut out of my shoulder was lying, pink and glistening, no more than two inches from my nose. We both stared at it for many seconds. "Oh dearie me," the nurse said cheerily, "you don't want to see that now, do you?" And with that, she flicked the lump off the bed with her right hand. I watched it fly through the air and land on the arm of a large lamp. It stuck. I have never been back into that room, but I imagine that the little bit of me is still there, as cleaners are not generally known for their zealous focus on nooks, crannies and arms of lamps. So now, in the back of my mind, I wonder if that was standard nursing practise. 'Nurses Handbook, Rule 342: The Disposal of Bodily Detritus (3cm and smaller): Position third finger behind aforementioned waste and flick toward wall or other non-human target. Note: Do not attempt with fluids.'

However, I am relieved to find not one jot of gunk anywhere, and I did inspect the arm of the lamp very carefully indeed.

We are then shepherded into the Holy Grail of labour rooms: the one with the birthing pool. Most of the pregnant women I have spoken to want a water birth, as they are meant to be much more relaxing and with less pain. I had not really considered it before, as I really do not fancy splashing round in a bath containing the contents of my womb for any length of time, but I can see the theoretical appeal. However, there is only one room with a pool so it is complete lottery as to whether it would be free when you need it. I think that a ticketing system like the one they employ at the deli counter would have worked a treat, but I guess they have already thought of that.

On our way back to the entrance, the midwife gestures to a locked door. "This is a private recovery room," she says, gesturing towards it. "You can pay a small fee to be in there after you have given birth. But it's much nicer to be with all the other girls in the ward." No, I think, it would not be nicer. Nicer would be to be on your own, recovering, without other people's relatives perching on your bed or peering into your baby's cot, or having to stare at the sartorial nightwear choices of complete strangers. I am seriously considering booking it on my way out, until she adds that paying for it doesn't guarantee you'll get it, in case there is an emergency. How very NHS.

Driving home from our tour, Mike and I discuss something that we have never touched upon before: home births. It never appealed to me until I saw the labour ward, but now it is looking quite an attractive option. However, we conclude that hospital is probably the better place to be. After all, we have just had new carpets laid.

TOUCH MY BUMP, I'LL SMASH YOUR FACE

I am not totally adverse to human contact, don't get me wrong. There is nothing I like more than a cuddle, a stroke or a handhold, from my husband, my family or my close friends. In fact I would go so far as to say I love it.

But there is a curious belief amongst people that they have the right to touch your bump and I find this quite disturbing. Moreover, the uninvited touching seems inversely proportionate to familiarity. People I barely know land a sweaty hand on my stomach only seconds after greeting me. I am not sure what they are trying to do, but whatever it is, it doesn't work. One even asks: "Can I feel it kick?" Oh yes, I'll just press this button on my side and I will get my little performing foetus to do a couple of somersaults for you.

I begin to stand a little further away from the people that I meet, not only to allow for the ever increasing rotundity of my belly, but also to ensure that said bump is out of arm's reach. Call me a grumpy old pregnant woman (a lot of people do) but no one felt compelled to touch my stomach when it was just full of pies, so why now? Weirdos.

USELESS ADVICE 3

A friend nods sagely at me. "Whatever you do before you give birth, make sure you go to the cinema." Now I must admit, this takes me slightly by surprise. Of all the bits of advice I have heard, this is probably the most left-field. I wonder whether he is about to tell me about a great new must-see blockbuster about childbirth (From Here to Maternity?), but no, it is just a general point about getting to the cinema. I ponder this advice for many days and come to the conclusion, when I consider possible life after Prawn arrives and the notion of diminished leisure time, that this is actually very sound advice in deed. Obviously, I ignore it.

NOCTURNAL PILLOW FLINGING

A curious and luckily short-lived pregnancy side effect occurs around this time. In the middle of the night, fast asleep, I grab my pillow and hurl it off the bed with some force, at which point I wake up. I always throw it out of my side of the bed and twice I manage to take out the entire contents of the bedside table, with lamp, clock and bottle of water all flying through the air on impact. Over the course of the couple of weeks, this happens quite frequently, to the extent that I start to leave some of the more fragile bedside accessories on the floor.

I have no idea if the nocturnal pillow flinging is in response to a recurring dream (a ten foot foetus bearing down on me with a murderous look in his eye, or that yellow birthing room, or perhaps our cup holder-less pram) or if it is something more physiological, but it is very strange indeed and I am mightily relieved when it subsides. I can't imagine trying to explain to the woman in the bed next to me in the hospital labour ward, who has my pillow stuck in her mouth, what has just happened.

MATERNITY CLOTHES

If ever an object provoked a reluctance to purchase, it is the maternity garment. You buy in the full knowledge that in six months, or sometimes in four, you will have no more use for it. Now I am aware of women who buy clothes seasonally, who keep up with the latest trends and use terms such as 'capsule wardrobe' but I have never actually met any in the flesh. Or in the rococo-print pin-tuck shift dress with matching gladiator flats. Personally, I tend to weep if I have to discard an item of clothing before I celebrate its tenth birthday, so to buy something with its life cycle already down to less than a year is a little hard.

It would be easier if I could don the aforementioned item and be transformed into a glowing, elegant vision of a pregnant woman. Unfortunately, it is more likely to make me look like a large whale that happened to swim through a capsized container of charity clothes. It is difficult to feel sexy when your trouser waistband is mainly constructed of heavy-duty ribbed elastic panels and your top seems to have been cut from a leftover hot air balloon.

However, I stumble across a rather marvellous invention, which saves me considerable money and clothes-buying angst. It is the simplest of things – a triangle of fabric attached to a short elasticated strap, which has a button type contraption that cleverly bridges the gap between the button and hole sides of your trouser waistband when they are no longer on speaking terms. Like a belly button modesty panel. Genius. It means that I can wear my normal trousers for months longer than I would have and for that I say hurrah. It does put me a little in mind of Christmas, when you sit down after gorging on three courses of lard with a few sprouts thrown in for good measure and pop open your trousers for a 'bit of breathing room'. Only with this, your trousers don't fall down when you get up in a hurry.

UNDER PRESSURE (WEEK 30)

I start to have a midwife check twice a week as my blood pressure remains high. I really should have taken more notice of what it actually is, but seeing as it is always expressed as '120 over 80' or the like, my mind just refuses to listen as it sounds far too much like fractions, and I was always crap at fractions.

The midwife checks occur in a newly-built wing of the local hospital. The planning for the aforementioned extension seems to have gone something like this:

"Let's build a new wing."

"Brilliant. Is this the sort of thing you had in mind?"

"Perfect. Can I colour it in?"

"Be my guest."

"Haven't we forgotten something?"

"Er, let's see. Door – check. Windows – check. Ridiculously high reception desk designed to make all patients feel about eight years old – check. Nope, it's all there."

"Great. Let's build it."

Five years later:

"So here it is."

"Lovely."

"Oh fuck."

"What?"

"I remember now, what it is we have forgotten."

"Oh?"

"Car parking."

"Oh crap. Just keep quiet, no one will notice."

No, no one will notice. Apart from the hundreds of drivers who morosely circle the small, hugely over-subscribed existing car parks, over and over again, with their will to live trickling slowly out of their arses. I swear they must have got a kickback from the mental health department who were desperate for more business.

So here I am, circling the car park, with my life force just a puddle in the foot well, my blood pressure slowly going from simmer to slow-boil as the time for my appointment approaches.

I finally experience some kind of divine intervention from the god of car parking and find a space, so rush into the hospital, stressed out, flustered and hot. This is not helping my blood pressure. The midwife puts the brown arm cuff on me and starts to pump. I hold my breath in a vain attempt to fool the machine, and try to think nice calm thoughts to bring my blood pressure down. I imagine a lovely, still pond on a warm spring day, but I can't quite settle on the image: Does it have ducks? Are ducks calming enough? Maybe swans. Just don't think about what's happening under the water's surface. What about trees in the distance? Oh yes, that's good. But would they rustle too much in the wind and spoil the tranquillity? Ooh, a boat would be good. Hang on, it won't be able to go anywhere without a breeze, so better get a breeze going. Which means the trees have definitely got to go. Hmm, looks a bit bare now. How about a cottage? Urgh, not thatched, too much of a pastiche and a bit of a fire hazard. So what about...

"Hmm, it's very high," the midwife says. Hang on, I want to say, I haven't finished constructing my calming image, you can't rush perfection. But instead I roll my eyes and mutter something about car parking.

Two days later I am back again, sitting on the same chair with the brown hessian seat and a couple of very dubious looking stains on it. This is meant to be a new wing, so how come the chair looks so dirty? Perhaps the furniture supplier offered the hospital a pre-stained seat fabric as part of their range, to save the dirty ones looking out of place. "So, you can have the vagina-leak motif in brown, forest-floor green or the ever-popular sky blue."

The midwife advances with the blood pressure cuff. I have heard of white-coat syndrome, where just the presence of a doctor or a clinical environment provokes a rise in blood pressure, but I think I have just invented a new syndrome: brown cuff syndrome. I will put money on this being a recognised affliction in years to come and I may well register *www.browncuffsareevil. com* right now.

As the unmistakable sound of Velcro being repositioned fills the room, my heart starts to race and my palms get sweaty. Think pond, I urge myself. Think cottage. Think a clear blue sky with a couple of fluffy clouds. Oh, that one looks a bit like a donkey with two heads...hmm, don't think about that... think about...

Not surprisingly, my blood pressure is still high. I may even have notched up a slightly bigger fraction. I blame the two-headed donkey. It is duly noted in my file and I leave, disappointed not to have confounded medical opinion and had my blood pressure miraculously return to normal.

HYPNOBIRTHING PRACTISE #1

Mike and I settle down in the lounge to do some Hypnobirthing practise. Mike, as 'birthing partner' reads calming scripts from the book whilst I put my feet up, close my eyes and work hard at getting relaxed. Now this is the sort of homework I can deal with.

Unfortunately, the session is about 95 percent giggling and 5 percent relaxing, as Mike initially adopts a slightly unnerving slow, low-volume drawl which is meant to be relaxing but puts me in mind of having a weirdo whisper secrets in my ear. He soon finds his hypno-voice, however and I float away on a tide of balloons that slowly drift out of my abdomen...ahhhh...lovely...

Until the next bout of giggles hits and we abandon the script again. Ah well, I am sure that this is all good practise for labour, as I imagine that giving birth is an absolute laugh a minute.

CONSULTANT CHECK UP (WEEK 30)

Circling, circling. Is she going? No, she's just putting something in her boot. Cow. Is he heading to his car? Difficult to tell with that limp. Circling circling. Back at the hospital, I am looking for a parking space. I have left well over thirty minutes to navigate through Dante's Inferno; at five past eleven, I pass through the first circle (limbo), by quarter past I pop out the other side of the fifth circle (wrath and sullenness) and am now cruising at five miles per hour through the seventh (violence). I'm not late for my appointment – yet - but banging my head repeatedly against the steering wheel isn't helping my search for a space. Just when I think all is lost, I happen across a man reversing out of his space who, not only blocks the angry queue of cars the other side of him allowing me to nip in, but also gives me his parking ticket with a couple of hours left on it. A double whammy of a moral victory; may the glorious sunshine of parking spaces always radiate golden light on his perfect little Peugeot.

It quickly becomes unclear why I had been worried about not turning up on time, when I overhear a patient in the waiting room asking a nurse how late the consultant is running.

"Oh, just a little," is her casual reply.

"How much?"

"Well...he hasn't actually turned up yet."

I decide against counting the number of people in the waiting room who have arrived before me for fear of crying and just settle down to my book.

After an interminably long period of time, I am called. Comb Over Consultant is back. We do the usual checks (baby kicking? Yes. Blood pressure high? Yes) and then I ask him about a few headaches that I have been getting recently. Are they pregnancy related? I enquire.

"Probably," comes the resoundingly expert opinion of Comb Over. Well, that's sorted that out then.

He does redeem himself momentarily by asking if I want a scan to see the baby. I eagerly hop onto the couch, whip up my tee shirt and wait in anticipation for the sight of Prawn. However many times I see it throughout my pregnancy, it is, quite frankly, never enough. It is like contemplating your own navel but a million times better. I could stare at that image of little Prawn all day, sometimes kicking, sometimes moving his hand, sometimes just being still with a flicker of pixels showing his tiny, delicate heart beat. It is ultimately fascinating to watch – I know in theory that what I see on the screen is inside of me, but believing this is quite another matter. I mean, I am aware there is something in there, due to the hugely inflated belly and the kicking, but that could be a case of over-zealous pie eating with the associated indigestion. To think that there is a tiny person in there, busy getting eyebrows and eyelashes and little miniature organs? How weird is that?

I stare at the screen. "Oh, this is quite an old machine," Comb Over apologises as a grainy image flickers to life. I wait for it to come into focus, but the screen remains undecipherable.

I enquire as to whether it is actually snowing in my womb, as all I can see is a blizzard of white dots. Maybe it is the batteries. 'There he is,' Comb Over proclaims, pointing vaguely to the screen. I look puzzled, so he points out a few key features. It is a bit like one of those 3D puzzles, where you tip the paper to see an image miraculously spring to life before your eyes. I tipped with the rest of them, never saw anything, but for fear of looking like a dolt, always acted amazed at what I was seeing. So I nod noncommittally at the Emperor's new Foetus and Comb Over turns the machine off. Rats.

PERI-WHAT?

I read in one of the many pregnancy sources that I refer to that I should have been applying perineum oil to my perineum. So all I need to do is find out where that is and I'm away. It turns out that it is the bit between the vagina and the bottom, or the bump between two holes, if you will. Damn. I was hoping it was somewhere more accessible.

So off I go to Mothercare and hunt through the shelves that look likely to be holding it. There are creams to rub on all sorts of parts of a pregnant woman's body. Stuff for your tummy so it doesn't end up resembling crazed marble, stuff for your nipples if they hurt, stuff for your nipples if they're cracked (I wince at this juncture). A pregnant woman is standing next to me, surveying the products on offer. We both gaze on in silence for a long time, thinking about the cornucopia of afflictions that we have had, might have or will have. I get to the sterile breast pads and sigh with resignation. The woman lets out a little sound, somewhere between a sob and a laugh. "I can't do this," she says in a quiet voice, puts down her basket and walks out. I am guessing she had passed the nipple balm and encountered the soothing post-birth vaginal pads.

I duly purchase my perineum oil and trundle home. It says on the packet that it should help stop the perineum from tearing during birth (cue another involuntary wince) by softening it up. I remember reading somewhere that olive oil would do the same job, but that just doesn't appeal to me. I think it is the thought of having people round for dinner, serving up some bread for dipping and having to apologise and shoot upstairs as the 'olive oil is in the bedroom'.

Crikey, it is a feat to reach that bloody perineum. You would have thought that Mother Nature would have planned this a bit more carefully. Maybe a flip-up perineum. But as I have already established, she is a cruel bitch, that one. Perhaps the product itself should have solved this problem, with a telescopic applicator that you extend downwards and dab on in a lady-like manner whilst gracefully lifting a leg onto a small ledge to facilitate the application. No. On all fours on the bed, face in the pillow, arm stretched round my big belly, bum in the air, grunting and pointlessly poking at various bits of my anatomy in the hope of hitting the target. Sod that. I imagine that a single application of the oil would not quite have the desired effect, but it will have to do. My arms and my life are too short for this.

HYPNOBIRTHING, DON'T MENTION THE P WORD (WEEK 31)

Mike and I attend our third session of hypnobirthing. We are well into the swing of it now, practising every night and knowing not to catch each others' eyes in the session when Bosoms comes out with her little pearls of wisdom.

The group are discussing natural birth. Bosoms mentions those African women who are always cited in these arguments. The pregnant ones who spend all day in the field, digging or chopping down trees or lifting mountains or something, then quickly squat down, pop out a baby, pick up their axe and carry on where they left off. Look, she says, all those women do it without feeling pain or needing pain relief. Funnily enough, Bosoms fails to mention that the death rate is ten times higher there than in the developed world. Well, why let a small thing like thousands of dead babies spoil an ill-informed argument?

Bosoms warns us all early on that there is to be no mention of pain. Even mentioning the word could bring on huge great spasms of the stuff. Okay, I exaggerate. But there is a hilarious resistance to this particular elephant in the room ("Excuse me Bosoms, there is a bloody great elephant in here sitting on my foot and it is very painful". "DON'T mention the pain! Oh, and what elephant?").

Every time someone inadvertently mentions pain, which, given that this is a class about childbirth, is about every six seconds, there is a sharp intake of breath from Bosoms and the perpetrator casts around in a futile manner for a word that *means* pain, but *isn't* pain.

"Turn it into a positive," Bosom urges.

"Ermm...the pain will end soon?" suggests one girl.

"No, think positively!"

We all look at Bosoms, each of us knowing that we just can't think past the pain, but wanting to for Bosom's sake. It all becomes a bit painful. Oops, I mean, slightly uncomfortable.

I ask Bosoms for the hypnobirthing approach to lowering blood pressure. She quotes one of her gurus who has advice for such an ailment: eat lots of beef and plenty of salt, along with a lot of eggs. What? Plenty of salt? Salt, as in the small white grains of condiment that have been scientifically proven to contribute to high blood pressure? What a pile of salty shit. I am presuming that this expert is now dead, of high blood pressure, or high cholesterol, or else he may have been shot by a pregnant woman who was trying to cure her high blood pressure.

YOU DO THE MATHS

I have no idea why it is de rigeur to state the length of your pregnancy in weeks. There is a very handy unit of time that is much easier to work with, called a month, but no one in the medical profession has cottoned on to this yet. It used to irritate me when I enquired of pregnant women how far gone they were, to have a meaningless number of weeks thrown back at me. Twenty-two weeks? How the fuck long is that? Have the hormones affected your brain, love? Tell me in months, like any normal bloody person would. I can't be doing with trying to work out what that is in months. I am shit at maths. I knew maths and me were never really going to rub along the day that Mr. MacGregor told us we were going to be having a 'bit of fun' in the lesson and, taking his position at the blackboard, began to explain that in maths, it is theoretically impossible for one car to actually overtake another. There were thirty-three people in that classroom. And thirty-two of them were looking at the other one, with his beard, tweed and elbow patches (yes, Mr MacGregor was an uber-cliche when it came to being a teacher, from his slightly balding crown to his need-a-polish brogues) and thinking: what the bloody hell are you talking about man? This episode was closely followed by my maths exam paper being returned to me in class. Mr MacGregor slid it onto my desk. "Very...neat handwriting," he said with a weak smile. You know you are in trouble when your artistry as a calligrapher is the most notable thing about your maths prowess.

And yet. Here I am, sitting with a friend, saying, "Oh, I am thirty-two weeks." She looks at me blankly and I realise that I have been lured over to the dark side. I roll my eyes. "Divide by four, that will tell you roughly," I suggest, not attempting something so complicated myself in public, of course.

I'M NO MIDWIFE (SO PLEASE SHUT UP) WEEK 33

My life is one long series of blood pressure checks, with a little bit of eating, sleeping and Prawn dancing thrown in when I get a chance. Today, I am at the medical centre for another routine check. So routine, in fact, that it appears the cleaner in a blue zip-up dress is considered qualified enough to take it. Oh no, my mistake, it's a nurse.

Dumbo pumps away at the armband, studying the dial. Her eyebrows rise. She takes the armband off and with a cursory, "I just need to see a doctor," she leaves the room. There is only one person at this juncture who really needs to see a doctor, and it is not her. Dumbo reappears and checks my ankles. Yes, I have two of them. She duly frowns again. High blood pressure and two ankles: what is this curiousness? She disappears again. I am beginning to think that it would be quicker for me to go with her. Finally, she returns.

"Have you got a urine sample?" These days, I never leave the house without one, and I duly produce a fresh one from my handbag. One day I would really like to bring it in a wine glass so they can swirl it round appreciatively, hold it to the light, have a deep smell and say "well, look at the legs on that". But no, I have my specimen in a small plastic tube, into which she dips a strip of paper and waits for it to turn an appropriate colour.

It seems, today, to be causing Dumbo a little consternation, as she holds the dipstick up against the chart on the pot. 'Hmmm, Summer Meadow or Buttercup Mountain?' she seems to be musing as she holds the stick closer to the window to shed a bit more light on the matter in hand. Finally she speaks. "You've got protein in your wee. I'm going to call the midwife team," and she picks up the phone. She seems to know how to use it, which is a pleasant surprise, but, unfortunately, all the midwives are out, probably trying to find parking spaces.

Whilst I ponder the significance of the fact that I have protein in my wee, Dumbo tells me that she will get an urgent message to them and that they will call me this afternoon, which is about four hours away. It obviously hasn't occurred to her that I may benefit from being told what is going on. After all, when she is sweeping her sponge round the toilet rim, she doesn't have to explain herself to anyone else.

"So," I venture, "what do you think might be the problem?"

"Well," she says, and then utters those immortal words. "I'm no midwife but... pre-eclampsia."

Now, I've heard of that. Pre-eclampsia was the bit in all the pregnancy books that I had skimmed over, as that was a Bad Thing, and my pregnancy was only going to be filled with Good Things. She does not look like she is going to elaborate, and by this time I am feeling distinctly upset, so I just leave.

I go home and fill the next two hours with the only option left to me: furious Googling of pre-eclampsia. I find a website that has a helpful list of side effects, which starts with the meek and mild (swollen ankles, high blood pressure) passes through the mildly alarming (vision trouble) and ends up with a fear-inducing statistic that one in an alarmingly small amount of mothers with pre-eclampsia die. At which point, with tears in my eyes, I feel around my desk until I find the phone and dial the midwife.

I tell them who I am. "Oh yes, we were all just talking about you." Oh my god. I could imagine them, huddled round my case notes, one of them already on the hot line to the ambulance service. My blood pressure notches itself up to 'furious boil'.

"We don't know why we have been asked to get involved. Your blood pressure is a bit high, but really, there is no cause for concern. None at all."

"So, I haven't got pre-eclampsia?" I ask. (i.e. So I'm not going to die today, then?)

"Not even remotely".

I put the phone down and sink into my chair, relief washing over me. The thought of marching down to the doctor's surgery, wrapping the blood pressure arm band around the neck of that nurse and pumping until her eyes hit the far wall crosses my mind, but I think better of it. I wouldn't want to raise my blood pressure now, would I?

YAWN (WEEK 33)

I am tired. Sleep is getting harder. And it is SO boring when you are staring up at the ceiling at 3am with nothing to do. I don't get out of bed, as that would be admitting defeat – and it is possible I might just fall into a deep, resounding sleep at any second. I stare into the dark grey shadows and try and decipher where the ceiling ends and the wall starts.

Prawn gives me a kick, just to remind me he is here, and also awake.

"Are you awake?" I whisper in Mike's direction. There is just the sound of his breathing. That deliciously slow, deep breathing of one who is fast asleep and dreaming the dreams of the un-pregnant.

"Are you awake?" I repeat, a little louder this time. Still nothing.

"Are you awake?" I ask in a very loud voice as I lean toward his ear.

"Umph...what?" mumbles Mike.

"Oooh, good, you are awake after all. I can't sleep and I am bored."

I believe this to be a good example of the Pregnancy Prerogative, whereby actions that would, in an un-pregnant state, elicit a slap round the face or at least a severe reprimand, provoke nothing more than a roll of the eyes and a vaguely – if somewhat strained - sympathetic response.

HYPNOBIRTHING HOMEWORK

Seeing as we have paid quite a lot of money to attend hypnobirthing, I feel I should really get my money's worth from the CD and listen to it, as instructed, every day. The trouble is, it is narrated by an American woman, whose voice is so annoying I would rather listen to nails being scraped repeatedly down a blackboard whilst watching a West End musical on a loop.

She blethers on about the positive affirmations, a variety of statements designed to put you in the right, receptive and relaxed frame of mind to encourage a natural, pain-free birth. These range from 'you feel overwhelming love for your baby' to 'it slips out of you with ease'. The latter affirmation keeps making me picture a helter skelter-shaped cervix, all pink and glistening, with a little baby whizzing down it, arms aloft, shouting "weeeeeeeeeeeeeeeeeeeeeeee" as it pops out of me and onto a waiting foam mat – and whilst a small part of me would love to believe that simply thinking this will make it happen, I am not convinced that this will, in fact, be the case.

PACKING (WEEK 33)

I make a list of what I will pack in my hospital bag, taking notes from various books and websites to make sure there is absolutely, unequivocally, not a cat in hell's chance I will forget something. I decide not to actually pack the bag – it seems to be tempting fate – so I gather all required items and make a tidy little pile in Prawn's bedroom *next* to the bag. I ponder over the packet of breast pads, and can't quite believe that I will actually have a use for them. Ah well, I suppose I can always use them to take my make-up off, just so long as I don't use the sticky side by mistake. My nose inadvertently wrinkles at the pack of disposable knickers. They are quite truly the most disgusting item known to man (let me correct that: they are known to very few men. No woman in their right mind would volunteer to show a man their disposable knickers, it would ruin sex forever). You know it's not going to be good when you can scrunch them up into a tiny little ball and use them as a Brillo pad. They are white, made of mesh and quite unappealing. I stuff them at the bottom of the pile and try to think nice thoughts.

It may be a little early to be thinking of packing, but I am not one to leave it to the last minute. In fact, with only seven weeks to go, I think I may be cutting it a little fine as it is.

PACKING #2 (WEEK 33 +1 DAY)

It's no good. I know there is an unfinished job upstairs, and I can't concentrate. I go up to the nursery and pack my hospital bag. I then rewrite the bag list, including only items that I have yet to pack – those perishable essentials, like Marks and Spencer flapjacks.

I then go downstairs and print out three maps – the route to the hospital from home, the alternative route if there is bad traffic on the first route, and the alternative alternative route if there is a major incident, such as all the tarmac melting on both dual carriageways, or an escaped herd of angry buffalo blocking our way. There is no way on this earth I am giving birth in the back of the car.

THE NCT SESSIONS (WEEK 34)

I am somewhat reluctant to join the NCT, as its reputation as a slightly hardcore breast-feeding-is-best and natural-childbirth-is-your-only-option-unless-you-are-the-devil-incarnate organisation was a little off-putting. However, the idea that a) I might learn something useful about the impending birth and b) I might find some other women in the same rocky, unstable boat as me spurs me on. So I sign up for the intensive three-day course, inform Mike that he has to attend for two of the days, which he was obviously thrilled about, and hope for the best.

I do have a last minute worry that I will have absolutely nothing in common with any of the other seven women on the course, but looking round the room on the first morning, with all of them splayed out on a variety of chairs, birthing balls (like space hoppers but without the handles or silly face, which I personally think is a shame) and sofas, each with a huge mound of baby belly, I realise that we all have a hell of a lot in common and most of it is curled up in our wombs.

Our facilitator turns out to be nothing like expected, which is all good. She is lovely – crikey, she even has (shock, horror) a sense of humour. One of the first tasks is an exercise where we have a variety of women's internal 'bits' and we have to stick them onto a cross-sectional diagram of a woman's torso. It is very much like 'pin the tail on the donkey' but without the blindfold – although based on my knowledge, a blindfold couldn't have made me make a worse job of it. But luckily, we have a GP in our group, so when I suggest that the cervix is a collarbone and she gently corrects me, I just pretend I am joking and fan myself with a handy uterus as I laugh.

It becomes clear that if you have read a few pregnancy books, the NCT class isn't really going to teach you a huge amount. But that isn't really the point. Despite being together for such a short time, we are already coming together as a proper group, brought close through a heady mix of shared predicament (sorry, I mean pregnancies), the desire to validate what you are experiencing by talking to others, and not a small amount of good, old fashioned fear.

Another exercise involves choosing from an extensive list - which activities you are committed to keeping up once the baby is born. Our group soon identifies what we feel are the essentials: washing yourself, washing your clothes, sleeping and eating. There is more discussion on some of the other activities: I, for example, am not that wed to housework as a critical activity but take the point that there is probably a tipping point where household bacteria stops co-habiting with you and becomes the landlord, so that goes on the list. One of the girls is adamant that gardening should make it through to the final count, which, I have to say, I find curious. I have never had a baby before, but I am imagining that if you do get time to wash, eat and sleep then you are doing a fine job as a new mum – but gardening?

"Darling, come in from the garden now, it's four in the morning."

"Yes, in a minute, it's just that the baby is due a feed in ten minutes and these rhododendrons really need dead-heading."

I can't see it myself, but her insistence and the group's politeness means that bizarrely, according to us, gardening becomes an essential activity to carry out once our babies are born.

We soon move onto the nitty gritty of it all: pain management. There is a large chart documenting the escalating potency of the pain relief options that we could be offered in hospital, starting with nothing (what I like to call the Nutter's Position), through gas and air, all the way up to an epidural (or Little Shot of Heaven).

We have to consider where we would like to be on this scale. There is no passing of judgement at any stage, but it does seem that the higher you creep up the scale, the worse a person you become. I wonder if you have to start at the bottom when you are in labour and earn your stripes by valiantly trying everything until you reach the top, or if you could elect for an epidural straight off, as you fasten your nightie and hop onto the bed. My default position is right at the hard-core end, but the weight of peer pressure means I notch it down a couple of rungs, so as not to appear a completely terrible mother-to-be.

We are talked through all the possible side effects of the various drugs ('short-term paralysis, you say? Ooh, smashing') and left to ponder. Most of us ponder for five seconds then go "la la la la la la la la" really loudly in our heads to stop thoughts of childbirth making us go slightly mental.

Lunchtime provides a chance for us to all waddle off to a local eaterie. We provoke a few turned heads, with eight pregnant women (so what is that: a placenta of pregnant women? An irrational of pregnant women?) waddling over the zebra crossing'together. It is like our version of the Abbey Road cover, but with more foetuses and fewer flares.

We settle into the local Italian. Our waiter instantly looks nervous and asks how pregnant we in fact are. I think he is mentally counting how many hot towels would be required. He dissuades us in no uncertain terms from anything with chilli in, in case this causes the on-set of labour, then hands out the wine lists just to tease us. No one orders wine, despite most of us secretly wanting to. It is one thing to have the odd cheeky glass in the non-judgemental comfort of your own home, but to flout such stringent medical advice in public? I dare not, in case one of the group is a closet pregnancy-despot but hasn't shown her true colours yet.

Back in the NCT class we move onto another of the exercises, which involves a Caesarean section scenario. One of the husbands lies down and pretends to be the mother and other people are told to stand round him, all representing the different people involved in the operation. Bloody hell, it is a cast of thousands – with that many people I would hope they would throw in a chorus of 'sit down you're rocking the boat' or something. I lose track very quickly, as there seems to be an inordinate number of people there. Someone to cut, someone to lasso, someone to mop, someone to operate the crowbar, someone to stitch, someone to do jazz hands, someone to applaud. It might be worth noting that these might not be the actual medical roles involved, but it is close. It does make quite an impression for a few seconds, but then

I remember that my labour and childbirth are going to be Absolutely Fine, so there is really no need to worry about Things Going Wrong as that's what happens only to Other People.

At one point in the afternoon we are handed an A4 sheet with a colour chart of poo on it. Studying baby poo is quite an art, it turns out, and is like the acceptable version of reading the tea leaves. Who knew that baby poo could be green when all they drink is milk? Or it could be brown with green flecks (like poo-tweed) or indeed jet black. All fascinating scatological facts. Apparently, it is very useful to study your baby's poo as it is a reasonable indicator of health and well-being, which makes sense. I stash the handout safely as I fear I will be referring to it a lot. Which gets me thinking about a better way of disseminating this information in our technological age. What about an iPhone app? You could simply scroll up and down the colour chart on your phone, comparing the colour with the poo your baby has just squeezed out, getting an instant answer to 'is orange poo normal?' for example. And should the inevitable happen and you use the wrong finger to scroll, you just wipe the screen clean. It could be called the Poo App. No wait. How about the CrApp?

GP CHECK UP (WEEK 39)

I am in front of Dr Scatty again for a check up. The parking at the surgery is a little less difficult than at the hospital, but my blood pressure is still high. She checks my legs. A little more stubble than I would have liked to expose, but quite frankly, getting down there to shave is almost a physical impossibility these days.

"Your shins are a little swollen."

Most of me is a little bloody swollen, given my advanced state of pregnancy, the warm weather and my daily intake of fruit pastilles. I think there are two types of pregnancy shape: those women who look like they have swallowed a beach ball and a perfectly round belly sticks pertly from their torso whilst the rest of their body changes not one jot from their un-pregnant days; then there is the rest of us, whose bellies swell left, right and centre, along with most other parts of our bodies. I am most definitely of the latter camp. Even my ear lobes seem bigger.

"Strict rest, and come back in 24 hours."

Buggar.

GP CHECK UP (WEEK 39 +1 DAY)

Not Dr Scatty today – she probably forgot to turn up or lost her car or something. A friendly doctor takes my blood pressure twice, giving me a chance after the first one to breathe deeply and try to stop the glass cover on the pressure dial from exploding. It improves but not significantly. She prescribes immediate and total rest for three days, at which point I will need to be checked again. I have effectively been placed under medical house arrest.

Imagine my glee when I realise that this has coincided with the Ryder Cup. I have Doctor's orders to sit on my arse and do nothing and my favourite sporting event just happens to be streaming live and direct to my sofa. Oh, the serendipitous joy of it all. This somewhat lessens the potency of the voice in my head that keeps saying 'this isn't good, this blood pressure thing'. It is being shouted down by the one whooping 'Nothing to do but watch TV and enjoy the golf! Woo hoo! In the hole!'

I decide that I want to keep an eye on my blood pressure, to try and be proactive about my situation and Mike, the ever-thoughtful man that he is, comes back from the High Street with not one but two blood pressure monitors. Ooh, gadgets: this weekend is just getting better and better.

I prepare to take my pressure, thankful that there is not a brown cuff in sight but a rather fetching pale blue one instead and I use the full hypnobirthing repertoire to try and calm myself into a coma-like state. I make a note of the reading and turn my attentions back to the golf.

An hour later, when there is a lull in play, I idly check my pressure again and note it down. Forty minutes after that, when they start to eulogise about the technical challenges of the eighth hole, I take it again. A further fifteen minutes pass before I pick up the blood pressure monitor one more time and take a quick reading, then again five minutes after that. Before too long, I am practically mainlining pressure readings, I have run out of space on my piece of paper, I have lost track of who it was that just birdied the ninth and I am not even bothering to remove the cuff between each go. The readings are steadily increasing as quickly as I fret that they are not decreasing. This is ridiculous. Finally, I throw the bloody thing under a cushion, where it stays for the rest of the day.

GP CHECK UP (WEEK 39 +4 DAYS)

I enter Dr Scatty's room, picking my way between the boxes and open briefcase to find a chair near her desk. I notice she has a ladder in her tights again, but in a different place to before. How can one woman have so many laddered tights? I worry that I am missing a key seasonal fashion trend for a moment, until I realise that the ladders are more likely to have been inflicted by the office obstacle course.

One brown cuff reading later, my blood pressure is high but not alarmingly so. I offer, in the interest of being proactive in trying to help my condition, to have another week's total rest, but Dr Scatty assures me that won't be necessary. Damn her.

BREAST OF FRIENDS

The NCT group with assorted husbands and partners are back together for the final session. It is an evening meeting dedicated to breastfeeding. I approach it with a certain amount of trepidation. I am not sure about breast-feeding. In concept, it is absolutely fine, but I have had a sneak preview at the reality of it through family and friends and I know it can be bloody hard, bloody painful and well, sometimes, just bloody. The sensation of 'my milk coming down' feels like my nipples are being scorched off, so I sense that I may struggle with the actual breastfeeding. The fact that it is so frowned upon not to breastfeed makes me want to try it even less. Call it petulance (or bloodymindedness, or immaturity, or a hundred other ways to label what is in essence a flaw in my personality) but if everyone is telling me, persistently and with the assumed moral high ground, that I have to do it, then suddenly I am not that interested in it. I get that it is good for the baby, but if it makes you weep with nipple pain or sends you slightly doolally in the process, then I am not so sure it is a good thing. But I try to remain open-minded, or at least not blow raspberries during every break in conversation.

We have a specialist in breastfeeding to take us through the ups and downs of the process. After the introductions, I am expecting Breast Lady to get down to the detail quickly, but instead she pulls a laminated sheet from her bag and tells us she is going to read us a poem. This already seems like a bad idea from where I am sitting.

The poem is written from the baby's point of view, except of course, it is written from *baby's* point of view, as the 'the' was unnecessary in such cloying, clichéd rubbish. It is written on pink paper, which should have been enough of a warning to take a loo break right there. It is a plea from the baby to its new parents to treat it with love, respect and understanding, to cherish it and care for it. Well, thanks for that, Breast Lady, I am sure there is no one in the room who could have worked that out for themselves. The trouble is, as the poem progresses, read by someone who seems to have left her backbone hanging on the coat hook at home, in a voice half way between patronising and imbecilic, I find it terribly hard not to laugh. I spend most of it staring intently at my shoes and trying not to listen, for fear of some untimely guffawing, so I don't quite get how the poem ends. It should have been: "so just pass that breast over here and give me some milk, will you mummy?"

but I fear it wasn't.

Finally we move onto more useful things. Not long into the session Breast Lady pulls from her bag a life-size, knitted boob. I stare at it, astounded, not quite sure which question in my head should take priority. How did I not know before today that knitted breasts existed? Who exactly knitted that thing? ("Hi gran, I was wondering if you could knit something for me?" "Certainly love, do you need another scarf?" "Errr...not exactly...") Why would you choose beige as the most appropriate colour for a woollen simulated mammary gland? Can you buy that knitting pattern from John Lewis? If you want a pair do you make an identical one or make the other one slightly different in size to be more realistic? Is it part of a range – if so, can I take a peek at the crocheted vagina? Can I get one with a nipple ring? And can I have a feel? By the time I have finished pondering, she has dispensed with the knitted boob and imparted the associated learning. I obviously missed the point she was making but I'm not that bothered. The image of that beige knitted boob will live with me far longer than the learning ever would.

It isn't too long before there is another revelation to behold: the breast shell. Bloody hell, all these inventions I never knew about. It is like stumbling into Aladdin's cave, if Aladdin had been less bothered about treasure and more concerned with the breast-based accessories of a pregnant woman.

The breast shell is a handy little device that you tuck into your bra or hold in place to catch the drips of milk. Apparently, your nipples are not like a tap – if they leak, you can't call your friendly plumber to come and tighten them up. Well, you could, and I am sure he would oblige, but that is something completely different. I am still reeling from the thought that I am going to be leaking milk from my breasts – I hadn't really considered the actual mechanics of it all before in such detail and I have to say, it doesn't really appeal. Rather than let your milk soak into a breast pad, you could catch it in a breast shell and save it, like a rain butt for your tits. What a marvellous invention. I presume that wringing out a breast pad to retrieve the milk is frowned upon, so breast shells seem to make sense and I add them to my ever-growing list of things to buy.

We get a chance to ask questions. "Does it hurt?" is the opening gambit, to which Breast Lady replies no. I suspect that this could be a lie. "How do you know how much your baby has drunk?" is a thought I have not even considered, to which the answer is basically: you don't, as they could be a sipper or a guzzler. Helpful. Then comes the question of the evening, posed by one of the husbands: "Can you feed on both nipples at once?" We all fall silent, trying to work out if he could possibly mean what it seems he means, then desperately trying not to picture him drinking milk from his wife's breast whilst his baby suckles on the other. It turns out that he is thinking about if there were twins involved, but we nevertheless all feel a little queasy for a few minutes.

Breast Lady passes round some pictures of breastfeeding in action. Most are as expected, with a baby sucking on a breast from a variety of angles, but one shows the baby getting squirted in the eye with a jet of milk from a near-by nipple. Brilliant. Photographer to mother: "Hmm, these shots are a bit static, could you liven it up a bit?" "How's this?" as she squirts poor Jacob straight in the right eye with a milky stream. "And that's the money shot!"

I am quite impressed that I will soon be in possession of two milk-laser guns – it makes me feel a bit like a superhero. 'Catch the Adventures of Lactation Lady! She can squirt the enemy down from twenty paces! And with her titanium breast shells she is invincible!' Breastfeeding doesn't sound so bad after all.

THE END OF HYPNOBIRTHING (WEEK 36)

We are taught the last couple of hypnobirthing techniques by Bosoms, who is practically delirious in her assurance that we are all going to have the most amazing, pain-free and spiritual births - even the woman who has been told by her consultant she has a condition that means she will definitely be having a caesarean. We are all slightly less convinced – Christ, we are still using the word 'pain' inadvertently about thirty times a minute, so what hope is there for us?

We start to practise our techniques and despite feeling like total idiots doing it in public, Mike and I get into the swing of it and start relaxing with the best of them. The room is warm and all I can hear is the quiet murmur of hypnobirthing couples. I feel so relaxed...

It is short-lived, however, as the couple next to us are having what can best be described as a bit of a to-do. The husband, Good Cop, is reading his scripts with diligence, counting his wife, Bitch Cop, into a state of relaxation. Well, apparently not.

"You're counting too bloody fast," she hisses.

"Oh, right. One...two..." he starts again.

"Now it's too bloody slow." I start to un-relax as this conversation is fast becoming quite compelling. There is nothing more fascinating than other people's domestics, particularly when they are conducted in barely-restrained whispers.

After much tutting and inaudible muttering, they eventually move onto the balloon exercise. "Imagine a red balloon..." Good Cop starts in a gentle voice.

"For god's sake, you know I don't like red balloons," Bitch Cop snaps.

Now if Mike and I got onto Mr and Mrs, and I was asked which colour of balloon Mike dislikes, I have to say I would be hard pushed to know the answer, so I felt that Bitch Cop was being a tad unfair here.

"Okay...imagine a big blue balloon..."

"Big? It shouldn't be big! Does the book say it should be big? No. Just read what it bloody says." Bitch cop spits.

Mike and I are now fully tuned in. I am trying to peek at them through pretend-shut eyes and we are starting to giggle. The phenomenal bickering carries on a pace. After a good five minutes of this, I am starting to feel very sorry for Good Cop, who is doing a valiant job in the circumstances. I whisper to Mike that I might invite him along to our birth instead of hers, as I don't fancy the chances of him surviving otherwise, and Mike agrees. It is only a shame that I can't lean over and whisper to her belly "if I were you, I'd stay in there."

As a parting gesture, Bosoms hands round a Tupperware box. Ooh, lovely, I think, sweeties. But it turns out that it is her collection of crystals, and we should all take one to give us wonderful births. Phew. Who needs a bloody epidural when I've got a crystal?

CONGRATULATIONS ON YOUR ENGAGEMENT (WEEK 37)

The midwife prods and pokes my belly and announces that the baby's head is engaged. I feel a thrill of excitement – oh my god, this is real after all, I am going to give birth – then slight consternation as I realise I still have three weeks to go. But Frenchie assures me that there is still some way to go before I'll be able to see his hands poking out to give me a wave (I paraphrase slightly) so I go back to just being excited.

She informs me that Prawn is head down and to the left, which is a perfect birthing position. God, he's good that Prawn, you can't teach that sort of obedience. Frenchie then goes on to advise me that I should try and lie on my left side to encourage him to maintain this position so I duly spend the evenings on the sofa turned away from Mike and craning my head back to the TV, as well as sleeping on my left side (I use the term 'sleeping' advisedly). If this baby moves from this millimetre perfect docking position, it is not going to be my bloody fault.

On my return for a check up a few days later, I see a different midwife. She tells me that Prawn now has his back to my right – not so good. Her advice is to lay on my left to help him turn back again. I duly heed this advice, despite Prawn obviously not agreeing – every time I turn on my side he springs to life like an angry ferret trapped in a sack. Now hang on a minute – if laying on my left was best for when Prawn was laying left and he subsequently turned, how can laying left when he is on the right work as well? It is like one

60

of those incredibly annoying logic puzzles: If Midwife A can only tell lies, and Midwife B can only tell the truth, and Midwife C can only make it up as she goes along, who do you believe?

THE BIRTHING PLAN (WEEK 37)

The NCT lady and Bosoms both recommended writing a birthing plan. I sit down to compose one but come a little unstuck after I have written "birthing" and "plan" at the top of the page, so I scroll through a few fonts, have a play with the font size and merrily pass ten minutes being busy not writing my birthing plan at all.

Eventually, I do what I should have done to begin with and Google it, so that rather than my two words, I now have hundreds of the bloody things to choose from. I cut and paste selectively, emphasizing that I don't want unnecessary pain relief. I then delete this, type "lots of drugs please" then go back to requesting no pain relief drugs if possible. I am not sure what has happened to my brain. Considering I was adamant that I wanted all the drugs lined up on the edge of my hospital bed so I could snort / swallow / inject them almost simultaneously, I am now contemplating trying to give birth with just my will power and a handy image of a helter-skelter shaped cervix. I momentarily feel distinctly not myself. No pain relief drugs? Really? I try to really focus on the question, to see if I am kidding myself. No, it seems that I do want to try to give birth without pain relief. I am either stupid, or have taken leave of my senses, or am just not thinking straight. Hang on, I'm pregnant - I could be all three.

THE GREAT VITAMIN K DEBATE

I have to suspend completion of the birthing plan due to cluelessness about the vitamin K injection. Apparently, it is given to newborns shortly after birth in case they have a deficiency, usually as an injection. There are some nay-sayers about this, so I do a bit of casting about on the internet to help me find out what it's all about. The theory goes that you can have a choice. This, it seems, is NHS choice – which means that somewhere, on some policy document, or maternity manual, or post-it note, it is written that mothers can choose. Which in reality seems to mean that your baby tends to get injected and you get little say in it.

It only takes ten minutes reading the mums' forums to impart the fear of god in me about what seemed initially quite an innocent little injection and now seems like Satan's sweat distilled into a syringe full of horror, but quite frankly, the amateurs on the topic are ignorant, or scaremongers, or can't spell properly, and the experts all disagree with each other vehemently. I lay my head on the desk for a while and wonder what to do.

When I wake up and peel an errant post-it note from my cheek, I decide that I will not give Prawn the injection, but have him take oral drops. Phew. Decision made, and it only took an hour and a half.

DR SCATTY STRIKES AGAIN (WEEK 38)

I waddle into Dr Scatty's office and plonk myself on the chair. A few nice-ties later (such as me checking she is looking at the right patient's notes) I make it up onto the bed to be Doppled. She administers the gel and starts to cast around for the heartbeat, dropping the Doppler once in the process. I can only imagine the carpet fluff that is then subsequently being spread across my belly.

"I can't find a heartbeat," she says, frowning.

Oh for fuck's sake, not this again. "Have you checked the batteries?" I ask, but she just stares at me blankly.

"Hang on, I'll just put a bit more..." she squirts another large dollop of gel onto me and gets to work once again, sliding around back and forth. Finally, we hear it. Thank god for that.

She leaves me with a few paper towels to get rid of the gel and I ruefully think back to my private scan, where they have eight Oompa Loompahs to do this sort of stuff for you.

She takes my blood pressure – still high – yawn, my medical predica-ments are even starting to bore me – and I plod back to the car. It is as I am putting my seat belt on that I realise I have a huge blob of gel slowly running down my left trouser leg. I scrabble around for a scrunched up tissue in the glove compartment and wipe it off, only to discover that I have another large blob on my elbow. I am running out of tissue now, and the absorbency of a month-old tissue is not great to begin with, but I scrape it off the best I can. And then I find a further dollop on my shoulder. For crying out loud, how did Dr Scatty manage to get it there? I find a discarded Fruit Pastille wrapper and try to remove the gel with that. She didn't so much gel me up, as bloody ice me. Is it too late, with a fortnight to go, to request a different doctor for my pregnancy?

THERE'S NOTHING WRONG WITH A WIPE-CLEAN BIRTH PLAN

Much to the hilarity of anyone to whom I mention it, I now have a laminated birth plan. People seem to find this hilarious, and I am not entirely sure why. It seems eminently practical to me, although my logic goes a bit hazy when I start to question my motivation for laminating it: do I really think that the midwife will be holding it in one hand whilst extracting the baby from me with the other? Will it really be so close to the action that it needs to be wipe-clean?

I would like to claim that it was the pregnancy brain that made me do it, but it is, I have to admit, something I was just as likely to do before I was pregnant. Hah, they'll all be laughing on the other side of their labour wards when they end up with placenta stains on their birthing plans.

UNDER PRESSURE (WEEK 39)

Another midwife check up. She takes my blood pressure and the news is not good. I have reached the critical level, meaning that she has to hand me over to the hospital. I feel like some kind of prisoner on the run, finally being caught and turned over to the authorities, but without the running or the crime (if you discount my pregnancy dress sense, that is).

I go home in a panic, and can almost feel my blood reach a fast boil. I call Mike, trying to be okay about it but failing miserably, grab my hospital bag (for no good reason as there is no way I shall not be coming back home) and call a cab.

I arrive at the fetal monitoring unit hot, flustered and miserable. They hook me up to a blood pressure machine – god, I have to wear that brown cuff constantly - and they get a heart monitor going for Prawn while they're at it. With all that beeping and rhythmic squelching of Prawn's heart I feel like I have walked into the middle of a space invaders game. The tiny ward with maybe only eight cubicles looks to be near capacity and I lie back, trying to think calm thoughts, listening to the cacophony of bleeps and heartbeats coming from seven other machines all in close proximity to each other. The woman in the cubicle opposite has her machine turned to eleven and it is very irritating, like sitting next to someone on the train who is listening to very loud, percussion-heavy music on their headphones.

I feel knackered and realise that with all the stress, I have not had anything to eat since breakfast. I weigh up the possibility of asking a nurse about some food, then decide I might as well wait until hell freezes over and take my chances then.

After an hour or so, I am moved to a separate room, which I take as a bad sign whichever way I look at it – either my blood pressure is so high they are frightened I will explode so they are trying to contain the blast, or they are thinking of keeping me in. The latter is unthinkable, so I concentrate on counting the tiles on the ceiling, then try to make recognisable shapes out of the stains, then forget that and focus on trying to work out just how the hell that many stains got onto the ceiling in the first place.

Mike arrives, which instantly makes everything a thousand times better. I bring him up to speed with a summary of the situation: "I may explode so don't sit too near."

Then a Registrar arrives. By way of introduction he snaps on a pair of surgical gloves. As an icebreaker, I have seen friendlier gestures. I immediately dislike him – not only because we both know there is only one place those hands are going to end up, but also due to the fact that he exudes arrogance. It is as potent as a cheap aftershave and twice as nauseating and I feel very nervous all of a sudden.

Without more than a couple of words of dismissive explanation, Arrogant moves towards me and gestures for me to widen my legs. Like a petulant child, I move my knees apart a fraction of an inch – he had not given me a sufficient justification as to why he was about to have a rootle around in my vagina and I am not happy.

"You're not going to do a sweep are you?" I ask. Thank god for the NCT classes - this *was* something that I had learned. It sounded like a fairly benign housekeeping chore ("my, my, look at that dust under your bed, would you like me to do a sweep for you?" "Ooh, yes please, and a cup of tea wouldn't go a miss.") Not quite, it transpires. To encourage the onset of labour the midwife or doctor can do a sweep, which involves sticking a finger up (or hand, or dust pan and brush, I am not quite clear) and passing it round the neck of the cervix.

I don't want the baby yet. It is not due for a week, I have not had time to pack my Marks and Spencer's flapjack and more to the point, I am going home this evening. End of.

The question provokes a barely disguised roll of the eyes from Arrogant, who gets down to business without a further word. Now, I have no idea if he did a sweep. Quite frankly, he could have got his Dyson out and had a hoover round in there, or laid a bloody patio, I have no idea. But he has a quick word with the midwife, throws his gloves in the bin and leaves.

I was already miserable and Arrogant has now really pissed me off. Okay, he may have been having a bad day. In which case, he can take a ticket and join the back of the bloody queue; I am way ahead of him on that one. No one forced him into a branch of medicine that means he spends all day with his hand inserted into the most private part of a woman's anatomy like some gynaecological glove-puppet-master and quite frankly, he should just bloody well cheer up a bit.

The midwife, who is lovely - though not difficult to have an astounding bedside manner when compared to Arrogant - informs me that I am to be staying in that night, and they would review me in the morning. I react to this news the way any pregnant woman would. I burst into tears.

ON THE WARD

At the very least I was hoping that I would be staying in that same room – one bed, plenty of space, a toilet. Oh no no no. That must have been the teaser room, to make me feel that actually, staying in for the night wouldn't be so bad. Instead, I find myself in a small communal ward.

Mike and I do a few minutes of looking on the bright side – "oh, great, a TV" "at least there is no one else on the ward at the moment, so that's good," "look, you've got a window! What a nice white pillow," then settle down into trying not to look too miserable.

Kicking out time for Mike is at eight, and so I decide I will get myself an early night.

THE FIRST NIGHT

I am not sure what the protocol is in terms of leaving the cubicle curtains open but I know there is no way I can sleep without them closed. As it transpires, it isn't the position of the curtains that is the problem. The bed is tiny and hard as a bloody plank. It may be ungracious to complain about the furniture in the NHS, and I wasn't expecting a luxury double divan with warmed sheets and a double-sprung mattress, but flipping heck, that bed is uncomfortable.

Having been warned by all and sundry that hospitals are kept at just below boiling point for most of the time, I had sensibly packed my lightest pyjamas. What I hadn't factored in was the air con on my ward – the window doesn't shut properly and through the huge gap between window and frame creeps an icy blast. I am freezing.

Add in the fact that the corridor a stone's throw away, down which the midwives' sensible shoes stomp every three minutes, coupled with scurrying couples entering and leaving, along with the door to the labour ward which, every time it opens, allows a partial scream or a snippet of an agonising moan to escape, and sleep is totally beyond me.

I am so desperate for a kip by 1am that I actually start to count sheep. But the sheep can't concentrate due to the noise and the cold and they all bugger off into an adjacent field.

HOSPITAL, DAY 2

I am just dropping off to sleep when the midwives decide it is morning; I get woken up at some ungodly hour feeling absolutely shit and I shuffle off for a shower. The bathrooms are a sight to behold. On every horizontal surface little pots of urine are scattered, like the medical version of pot pourri: everyone is giving samples like their lives depend on it.

Having completed my ablutions, I wait for the breakfast bell. When it rings, the occupants of the labour ward all make their way slowly to the serving room, like a herd of slow moving cows, where we feast upon the delights on offer. A bowl of cereal with warm milk, or some square items that have been chopped from one of the hospital beds. Oh no, my mistake, it is toast. How they managed to get it quite so hard and quite so cold is a mystery, but I take a slice and return to my bed.

A midwife appears to start the day's monitoring. Approximately three seconds into our conversation I ask when I can go home, to which she makes a non-committal non-promise. My blood pressure taken (unsurprisingly high), I am then hooked up to the baby heart machine. It is quite amazing that someone has invented a machine clever enough to track a tiny heartbeat whilst still in the womb. Unfortunately, it seems that their inventiveness was all used up on the main event.

"Right, so we have the monitor all designed, and it works a treat."

"Yep, all good. Heartbeat coming through loud and clear."

"Jolly good indeed. So, job done?"

"Errr, not quite."

"Oh buggar, I was about to go down the pub."

"Well, the monitor needs to stay on the woman's tummy for up to thirty minutes at a time. How is the sensor supposed to stay on?"

"Bollocks. That's a tricky one...errr, sellotape? No, that won't work. Let's think...nope, nothing comes to mind. Oh sod it, get some elastic strapping and fashion a buckle out of...errrr...here, this paper clip. That should do the trick."

It is like some comedy pair of braces with a hair trigger. When the midwife finally finds a position on my hillock of belly where she can pick up the heartbeat, she positions the strap around me (I would say around my waist, but I haven't seen my waist for many, many months now) and clips it in place - but if either of us breathe, or a woman in the next ward sneezes, off it pings. The midwife gives it a few valiant attempts, trying really hard not to swear in front of the patient, then sighs.

"Here, put your finger here," she says, nodding at the clip. Obediently I do as I am told, waiting for her to adjust it again. But instead, she walks off. So I spend the next half an hour with my forefinger pressed against the strap clip, my hand slowly going numb.

Finally, a midwife returns and unstraps me, and whilst I painfully try to encourage a little bit of blood to flow back into my finger, she studies the print-out from the heart monitor, a huge long curly receipt-like piece of paper with a wiggly line down the middle, that spirals its way almost to the floor.

"Hmmm, you have a lazy baby."

Now just hang on a minute. A lazy baby? How dare she. Prawn is certainly not lazy, I can bear testament to that with all the nocturnal kicking he does.

"He doesn't have a very strong heart beat," she adds, just in case I am not feeling bad enough.

I think perhaps Prawn is just so busy knitting himself some eyebrows that his heartbeat is not as active as it could be. Give the Prawn a break.

"Are you taking any drugs?"

"No," I reply sulkily, still not having forgiven her for insulting my foetus. But I bloody wish I was.

THE PLUMBER'S WHISTLE

I get a new style of bedside manner today. A midwife comes into my cubicle to join a colleague of hers, who is unstrapping me from the baby heart monitor and doing my umpteenth blood pressure check. As they move to the next cubicle, drawing the curtain behind them, she asks her colleague what my BP is. The first midwife checks her notes and tells her. The second midwife, let's call her The Whistler for arguments sake, lets out a long, drawn-out, low whistle, exactly the sort you get in response to telling a friend you've just paid £9,000 to have your heating overhauled, or the sort that plumbers give you when you ask them if they could possibly get that tap fixed by three weeks on Friday. A sort of a disbelieving, well-I-never, you-have-to-be-kidding, kind of response. Quite frankly I am not sure that this was part of the midwives' training. I can't imagine the chapter on 'Bedside manner' including a para-graph about either a) talking about a patient whilst still in their earshot or b) a plumbers whistle needing to be perfected before qualification is granted.

Perhaps no one had ever disabused her of the childhood belief that if you can't see someone – say, when you have stood behind the lounge curtains – they are not actually there. I was highly irritated. No change there then.

HOSPITAL, DAY 3

"Can I go home today?"
"We'll see."

BLOOD PRESSURE PALAVER

I have my blood pressure taken on a very regular basis. Whilst each check doesn't take long in itself, the entire pantomime seems to take forever. A midwife turns up at my bedside.

"Right, I'm here to take your blood pressure." She looks around on the off-chance a monitor will miraculously appear. "Oh, I'll just find a machine."

Her departure can last anything from five minutes to three quarters of an hour, depending on a complex series of events, including: the location of the machine, whether it is currently in use and whether the midwife is due a tea break.

Finally, the midwife reappears, wheeling the monitor to my bed. She cuffs me and starts the machine going. Nothing.

"Hmmm. Batteries are probably dead," she says and rolls her eyes.

Bloody hell, does the whole of the NHS run on sodding batteries? We are not in the middle of a field, there are power sockets not ten inches from my bed, so why does it run on batteries?

Off she goes to hunt another machine down. It appears that there are three blood pressure machines in the entire hospital, one of which we have already established is out of batteries, leaving two machines. I imagine the midwife storming into intensive care and yanking a cuff from a patient. "Sorry love, our turn."

HOSPITAL, DAY 4

"Can I go home today?"
"Don't ask me love, I'm just the tea lady."

SLEEP, SLEEP, WHEREFORE ART THOU SLEEP?

I feel like total shit. But I have found out what NHS actually stands for: No Hope of Sleep. I haven't slept for more than about two or three consecutive hours since I arrived. It is at this point that I wish my friend's advice about stockpiling sleep had been true, as I would have cracked open a six-pack right then and there.

Last night I *had* been asleep, sleeping the sleep of someone who knows it won't last and can never quite forget that one wrong move will send me toppling off my bed-plank and onto the floor before you can say "squashed Prawn", when I am awoken by a shout.

"BEV?" shouts one of the midwives, right outside the open door to my bit of the ward.

"BEV?" Shouty wails again, louder this time so she really gets her screeching voice bouncing off the walls.

Bev doesn't answer.

"NATALIE, HAVE YOU SEEN BEV?" she yells. Natalie's reply is not given at 3000 decibels, so I don't hear it.

"BEV?" Shouty shouts again.

Bev has obviously left the country, otherwise she would have heard Shouty bawling.

"BEV?"

For chrissakes. If Bev does not make herself known to Shouty soon, I will bloody well get up and track her down myself.

And that was the end of my sleep for that night.

SLOP

The food at the hospital is a revelation. Not in a good way but in the way that you might find out you have a serial killer living next door to you. The first evening –well, I say evening, they serve dinner at about 4.30pm, presumably so that they can get all the washing up done before Eastenders starts – I am hopeful. Pork hot pot is on the menu – not winning any awards for presentation, but I am starving so forgive them a missing sprig of parsley or two. Tucking in, I find the potato topping rock hard and yet curiously soggy. They must have commissioned years of research by a top culinary physicist on that topping in order to create a hard potato / mushy potato duality that is usually only found in waves and particles. The pork (let me clarify as that suggests a multiple: there is one solitary piece of pork on my plate the size of pencil sharpener) closely resembles carpet underlay in taste and texture. Soggy onions make up the rest of it, flopping forlornly round in a brownish liquid that could have been resold on its own as the original primordial soup.

Ever the optimist, I try two further dishes: firstly, pasta with broccoli in a cheese sauce. This has fewer ingredients than I have fingers, how can they possible muck it up? The first forkful confirms that yes, it is possible to make broccoli pasta inedible, by making both the pasta and the broccoli *exactly* the same texture, reminiscent of slippery, soft rubber. It is truly rank.

Finally, one dinnertime, I try a vegetable country pie. I presuppose lots of vegetables, freshly dug from the countryside, cooked to perfection in a tasty and healthy broth. Obviously the lack of sleep is affecting my critical faculties. It is actually a spadeful of countryside, dug up, chucked in a pot with some water, and boiled until it resembles a shitty puddle.

Ah well, I think, as I push my country catastrophe to one side, I shall console myself with some ice cream. Sorry, did I say ice cream? I mean expanded lycra soufflé. In its former life it had been cavity wall insulation, I swear. I have never, ever in my entire life, not finished eating a portion of ice cream, but I push this to one side immediately. Curiously, in the hour I stare at it on my tray, it doesn't actually melt.

The dinner bell soon reminds me of the death knell. All it needs is the Grim Reaper to be wielding the spatula behind the counter and the food would do the rest. So I end up eating vicariously through Mike, who regales me of his dinners and brings in anything that will survive the journey in a bit of tinfoil.

Now I am not ill, just pregnant. But it does make me think about the other residents of the hospital, who are in various states of poor health. How the hell is this slop supposed to aid the healing process? Granted, the ice cream could probably shore up a nasty flesh wound, but really. I wouldn't feed it to next door's cat. Actually, I *would* feed it to next door's cat, as it keeps pooing on our bloody garden and that would be a sure-fire way to kill it. Jamie Oliver, you are wasted transforming school dinners. Get yourself to this hospital and make this food edible before everyone dies. Christ, I'd even welcome in 'show me your pepper and tomatoes now, dears' Ainsley Harriet.

MIDWIFE SPEAK

As this is my fourth day on the maternity ward, I feel I am finally getting to grips with Midwife Speak.

"I'll just hook you up to the baby heart monitor for 20 minutes." Translation: "I'll come back in two hours when your bum's gone numb, your limbs have all seized up and you are about to wet yourself."

"Sure, I'll get it for you now." Translation: "I will forget you ever existed as soon as I draw your curtain."

"The doctor will see you at 3.30." Translation: "Doctor? What Doctor?"

"Well, everyone is different so it's hard to be precise." Translation: "I have no fucking idea. "

"I'll check on you again in fifteen minutes." Translation: "No I won't."

"This machine is faulty." Translation: "Has anyone got any batteries?"

"You're our number one priority for a bed on the labour ward." Translation: "You are now the only one left waiting to get into the labour ward."

"This won't hurt." Translation: "Prepare yourself, you are about to experience pain the likes of which you have never before encountered."

AN INDUCEMENT

A woman takes residence in the bed next to me. How dare she? This is my ward. We swap notes: it seems that she is here to be induced, and the midwives get down to business swiftly. As there is absolutely nothing else to do whilst Mike is not here, I listen closely to what is going on. So whilst I do not see the induction process with my own eyes, I certainly hear it at close quarters in Dolby quality surround sound through the bay curtain as she experiences it. Imagine listening to a horror film with your eyes closed. When she has the pessary inserted she yells like a banshee and moans like a...well, a pregnant woman. Her mother is on hand to dispense helpful advice and encouragement – directly after the pessary insertion and associated scream-ing, the mother says "Well, if you think that was painful, you just wait." Nice. Everyone needs advice like that when they've just had someone's hand thrust up their vagina. Listening to the whole episode makes me wince numerous times and once I have forcibly uncurled my toes, I thank my lucky stars that I am not being induced.

I have an afternoon visit from the consultant, who turns up at the foot of my bed flanked by his bodyguards - sorry - midwives, who are carrying all the paperwork for him. He asks me how I am. "Oh, super," I lie, as he lifts my trousers and gives my shins and ankles a good, hard poke.

"Yes," I laugh breezily, "they are a little swollen." My feet are so huge they look like inflated Marigolds and I am just thankful that my trainers have full-frontal Velcro openings, otherwise I'd have to resort to wearing shoe boxes.

The consultant refers to my notes. "You possibly have mild pre-eclampsia," he tells me. "So I think we should induce." Which really means: "You have been cluttering up my ward for far too long, it's about time we got rid of you." It is at this point that I realise there is no way I shall be going home, not until I have Prawn on the outside rather than the inside. I feel desperate that my hope of returning home a pregnant woman has finally been well and truly dashed, but also a tad relieved that at least I will be leaving this hellish stasis for something else. I don't want to think too closely about what this something else is, and employ the 'la la la' technique for a while until I am distracted by the fact that the consultant has subsequently moved on and I am lying there alone, trousers hoisted up attractively round my knees.

My lucky stars have obviously fucked off on a day trip to Margate, as half a day on and I am starting the induction process. The midwife turns up with my pessary, explaining that she will be inserting this into my vagina and that I should relax. Yes, I find I am at my most chilled out when a stranger is rummaging around in my cervix. But I remember a breathing technique from hypnobirthing and remarkably the process is totally pain-free. She does have the boniest hands known to man, which means they are thankfully small and easy to insert, even if it is a little like having a bag of protractors pushed up there, but on the whole I give it a nine out of ten for lack of pain and five out of ten for artistic impression.

Mike and I are now on tenterhooks as things are Definitely Happening. Well, actually, nothing at all is happening, but surely it wouldn't be long now as I have officially been induced. We go for very slow waddles around the hospital grounds, read the mountains of papers that Mike brings in, do the crossword, I have a little cry now and then (I have no idea why, but it passes a bit more time) and generally try not to think about what is coming next. I still cannot quite comprehend that, at some point soon, I will not only have a baby pop out of my womb, but I will be a mummy and Mike will be a daddy and we will have a little person who is utterly dependant on us. It is just too weird to contemplate.

BOSCASTLE REVISITED

I hop (relatively speaking) off the bed to go somewhere when all of a sudden my waters break. Now, I had hoped, somewhat erroneously it turns out, that there would be teaspoonfuls of fluid to be discharged - that was the rumour. As my pants alarmingly fill up with amniotic fluid, I realise that *teaspoons* really doesn't cover it. Mike jumps into action to find a receptacle that will stop the ward becoming awash with the contents of my womb and to locate some method of trying to mop up what has already escaped. As I whip off my trousers and pants with an agility usually quite beyond someone who is nine months pregnant, Mike returns with an armful of paper towels and a small kidney shaped bowl which I place on the floor and straddle, legs unceremoniously apart, naked from the waist down. Well almost - it is at this point that I realise I have forgotten to remove my socks, which are now soaking wet and adding a certain cold squelchiness to the proceedings.

And still it comes. Any minute now, it will stop, I reassure Mike, uncon-vincingly. We get the giggles at the absurdity of the situation, as Mike throws down more and more paper towels, only to have them disappear seconds later into the soggy pile beneath me. I stand, socks soaked, in a puddle of my own waters.

Fortuitously, at that moment, Calamity Student Midwife arrives.

"My wife's waters have broken," says Mike, gesturing toward me with a fistful of paper towels. I am partially hidden behind a half closed curtain and, without glancing at me, she turns round and leaves the ward, presumably to call for reinforcements (and an industrial flood pump). And still the waters come. It is starting to remind me somewhat of that Cornish village, Boscastle, whose river banks were breached in the floods of 2004, sending tons and tons of water crashing down into the village. I half expect to see camper vans, parked cars and a few crumpled tents bobbing into the corridor on a wave of my womb water.

Now here's a curious thing: text books say 'your waters break'. Break. As in a moment in time. As in: one moment, they are *not* broken, and then, whoopsidaisy, they are. As in: this mirror is not broken. Crash. This mirror is broken. Two distinct states, with the transition between them being measured in milliseconds. But not my waters. My waters break continuously, like a rolling mini-tsunami of amniotic fluid, and they continue to do so, for tens of minutes. Minutes that stretch on as nobody comes to help. Still we have the giggles, which isn't actually helping much, given that they are causing convulsive waves to fall into the kidney bowl, the meniscus of which is starting to strain at the rim.

I hear someone approach and give a sigh of relief, until I realise it is the tea lady.

"Cup of tea, love?" I grab the curtain in a vain (in every sense of the word) attempt to spare my blushes, or maybe hers.

I smile apologetically. "Err, no I am a bit busy at the moment. But I could offer you some water if you are running low?" I wonder briefly if it is in her job description to offer a cup of tea to every single patient, no matter what medical predicament she may stumble across (or wheel into). Perhaps her bonus is tea-offer related. As I wriggle my feet in my soggy socks, she leaves us to it, seemingly disappointed that there is no tea dispensing to be done. Twenty minutes pass and I wonder what the hell Calamity is up to.

Eventually she returns and looks with utter astonishment to find me astride a small bowl, standing in a large puddle with wet socks, *sans* trousers and pants, dripping. Her astonishment is a little confusing until she claims that she hadn't actually heard Mike say that my waters were breaking. I never got to the bottom of what she did actually hear, or what she had been doing in the meantime. Probably looking for batteries. She disappears again, promising this time to come back before the weekend.

With all the excitement, Mike and I have completely lost track of time and it is well past the eight o clock curfew for visitors. Stupidly I assume that seeing as I must be close now to Birth 'o' clock, Mike might be able to stay - but no, rules are rules. Forlornly, as my waters diminish to a dribble, I hand over my soaking trousers and pants with a reminder to him not to leave them festering in the bottom of the rucksack until next year, and off he goes. I cut a sorry figure, waving goodbye, still wet from the vagina down, waiting for the cleaners to come and sort out the small reservoir of baby soup on my bed and mop up the floor.

I am stuck. I can't really go padding about the ward with just wet socks and a tee shirt on, I can't sit down as the bed is soaked and whilst my waters have slowed down, there is still a definite occasional trickle happening, so that, if nothing else, my socks remain delightfully sodden. It is about now that the air con kicks in as darkness falls and the cold breeze from the faulty window does a good job of making me feel just super.

Ah! A brainwave. I fish around in my bag and pull out the Breaking Waters survival kit - a heady combination of disposable knickers and maternity pads. I put the pants on, trying not to think about how the stringy mesh feels as it scrapes against my damp skin, and position a pad (roughly the size of a single mattress) in place. At least I feel now like my socks have half a chance of drying out. For reasons only known to my heavily pregnant brain, it does not occur to me to remove them.

After another very long and moist half an hour of standing next to my sodden bed, the cavalry arrive and start operation Dry Out. There is nothing more embarrassing than watching two strangers clear up your bodily fluids. They unfurl what can only be described as a sanitary towel for beds, a huge long padded affair (disappointingly without wings) so that my leakage will be contained.

On their departure I lie down and think that I ought to try really, really hard to get some sleep. I have had three nights of practically no sleep with terrible food, which I am guessing is not putting me particularly in the best state for childbirth.

I hunker down (gingerly) and lie there, damn exhausted and sure I will sleep. It is then that I realise I am in fact now lying in a small puddle of my own making. It is like trying to sleep in the damp patch of a post-coital bed, with none of the preceding pleasure and all of the grimness of the patch being able to regenerate itself whenever it looks like it might dry out. Nice.

STUPID 'O' CLOCK (DAY 5)

I must have finally resigned myself to sleeping on top of a large, wet sanitary towel, because the midwife comes to wake me up. It feels like I've only had a few hours sleep. "What time is it?" I ask groggily.

"It's one 'o' clock."

One 'o' clock in the bloody morning? Bloody hell, I *have* only had a few hours sleep. What sort of hellish time is this to be woken from a rare slumber? If my toes are not on fire or if the sky is not falling down I will be mightily pissed off.

Apparently, the next most unlikely thing has happened: there is a bed free on the labour ward, there is a midwife who is not busy or looking for a blood pressure monitor and it is my turn.

I call Mike, tell him to forget all thoughts of any more sleep for the foreseeable and then go and grab a shower (because perish the thought I might not be squeaky clean for my labour). Finally, it is happening.

SETTLING IN (2AM)

Mike and I enter the labour room and get prepared. The plinky-plonky, airy-fairy hypnobirthing music goes on, I try and get used to wearing a nightdress which I haven't done since I was about ten (there are places that a girl just does not want a breeze, thank you), and I hand over my laminated birth plan to the midwife. All credit to her; she doesn't laugh.

Then a nurse spoils the atmosphere by putting a drip in the back of my hand, which is blinking painful and then just weird so I don't look at it. I keep that hand as far away from the left side of my body as I can, as I am suddenly paranoid I shall give an involuntary spasm and knock the bulky contraption that is emerging from my skin. I feel excited, and slightly terrified, as I lie on the bed. The room settles into quietness, and Mike and I are trying to follow suit, but the palpable sense of anticipation and a strange feeling that the calm is teetering on a precipice, below which lies barely contained chaos, is making it a tad hard to be relaxed. The Syntocinon starts to flow into me with a curious and not particularly pleasant icy-cold sensation in my vein and they hook me, or rather Prawn, up to a heart monitor on the other side. I am well and truly tethered to the bed; so much for moving around freely and having an active labour. Don't get me wrong, I wasn't anticipating some light jogging or press-ups, but it would have been nice to stretch my legs occasionally. It is explained that they will gradually increase the amount of Syntocinon they are giving me, up to a maximum of 48 (I wasn't sure if this was parts per millilitres, bucketfuls or minutes, but decide I am probably best off not knowing) until the baby pops out, or words to that effect. So far, so straightforward. Mike and I start the Hypnobirthing techniques and the midwife pretty much leaves us to our own devices.

OH GOD, NOT HIM AGAIN (5AM)

All is calm in the labour room. Mike has hardly paused for breath whilst reading the hypnobirthing scripts (did I mention that I had laminated them?) and gentle contractions are well on their way. I feel fine. Prawn's heartbeat is still quiet, so every time someone comes to check on the read out, I pre-empt it with a resigned: "Yes, he's the lazy one." It is all very well having to make excuses for your child's behaviour, but doing so before he even emerges from between my legs is a bit galling.

Then Arrogant appears. Just sodding typical that he is on shift. He has lost none of his charm or bedside manner and snaps on a pair of surgical gloves to do an investigation. I have no idea what he is looking for, maybe he left his sense of humour in there the last time he visited.

He has a feel around, reminding me slightly of one of those game shows where the contestant is blindfolded and made to put his hand in a series of boxes containing random objects. "Errr...it's a hair brush..and this one is... oh crikey...a piece of steak?....Now this one...oooh, hang on, I think I know this...a cervix?"

"Not all the waters have broken," Arrogant says to the midwife. Apparently, I don't qualify to be part of this conversation.

Not all the waters are broken? You have to be kidding. It seems as if I have emptied the contents of a small swimming pool from my womb in the last ten hours - how much more can there be?

He then utters the immortal line that will be etched in my head forever: "Pass the hook."

If I had not been tied to the bed by a drip and a heart monitor, I would have run for my life at this juncture. The hook? All I can see in my mind's eye is an old, rusty coat hanger, straightened out then re-fashioned into a viciously sharp implement. Surely, whatever nastiness The Hook was designed for, there was never any need to christen it The Hook. What about the Stroker? Or, at worst, the Gentle Chafer?

The midwife explains to me that there is still a sac of amniotic fluid that has not burst, and The Hook is just the tool for the job. Oh good, I am so looking forward to this.

As the midwife searches for The Hook (please, please, don't let it be battery operated) I console myself with the thought that, if this is really painful, I can accidentally on purpose kick Arrogant in the face, or at the very least, crush his swarthy little head between my knees and blame a spasm of pain. As it transpires, the hook really should have been called The Soft Prodder, as

I feel very little apart from another bucket-load of water releasing itself onto the bed.

"There is meconium in her waters," Arrogant tells the midwife, who comes over to have a look. Hang on, I know this word...I think back to all those books I have read. Ooh, I know, I know...it's baby poo. Oh. That's not good, is it?

I suddenly can't swallow and forget about my contractions. Mike and I exchange glances, and look back at Arrogant and the midwife.

"Well," begins the midwife hesitantly, "I am not sure there is, actually."

I'm with the midwife. I can't see what's going on, but let's look on the bright side. Prawn's probably spilt his hot chocolate or something.

"Of course there is," Arrogant snaps back. I feel like waving my arms around in front of his face shouting "Cooo-eeee, I'm over here," as he seems to have forgotten I am still in the room, but resort instead to waggling my knees about. This is duly ignored and only provokes further baby juice to escape onto the bed.

Eventually, he turns to Mike and I. "There is meconium in your waters. I recommend a C-Section," he says very matter-of-factly.

Holy shit, a C-Section? We've only been going three hours...a C-Section? A C-Section? A C-Section? I instantly lose the ability to think past this phrase and look, panicked, at Mike. It isn't supposed to happen like this.

"Well?" asks Arrogant, looking at us both. Oh god, he wants us to make up our minds right now. We haven't even conferred. Can't we phone a friend? I want to cry but am so confused that I have momentarily forgotten how to. Mike and I look at the midwife.

"Well," she starts, diplomatically, "the consultant is due round soon, and there is no absolute urgency at this point...so why don't you talk it over with him?" I feel like crying all over again, out of sheer relief. The midwife has waved a get-out-of-jail-free card and we snatch it with both hands. I want to hug her but am restrained by my medical manacles.

Arrogant has obviously heard enough. He yanks the gloves from his hands and leaves without another word.

The midwife, Mike and I watch the door slowly swing to a close, and have a simultaneous, single thought: Wanker.

AND SO IT CONTINUES...

I have no concept of time. There are no windows in the labour room and the only clock is behind me on the wall, involving far too much effort and shifting of medical apparatus to warrant a look. Was that a minute that just passed, or an hour? I consider this briefly, but decide no news is good news and focus on those balloons instead, swelling and releasing, swelling and releasing. We are still hypnobirthing like our lives depend on it, and although they are steadily pumping more Syntocinon into me, I am calm and in control.

The consultant has been and gone, dismissing all talk of a C-section, and I imagine myself sticking that bloody Hook up Arrogant's nostrils and telling him never to darken my vagina again. The contractions are getting harsh and, in between balloons, my mind wanders into pain relief drug thoughts. Damn those midwives, they have obviously taken my birthing plan to heart and don't want to offer me anything. Asking for it seems like I will have failed in my task, but if it's offered, well, that wouldn't count. It's like chips from someone else's plate: everyone knows they don't contain any calories, it's a guilt free option.

We are through a shift change now, and a new midwife joins us. On entering the room she is slightly taken aback by the lack of shouting, groaning and general fuss from the bed, so we explain the Hypnobirthing and she leaves us to it.

At one point I force Mike to go to the canteen to get something to eat, threatening a thousand cuts by a laminated Hynobirthing script if he doesn't leave. He is not, I am sure, the first person who has had to be threatened with physical harm to make him eat there, but reluctantly, he does, and I tuck into a flapjack in his absence. Despite not having eaten since...well, a long time ago, I am not actually hungry. I am very slightly nauseous, which could be just a heady mix of excitement, anxiety, the Syntocinon and the after-effects of dealing with Arrogant, but some part of me (my stomach, I would guess) is telling me to eat something.

The midwife then informs me that it is time to go for a wee. Personally, given that I am lying in my own amniotic fluid, I would be perfectly happy to save everyone the hassle and just pee myself then and there, letting the four foot sanitary towel prove its worth, but no.

With much difficulty and cries of 'hang on dear, your arm is wrapped round the drip' and 'wait a second, the heart monitor is caught in your hair' I manage to get upright. Sorry, did I say upright? I meant bent over like some arthritic eighty year old. Myself and the midwife then start the long, slow procession to the toilet. I cling onto the drip stand and take tiny, laboured steps down the corridor. Every time a contraction arrives, I am forced to stand still and just wince my way through it. I promise myself each time that I will not stop when the next one comes, but it is impossible to make my legs work when it does appear. I am aware in my peripheral vision of doors opening and closing to other labour rooms, and I stare intently ahead, desperate not to see what is going on, but I can't stop my eyes having a quick flit sideways, which does nothing to lighten my mood. I swear there is a cow bellowing in one room. And someone has spilt rather a large amount of tomato ketchup in another. Step by step, inch by inch, the toilet door gets nearer. Please don't let there be someone in there - that would be too much to bear. My midwife has the patience of a saint. If I were her, I would be compelled to give me a little nudge to chivvy me along a bit, or pull my drip along in front of me, employing the successful 'carrot' incentive to make me get a shift on.

I finally arrive and sit on the toilet, knackered from the marathon six metres that I have covered. It is a shame that I pee enough wee to only fill a thimble, as after that herculean effort I am hoping for something more along the lines of an elephant relieving itself, complete with a copious amount of steam and splashback, but a tiny dribble is the only reward. Christ, I really could have just let that go on the bed and no one would have noticed. Already, I note, my dignity seems to have packed up and left in disgust.

Three days later (or some possibly shorter amount of time, I have no idea) I make it back to my room and get strapped back up to the heart monitor. It is reassuring to be rejoined by Prawn's heartbeat, that slightly squishy rhythm from inside me.

Mike returns shortly after and regales me with tales of hard jacket potatoes and rancid coffee, which passes some time, and then it is back to the Hypnobirthing.

YOU COULDN'T GET A GOLF BALL UP THERE (8AM)

The consultant arrives to check my dilation. I have been in labour for six hours and feel like the end should be near. I am bloody tired and it hurts (I think these are both what are called in the trade 'sodding great understatements').

He gets down to business to check out what is going on and to find out how dilated I am. I pray repeatedly to the god of wide openings for at least eight centimetres. I could probably just about cope with seven. Come on, my lovely helter-skelter cervix, don't let me down.

"You are two centimetres dilated," he announces. Fuck. Two centimetres? Two? Twenty bloody millimetres? Are you sure you are not measuring my poo hole by accident?

"So technically, you are not really in labour." The consultant means well, but I am on the verge of repeating those immortal words 'pass the hook' so I can gouge his eyes out and stick them up his nostrils, which are about as wide as my cervix is at this point. I have just experienced six hours of hard labour and really, I haven't even started.

Weirdly, seeing as over the last four days my tear ducts were capable of being triggered by pretty much anything, from a storyline on the regional news about a cracked paving stone to a very hard crossword clue, I don't cry. It is probably a subconscious attempt to conserve whatever energy I have left. We talk it through with the consultant, and Mike and I decide to keep going. After all, six hours isn't long. Although try telling that to my pain receptors.

GAS AND AIR

Shortly after my spectacular two centimetre dilation was confirmed, I ask the midwife for some gas and air. I can safely say I have just about had enough of the pain and want some help. Now.

I breathe deeply from the snaking tube of loveliness, waiting for a little less pain. I breathe some more. And then a bit more. I am beginning to feel a little light-headed from all this excessively deep breathing, which is maybe what this gas and air thing is all about, as there is definitely not one jot of difference to the contraction pain I am experiencing. I feel cheated. I waited six hours for this? I persevere, but really, it is ridiculous. I might as well have been sucking on an empty toilet roll.

Using gas and air does have some benefit though, as the mouthpiece is fantastic to bite down on when the contractions arrive. And god do I bite down on it. It isn't long before I have toothache and jaw ache. I mentally add it to the ever-growing list of pain: cervix pain from the contractions, backache from god knows what, bum-ache from laying down too long and eye-ache from not having slept for three nights. It is quite a little collection I am gathering. All I need is toe-ache and a twinge in my chest and I will be able to shout 'house' and claim my prize.

KEEP IT PUMPING (10AM)

I look at the digital read out of the Syntocinon levels and the midwife turns it up once more. I dread it every time they do this, as the contractions get that little bit more painful and a tiny bit more frequent, but seemingly not enough to trigger my cervix into opening its hatches and letting Prawn out. The level is nearing 48 which the midwive had informed me was the maximum dose. At the point at which we actually reach the maximum, I have no idea what happens. Perhaps The Plunger is called into action.

It is around this juncture that I realise the mouthpiece to the gas and air machine has become unattached and for the past god only knows how long, I have been sucking hard on nothing more than oxygen. It is a testament to the ineffectual nature of the gas and air that it took me so long to notice. Not long after, I dispense with it all together.

ON AND ON

It could be day, it could be night. I have no idea and I am not sure that I care.

STILL HERE (12PM)

We are on our third shift change and yet another midwife takes the reins. She is being shadowed by a trainee. I am annoyed by this, but have no idea why. I am certainly not going to say anything, because a) talking takes too much brain power and energy and b) if I have learnt one thing in the last ten hours, it is that the midwife in the labour room is my best friend and it is more than a little foolhardy to jeopardise this relationship with an irrational hatred of a woman with blonde plaits.

However, it isn't long before I realise why I am annoyed with Plaits. The midwife announces that she needs to take some blood. At this late stage, I am not sure what they are testing for. Perhaps the midwife feels a little under utilised, what with Mike and I getting on with the Hypnobirthing and not taking any notice of her, and so decides it would be a good way to get involved and pass the time.

Plaits comes over to take the blood, under the somewhat hands-off supervision of the midwife. Unlike most times I have blood taken, this time I do not get sweaty hands or fear of the needle – after all, I have been having chemically-induced contractions for what feels like a week – the pain of a needle slipping into my skin in comparison to that will be a mere whisper of a sensation. Wrong. Wrong wrong wrong wrong wrong. Rather than the more conventional technique of finding the vein visually, picking the entry spot carefully, putting the needle in, then taking the blood, Plaits seems to be free-form injecting. She sticks the needle into my arm immediately, and only when it is good and submerged does she start prodding around for a vein. Good god it hurts like buggery.

She looks up at me and smiles apologetically. "Nearly there."

Nearly where, exactly? My bloody armpit?

But on the up side, I don't think about my contractions for a whole minute and a half.

STILL HERE. STILL.

Oh fuck, this can't still be happening, can it?

MAXED OUT

Mike is practically hoarse from the continuous reading of the Hypnobirthing scripts. He dives out very occasionally for a wee or a drink, or to phone my parents to keep them updated with more 'no news' but he has hardly stopped in eleven hours. I keep trying to persuade him to take a longer break and that I will be fine without him, but luckily, he sees through my lies and stays (It must be the fact that I shake my head vehemently with a look of panic in my eyes as I ask).

The midwife cranks up the Syntocinon again. Christ, we are nearly on 60! How come we have broken through the magical ceiling of 48 without so much as a murmur, let alone the emergency alarm being sounded? Now I am concerned that my body is nine parts Syntocinon and one part pain. Can you overdose on this stuff? What if...another contraction strikes and all thought stops, apart from one: fuck, fuck fuckity fuck.

OUCH

Question: On a scale of one to ten, how knackered am I? Answer: One hundred and ninety three.

WHERE DO I SIGN? (3.30PM)

Thirteen and a half hours. I have never done anything in my life for this consecutive number of hours, apart from breathe. It is time for another consultant check and he gets out his highly technical precision cervix-measuring instrument (otherwise known as fingers).

Okay, after this length of time, I must be nine and a half centimetres. In fact, I will be surprised if he doesn't make eye contact with Prawn whilst he's down there.

"Hmmm, about three centimetres."

I am numb. No, I am not numb in fact, as another contraction hits. Bollocks. I bloody wish I was numb. I think it is just my brain that is numb. It is flashing up 'Does not compute' every time I try to feed in the information that I have dilated one more centimetre in the last seven and a half hours. Tectonic plates move bloody faster than my sodding cervix. I need an emergency swear word. I need a swear word so heinous that it is kept behind glass with a small hammer hanging beside it, not to be used unless in the direst of circumstances. It is at this precise point that I would break that glass and scream the word repeatedly at the top of my lungs until there is not one iota of breath left in my body.

The consultant presents Mike and I with our options. We can either carry on, as although the baby's heartbeat is not as strong as it should be, he doesn't seem particularly distressed (at least that makes one of us), or we can have a C-Section. Then he adds, somewhat too nonchalantly for my liking, that carrying on would mean at least another four to six hours to make any meaningful progress.

"What shall we do?" I whisper to Mike as the consultant leaves us for a few moments to decide.

"What do you want to do?" replies Mike.

Many things that I want to do flash through my head, comprising:

Be anywhere but here

Be anywhere but here

Be anywhere but here

"I don't know." I think I do know, deep down, but I want this to be a joint decision. After all, it may be hard being the one full of foetus, but Mike's past four days have been no bloody picnic. Before this sounds a little too caring and altruistic, making a joint decision does also leave the "what did you make me do that for?" card in play.

"I think I want the C-Section," I whisper as I start to cry.

"Then let's do it," Mike replies.

FORM, RAZOR, ACTION (4.00PM)

We inform the consultant and midwife that we'll take the C-Section please. Mike packs away the hypnobirthing scripts and the consultant, armed with his form, starts to talk us through the procedure. He lists all known side-effects of the epidural I am about to undergo, along with possible complications that the surgery can have. I have no idea what he is actually saying, he could be telling us that there is every likelihood that my head will fall off as a result of the operation and I would still sign that form.

As he talks, I begin to shake uncontrollably. I sit on my hands to try and look a bit less like someone is passing 240 volts through me, but it feels like every single muscle in my body is trembling violently. It is so ridiculous that I laugh, which is no mean feat when a contraction is hitting your abdomen with the force of a small tornado. Being a polite kind of chap, the consultant does not pass comment on my juddering limbs; there is no 'hey Jerky, sign here please'. I have no idea why this is happening, I assume that, having spent the last thirteen and a half hours hypnobirthing, keeping my body on a very tight leash with just the aid of my brain and some imaginary balloons, it is now wreaking revenge on me good and proper. Signing the form becomes a game of drunken pen darts, with me desperately trying to make contact with the paper at the precise moment the nib passes over the dotted line. I think I may have ended up signing the side of his clipboard, but he accepts it – probably because he knows he only has three hours left on his shift to get this C-Section done.

Now it is the turn of the anaesthetist. He comes in and sits on the bed, and slowly and gently talks through the mini epidural I am about to have. I am not clear why it is a mini one – personally at this stage, I am all for a Super-Max-Deluxe-King-size one with extra fries, but he assures me that a mini one will be just fine. A contraction hits and I yelp with pain and cling to Mike.

"That will be the last contraction you will feel," he tells me and I instantly fall in love with him.

"Okay, you just need to be still whilst I administer the injection." Hmmm, easier said than done when I am shaking like a windsock in a hurricane and I start to fret about moving just at the moment of impact, but before I can formulate an appropriate level of anxiety, he tells me he has done it and I should start to feel the effects shortly. I fall in love with him all over again.

The midwife then steps forward and tells me I need a shave. Now, I realise that I have been in this bloody room for a long time, but surely I haven't grown a beard? No. They are going to shave my pubic hair off. Mike is whisked away – as if they have decided that whilst he can sit through labour and childbirth, watching his wife's pubes get shaved off in a way reminiscent of a boarding-school-style prank would be too much for him to take. The midwife and Plaits divest me of my pubic hair, with little ceremony and no offer of being able to take my pubes home in a little drawstring bag, which I thought would be part of the ritual of the first haircut my pubic region had ever had.

Then I get wheeled to theatre. This is a strange experience indeed. It is the most clichéd fifteen seconds of my life, staring up at the ceiling, watching the fluorescent lights slide by, hearing the whoosh of the swing doors parting as my trolley forces them open and the slam as they meet again somewhere behind my head. I feel like I am in any one of many hospital TV dramas: "Just film the ceiling lights sliding by, it's cheaper than trying to film the trolley career down the corridor."

I am wondering if I should not be having thoughts of a more serious nature as I glide toward a fairly major operation, but I think I am slightly delirious about not being in pain.

I am rejoined by Mike as I enter theatre. His green surgical trousers leave little to the imagination, which cheers me up no end. I may be about to be cut in two, but boy, does he look amusing. A green cloth goes up over my chest, which I like to assume is so that I can't see the business end, but is probably more to do with containment of splashing. The anaesthetist's head appears from behind this screen and he talks through what is about to happen, slowly and clearly and with a smile. For the third time, I fall in love with him. I am sure he must have spiked my anaesthetic.

Mike hunkers down next to my head and starts to talk to me, about what exactly I have no idea, but it is fantastic. It is the 'la la la' technique made manifest and it works a treat – for a long time I let the assembled masses do what they have to do down there without so much as a second thought.

On one of my previous perusals of baby and pregnancy websites, I had read an account of a C-Section by a new mum. She had described it as feeling like someone washing up in your stomach. So as I lay there, I am anticipating this gentle sensation, akin, I imagine, to a little light rummaging.

What a load of tosh. There is a four man tug-o-war going on down there all of a sudden, and I wonder if they are trying to pull a baby or my entire spinal column out of there. Washing up? Does that bloody woman wash up in a cement mixer? I swear one of them puts their foot on my hip to gain some traction at one point, although given the state of my head, I admit I may have been mistaken. There is absolutely no pain, which in itself is a little perturbing, as I know by the way my body is moving involuntarily the voracity with which they are attempting to extract the baby.

"Here he is," says one of the masked womb raiders, and holds up Ellis over the screen. He is scrunched up like an angry little puce fist and immediately blows a big bubble from his mouth. I smile at his bubble-blowing party trick and at the sudden sense of it all being over. I am secretly hoping that they don't pass him over the screen to me as he looks like an extra from a low-budget horror film, covered in gunk, blood and dripping with ectoplasm. Or placenta juice. Or some other bodily fluid that I would rather not have to kiss. I am no Earth mother. I'll take my babies scrubbed, cleaned and lightly fragranced, thank you. Luckily, they whisk him away to clean him up; I am hoping they have the services of an industrial pressure washer. Mike and I seem to be holding our breath, and then Ellis cries. We exhale and smile.

Mike is called over to collect Ellis. Ever the attentive wife, I remind him of a sage piece of advice we received from the NCT class – in exactly this scenario, don't let the husband get the baby, then turn round to head back to you – he will come face to face with the insides of your abdomen and he may not be able to look you in the eyes again, or at the very least, will cover your new baby in vomit. So with averted eyes, Mike goes to collect Ellis and returns to my side, holding him next to me for a few minutes. We stare at him, cocooned in a white towel. Our baby. We say nothing, just stare a little more before Mike and Ellis are told to leave whilst I get "tidied up", a gentle euphemism for what I imagine is quite a repair job. Off go my husband and my son, and I am left alone. My first thought in the silence that follows is to wonder if it is appropriate to ask the surgical team to maybe do a quick nip and tuck on my belly before they stitch me up, to go some way towards counteracting the Fruit Pastille fest I have been on, but fear it would fall on deaf ears. There seems to be quite an engrossing conversation happening about arrangements for their night out, so I turn instead to the momentous occasion that I have just experienced: the birth of our child. How do I feel, I ponder? Totally and utterly knackered, I answer. I don't feel different. I don't feel whole (who would though? I am pretty sure half my insides are lying outside of my body at this point in time). I don't feel elated. I don't feel infused with a love profound and deep. I just feel relief that it is all over. It is not the most poetic of emotions, relief. It doesn't make the heart soar, nor the soul sing, but it will do me just fine right now.

THE RECOVERY ROOM (8.30PM)

I am wheeled into the recovery room where nurses check me, prod me, do things to me I have no recollection of and I lie there, still relieved. Mike and Ellis appear and a midwife suggests that Ellis is put on my breast to see if he wants to suckle.

We duly oblige and Ellis quickly latches on. Well, I think, all those people who moan about how difficult breastfeeding is, what a bunch of liars. This is easy. Saying very little, Mike and I watch Ellis. We touch him as lightly as we can, not wanting to inadvertently crush something seemingly so fragile.

We have a son. It feels strange. All that waiting, and now he is here, outside of me, with us. I look at his screwed up face, red and blotchy, and stroke his matted hair with one finger. The recovery room is quite dark and quiet after the last chaotic, crowded eighteen hours, and is a perfect way to just be with Ellis. Even though I had been tethered to a labour bed for nigh on fifteen hours, there had not been one moment of stillness. Now there is, and I just watch Ellis, looking at Mike from time to time, too tired to think anything, too feel anything.

A nurse reappears holding a glass with a long straw poking out of it. Ooh, lovely, cocktails. Not quite, but I have to take some large sips of water for the final test to ensure that I have survived the C-Section intact and so that they can make sure the consultant didn't accidentally sew my bladder to my belly button. There is no sign of water spurting from my tummy or any other inappropriate hole, so I am okay to be put on the ward. Before we leave, the nurse picks up my camera and takes a few of shots of us. Oh yes, lovely – I have not slept properly for four days, not eaten for most the day, have just undergone 15 hours of labour and an operation and Ellis still has patches of womb juice and other things I dare not contemplate over him and my breast is on full display. That one is bound to make it onto the mantelpiece.

THE WARD (EVENING, DAY 5)

I am wheeled into place, with my must-have accessory of the season, my drip, into a slot at the end of the ward. Oh good, another window seat, I do hope this one comes with air con too. A midwife comes to tell us that, seeing as I have just given birth, Mike can have another ten minutes with us, but then he will have to go as it is way past kicking out time. If I had any energy left, I would be bloody furious. How mean is that? Mike has only just met his son, I am in no fit state to do anything, and he's being chucked out. I think wistfully about that private room that we could have had. At least in there Mike could have hidden under the bed and then we could have stayed together a bit longer.

But Mike has to go, and Ellis is put in a plastic wheelie cot at the end of my bed. I am very keen to get up and look at Ellis some more, but the fact that I still can't really feel my legs properly, let alone make them work, and I am tied to a drip-leash, means that Ellis-gazing is off the agenda.

A heady mix of exhaustion and super-max strength pain killers I have taken means that I fall into the duvet-soft arms of sleep. For the first time since arriving at the hospital I do not notice the plank I am sleeping on, nor the cold, nor the noise.

ELLIS' FIRST DAY (DAY 6)

I am woken up by the midwife who says something about breakfast. I try and sit up but fail. Who the hell looked after Ellis in the night? Did he not need feeding? What about a nappy change? Did he need one? How often does it need doing? Did he cry? Did I wake up at all? Was my baby crying and I slept right through it? Is he still there? I manage to lift my head up enough to see him, still in the cot.

"Hello," I say, then collapse back onto my pillow, thinking that this is not the most auspicious start to a lifetime of nurturing my offspring and firmly resolving to be less of a shit mother.

A midwife appears from behind the curtain with a plate. Blimey, I am hungry, I suddenly realise. She pushes the side table a little closer, and places the emergency call button on it.

"This is only for absolute emergencies," she announces with a frown and then puts the plate down next to it. She seems at pains to explain that I am only getting waitress service because I am a C-Sectionner. I am not sure if she is angling for a tip, but she fucks that right up by leaving the toast unbuttered on the plate, and the plate just far enough out of my reach that I can brush the rim against my finger tips, but not do anything useful with it. My drip is at full stretch as I try desperately to reach the toast but it's no good. Anyway, I realise, getting the toast is one thing, buttering it with one hand is quite another. In fact I will give the midwife a tip after all. Don't be such a bloody idiot. I wonder if I should use the emergency button. Does not being able to reach your breakfast constitute an emergency? I decide that, sadly, it doesn't and resign myself to waiting for Mike to bring in one of his lovely food parcels.

WHEN CAN I GO HOME?

A little later, another midwife arrives.

"Oh, didn't want your breakfast, dear?" she asks. I am too tired to argue and just take the multi-coloured collection of pills she gives me. I have no idea what they are, but hey, when in Rome.

"When can I go home?" I ask.

"Oh, not until Friday," she replies cheerily. My blood runs cold. Friday? That's two days away. Another forty-eight hours in here? I feel a relapse coming on.

THIS ISN'T HELPING MUCH, YOU KNOW

A midwife appears.

"Right, time to feed your baby."

Oh yes, I knew there was something I needed to be doing. I really must get a grip on this whole mothering thing.

She helps me wriggle my way to a vague sitting position and places Ellis on me. I manhandle him into position, nearly garrotting him with the drip line more than once, but eventually manoeuvre him close enough so that his lips are touching my nipple. So now bloody what?

Ginger McWitch looks at me expectantly, so I waggle my breast about a bit and try to get Ellis interested. He is blatantly not; I may as well be waving a beige knitted boob in his face. I prise his lips open with my nipple like some kind of fleshy, puckered, button-shaped interloper and give it another wiggle. Nope, nothing doing. I fear I may have been a little previous with my self-congratulations about how easy this is.

McWitch is obviously getting a bit irritated with my ineptitude. She suddenly leans over and grabs my nipple in her crab-like finger vice and somehow attaches Ellis' mouth on.

I am so taken aback that I am silent, and watch as she starts to squeeze my breast, a manoeuvre so precise and excruciating it must have been honed over many years of practise. Her hands resemble a pair of red-hot steel pincers and the sensation makes my eyes water profusely. Now given what I have been through of late, the pain is relatively manageable, but quite frankly, I was really kind of hoping to avoid any more pain for a couple of days and eventually I have to protest.

"Ow!" I say loudly and wince theatrically; just to really make sure she gets the message.

"Ellis!" she scolds, looking at my son. "Don't do that to your mother." And she tuts.

Hang on a minute. I may be mistaken, but I could have sworn it was *her* crabby little hands that were trying to puncture a hole in my left breast, not Ellis'. What the fuck is she on about?

I look at her, puzzled, and she rolls her eyes and gives me a look as if to say 'huh, kids, eh?'

IT WAS YOU, YOU STUPID BITCH, I want to shout. But I don't. She is called away, no doubt to grasp some other poor woman's breast until the nipple explodes. It was a very strange exchange and feels to me like someone wearing a glove puppet, punching you hard in the face with it, then turning to the puppet and telling it off.

SPLISH SPLASH

Later that morning, as Mike and I are indulging in a spot of Ellis-gazing, two more medical types arrive in uniforms of a shade of blue I have not yet encountered. They are either really important, or really...not.

"We've come to help you out of bed," one tells me. Ah. The Getting out of Bed team. I guess they are above the Put Large Sanitary Towels On Beds team, but only just.

The thought of actually moving is a curious one. I would quite like to move, as it does seem I have been lying on my back for about a month, but when I actually contemplate moving my limbs... I am not so sure.

They advance into position, relegating Mike to the end of the bed.

"Try not to tense your stomach up," one advises, as they wrestle me to a semi-sitting position. Have they tried sitting up without using your stomach muscles? It's about as feasible as having a poo without using your bum.

I – well, I say I, as I fear the two helpers did most of the heavy work – swing my legs off the side of the bed.

"Ready?" They each take one of my arms and brace themselves.

"Errr..."

"One, two, three..."

In a second, I am standing. In approximately the following second (but I am guessing) three gallons of blood and post-operative gunk releases from inside me and hits the floor like a storm wave hitting the shore. The splash back is quite impressive. Both helpers now have a shiny patina of my liquid insides covering their tights and shoes. The three of us stare at the bloody puddle on the floor. Well, I certainly wasn't expecting *that*. Perhaps they should have dispensed with the sky blue uniform and opted for the thigh length waders and matching sou'westers instead.

Hang on, what's that, in the middle of the puddle? Oh yes, look, it's the last remaining shreds of my dignity.

"Whoops," I offer, perhaps the feeblest apology for covering two complete strangers with post-operative goo ever uttered.

One of them disappears off to hose herself down and find a mop, and I look at Mike. He looks a tad pale, but seems mostly relieved to have been just out of blast range. I am not sure he would have forgiven me if I had put womb blood on his shoes.

The helpers get to work on Operation Sluice Down. There is something uniquely humiliating about having two people on their knees in front of you, wiping down your inner thighs with damp paper towels. I have no previous experience to call upon regarding etiquette in these circumstances. Should I try and make polite conversation? 'Well, this is nice,' doesn't seem quite right as an opener as one of them has just started dabbing my bum cheeks. 'Looks like there could be rain later, seems a little trite and I think 'Do you come here often?' may get me slapped. So I wait in silence, legs apart, staring out of the window until they finish. Credit where credit is due; they don't moan, they don't tut and they don't take a pile of blood-soaked paper towels and rub them in my face, which is what I would have been tempted to do if I were in their shoes. And judging by the current state of their footwear, I am bloody glad I am not.

Eventually, they leave and I take a few tentative steps to the cot to look at Ellis. Mike and I stand over him, staring. There seems to be a lot of staring going on since I gave birth. I didn't realise it was such a huge part of the early days. Even fast asleep, Ellis is fascinating. We study tiny ears, tracing the nest of pink curves with our eyes. We contemplate his tiny snub nose, which I fear he has inherited from me. We consider his little lips, quivering slightly as he sleeps. We gaze at his hands, which still look like he has spent far too long in the bath, all wrinkled and dry. He has the face of a one-day-old and the hands of an octogenarian.

ALL CHANGE

At one point Mike and I summon up all our courage and decide to change Ellis' nappy. We line up everything on the bed that is required and start the procedure. Why don't nappies come with sodding instructions? We fumble around, trying not to break anything (such as Ellis) and talk in earnest about how tight the nappy should be, have we remembered to poke his willy down-wards and how much cream to use. It takes us forever, and we think we are on the home straight when the mighty task of getting him back into his baby grow looms. How can you possibly get his limbs back in there without snap-ping one? Grimacing, we gingerly poke an arm into a sleeve, then feed a leg into the garment whilst praying it ends up where it should. The whole thing seems to go on for hours. How are you supposed to do anything else with your day when a nappy change takes this bloody long?

SLEEP, GLORIOUS SLEEP

Both Ellis and I spend a lot of the day asleep. At one point a nurse arrives and administers a dose of liquid morphine by squirting it directly into my mouth. That stuff is nectar of the gods, I swear.

FINALLY, SOME INSTRUCTIONS

We are paid a visit by a nursery nurse who has come to help us learn how to breastfeed. Obviously McWitch tipped her off that there was an incompetent mother in bay three.

She is Lovely. I don't feel like half a mum all of a sudden just because Ellis won't latch onto my boob and she talks about breastfeeding like it is a skill to learn rather than an inherent talent that any woman with one speck of motherliness in them should be able to do with their eyes closed. She comes with boob technology too: an industrial sized breast pump. Oh my god.

But we start with the basics: as a C-Sectionner, I am better off holding Ellis like a rugby ball to save the pain of him pressing down onto my wound. Not being a rugby fan, I have visions of spinning him on my middle finger from his pointy end, but in fact Lovely tucks him under my arm. Oh, the roll of carpet hold, I get it now.

After several hundred attempts at latching on, we finally get there. It is at this juncture she tells me that, as a C-Sectionner, it is more than likely my milk is not ready so there won't be much for Ellis to drink. Bloody hell. I have been lying in hospital for a week, you'd think my body might have utilised the time a bit more productively and got some milk ready.

She suggests that we give Ellis a little bit of formula to keep him going, as well as getting him on the boob to encourage the milk. This sounds eminently sensible to me, so we give Ellis a little bottle of formula, which he guzzles, as if to say 'thank god, no more of that weedy boob stuff, just this will be fine thanks'.

She then wheels the Turbo Nipple Sucker forward and explains that, initially, I should express every few hours to encourage milk production. Then she shows me how to position the funnel over my boob. As the machine kicks into action, I am relieved to find that is doesn't hurt, but it is like nothing else I have encountered. I watch with morbid fascination as the end of my boob gets momentarily moulded into the shape of the funnel, then released, then sucked in again. This soon becomes like watching paint dry and we all chat on for a while. If someone had told me nine months ago that I would be sitting with my tee shirt hoisted up round my neck, having a chat with a complete stranger whilst my boob gets sucked within an inch of its life by a pale yellow machine, I would have seriously questioned their mental health; now I just fear slightly for mine. I glance down into the bottle expecting to see at least half a pint sloshing around, and am dismayed to see that, after twenty minutes hard expressing, I have produced what I can only optimistically call milky condensation on the inside of the bottle wall.

"I think my boob is broken," I say, disheartened and ready to pack it all in.

Lovely reiterates that it will take some time, and I glumly switch boobs to see if the other one has bucked its ideas up yet.

"Don't worry," she says as it becomes apparent that I have the most reluctant breasts in the history of motherhood. "Give it a week and you'll be hitting the window from twenty paces."

Now that, I like the idea of, so we fastidiously express regularly through the day, with Mike diligently saving my milk droplet (singular) in the fridge and sterilising all the bottles, lids and funnels (being slightly incapacitated does have its advantages). It may take me three months to collect enough to constitute a teaspoonful, but I am not ready to wave the white flag just yet.

WILL THIS HURT?

More joy abounds, as I am told by a midwife that she has come to remove my catheter.

"Will this hurt?" I ask immediately.

I have just given birth via the sunroof after a long, hard labour. What a bloody ridiculous question.

NIPPLE CONFUSION

A midwife, when I tell her I am considering giving Ellis a bottle for one or more of the feeds, twitches nervously. "Well, you don't want to give him teat confusion," she warns. "Why don't you put some milk in an open cup and let him lap at it?"

I don't know, let's see. Oh yes, that's right, because he's not a fucking cat. Anyway, it is a bit late for nipple confusion. When Ellis is hungry and he's on my shoulder he turns his head to my face, latches on to my chin and begins to suck hard and fast, waiting for the milk to arrive. If he's confusing my chin with my nipple, then quite frankly there's no hope for him, and I might as well give him some milk from a bottle. And whilst on the subject, I am none too pleased that Ellis can't tell the difference between my chin and my nipple. I don't know which to feel more sorry for, my face or my breasts.

THE MORO ECHO

There are six babies in my ward room, all mostly sleeping to try and recover from the shock of being thrust into this world. The occasional yet unmistakable sound of babies' knuckles hitting the side of the plastic cot can be heard from every bay – it is the Moro reflex, if my memory serves me correctly, although I won't put money on the reliability of anything that comes out of my grey matter at the moment. These arm spasms happen when they are sleeping and Mike and I comment that Ellis must be dreaming of chasing rabbits, as it is not dissimilar to the leg twitches of sleeping dogs. In all likelihood, Ellis is actually dreaming of fending off the masked men who ransacked his womb and plucked him out.

I am not sure why I find the soft 'thwonk' of day-old knuckles hitting plastic entertaining, but I do, it makes me smile every time. Mind you, I giggle every time I hear the 'donk' of bumble bee against glass as a dozy creature flies headlong into a closed window, so I am not sure I am the most reliable arbiter of what constitutes entertainment.

SEPARATED AT BIRTH?

It is already that dreaded time when Mike has to leave and Ellis and I are left alone. Shortly afterwards, Ellis starts to cry and I fear he needs his nappy changing. I shuffle out to the corridor and collar a passing midwife, explaining that my wound is very painful and could she help me change Ellis? Okay, it isn't that painful, but quite frankly, I have worked hard and endured much to get this first class maternity ward ticket, and there has to be some bloody perks of a C-Section apart from cold toast delivered to your bedside – those in economy could change their own nappies, I am still not sure I have the hang of it.

One change and some half-arsed breastfeeding later, Ellis is asleep. I take the opportunity to go to the adjacent ward to visit my friend from the NCT class who has also just popped. I peer into her plastic cot and Ellis is there, asleep. What? I just left him, he can't be...I look again. Oh no, it's not Ellis. For a start, it's a girl. Bloody hell, it really is a damning indictment on your maternal instinct when you can't tell the difference between your baby and that of a friend's. I mentally add it to the list of mummy-type things that I am slightly rubbish at and we swap edited highlights and lowlights of our birthing experience, grimacing and oohing in the appropriate places.

I return to my bay, swiping a baby blanket from an empty cot on the way as the open-window air con is working a treat and Ellis' hands feel like ice. I double blanket him, put on a hat and mittens, and wish I had asked Mike to bring me a blanket, or at least a bloody draft excluder.

THE LONGEST NIGHT

I wriggle gingerly down under the gossamer thin blanket and try to sleep, thinking intently about anything but the cold and the noise, and as a result, end up thinking solely about the cold and the noise.

Slowly, slowly, I start to drift off and as I am teetering on the precipice of sleep, the baby in the next bay starts to cry. My eyelids spring open and my first thought is: is that Ellis? I decide it is not, so my second thought is: will someone shut that fucking baby up please, some of us are trying to sleep here.

The woman next to me picks up her baby and, cradling it, returns to bed. Her curtain is almost closed, but I peek through the gap to see her rocking it back and forth to try to comfort it. It is then that I notice the mother is making the most curious noise. Every time she rocks forward, she emits a low grunt through her nose and as the baby's crying increases, her grunts do too. I close my eyes and try to block it out, which is when I realise that she sounds like she is building up to have some kind of orgasm. Now I know that is not the case, mainly due to the fact that she has just given birth, as well as the small fact that she is lying in bed in a hospital ward, but once the thought has occurred to me, that is it. I desperately want to unthink it, but I can't concentrate as it sounds just like there is some kind of low-grade porn movie being enacted in the next bay. I have never wanted a baby to stop crying more in my entire bloody life.

Some unspecified time after hope departs my bay, her baby seems to go quiet and I try once again to get some sleep. It is then the turn of a woman in the bay opposite. It appears that she holds the world record for the loudest snoring. Oh the joy. It would have rattled the windows if the window actually made contact with the frame at any point. It is like having a Harley Davidson revving up in your bedroom – in fact, she should team up with Orgasm Lady, it might spice her porn scene up a bit. I have never heard snoring like it. It is bad enough that the noise means I can't sleep, but it is just rubbing my nose (or ears) in it that the snoring represents someone else having a marvellous night's slumber. If my fairy godmother had arrived right then and given me three wishes, all three of them would have been spent on causing the Snorer grievous bodily harm.

The Snorer must have turned over, or her pillow must have accidentally fallen into her cavernous mouth, as the decibel level drops a little and I start to feel sleepy. Suddenly a baby cries: shit, that's Ellis! I jump out of bed and then immediately collapse back. I really must remember that I have just had surgery before I attempt any more leaps from a lying start. With renewed pain and fresh resignation, I take Ellis in my arms and rock him. This is the extent of my 'getting a baby to sleep' repertoire, so when it doesn't work, I do it some more. I try him on a boob, which diverts him for a few minutes, but then he starts up again. Now what? I check for poo, quietly impressed with myself that I actually remember to do this. Hmmm, no poo. So what next? Oh, I know, some more rocking. I ad lib some gentle 'sshhing' and eventually, he falls asleep again. Lucky bastard.

At some indeterminable point in the night – it is so difficult to tell, given the delightful low-level fluorescent glow that all hospital wards have when everyone is trying to sleep – I realise that I was told whilst in the recovery room that Ellis had been given the Vitamin K injection, rather than the drops as I had requested on my birthing plan. They are no fools. They could have said 'oh, just to let you know, we have taken out your baby's brain and inserted a three day old cauliflower and I would have just nodded. Birthing plan. Pah. I wouldn't even wipe my arse on it. Particularly as it is laminated, I could get some very nasty cuts.

It is misery 'o'clock in the early hours. The night is one long round of a snoring soundtrack, on top of which is the unmelodious noise of a baby crying, which triggers the one in the next bay to wail, and so on, until it gets round to Orgasm Lady, where the cacophony is joined by the rhythmic bass of pseudo-sexual grunting as she tries to placate her screaming child. I am in and out of bed with Ellis, either comforting him when he cries, or getting up thinking I have heard him cry, or getting up to check I haven't left him face down by accident. I am so exhausted I have lost the will to live and what-ever I possessed of my mothering instinct seems to have dribbled out of an unspecified orifice. I don't want to be here. I don't want to keep getting up. I don't want to be feeling like a road accident victim. I just want to sleep. AND WILL SOMEONE SHUT THAT FUCKING SNORING BITCH UP RIGHT NOW.

HELLO? IS THERE ANYONE THERE? (DAY 7)

I am awoken by the midwives rattling curtains and talking in voices that are overly cheerful and slightly too loud. They are the voices of people who have had more than two hours sleep and I grit my teeth hard. Oh good. Is it morning already? Ellis is asleep, so I take the opportunity to lie there and plot my escape. After last night, there is no way on god's earth that I am staying in this hellhole for one more night. I will dig my way out using just my teeth and a used sanitary towel if I have to, but enough is enough. I decide that the trick is to look well.

Just as I am wondering about the whereabouts of my hairbrush, last seen when I wasn't a mother, Ginger McWitch appears. I flinch involuntarily and shield my breasts as she picks up Ellis and comes to the side of the bed, pushing the table away and plonking Ellis on me.

"Right," she says brusquely, and I suddenly fear for my nipples, but an urgent shout from another ward sends her rushing away at full speed. Thank god for that, saved by the emergency bell of someone else who probably can't reach their toast but has a more liberal approach to the use of emergency buttons.

I lie there, staring at Ellis as he sleeps. I take gentle, tiny breaths for fear of waking him and enjoy some time, staring. Minutes slip by, and I take pleasure in the peace and just being with my son. I place my mouth and nose gently on his head, so I can feel his silky fine hair against my lips and breathe in his smell. Everyone talks about the adorable 'baby smell'. I imagined the fragrant smell of talcum powder or the scent of fresh linen. Not quite. Ellis smells a lot earthier than that. I love his smell, it is his smell, but there is no pretending that it could be used as a fragrance in a washing powder. He has a small, round, rough patch on the top of his head, reddish brown and scaly. I have no idea what it is but rub my lips over this little imperfection repeatedly.

More time passes, and I start to think about the pins and needles in my right arm where Ellis is laying. Even more time passes, and I come to the conclusion that Ginger McWitch has forgotten all about me.

Well, I think, it's no good, I suppose I better get up and start Operation Get The Fuck Out of Here. With Ellis lodged firmly in the crook of my arm, I position my left hand on the bed in an attempt to lever myself up. But I just can't do it. I try again, keeping my eyes on Ellis in case he starts to tip, and attempt and sit up without over-taxing my stomach muscles. I lurch alarmingly to the right and squeeze Ellis even tighter. It really wouldn't be an auspicious start to motherhood: "Mummy, why is my face so flat?" "Well, dear, Ginger McWitch left me stranded so I was getting out of bed one-handed and sort of… well… dropped you."

I check my watch. It is getting on for an hour since I was handed Ellis and then abandoned. I have to get up, I could be here all bloody day before someone notices. I try to get upright again, but fail, now convinced that I have just popped my stitches. Forget it, it is not going to happen. These days, getting upright is definitely a two-handed job.

I eye up the emergency button. This is surely becoming a legitimate emergency, what with me being stuck in bed and Ellis stuck on me. But McWitch has shoved the button way out of reach, as it was on the table that she moved. No doubt on purpose. Great. I am well and truly stuck. I eye the time again. Can I last here until Mike arrives? Shit, that's nearly three hours away. I am getting desperate and am just contemplating shouting for help when another midwife appears at the end of my bed with a breakfast tray. Thank the lord for my first class ticket. I get her to help me sit upright, from where I can slide off the bed and put the sleeping Ellis back into his cot whilst I saw my way through a piece of cold toast and slurp a cup of lukewarm tea. Delicious.

I'M A C-SECTIONNER, GET ME OUT OF HERE

Having been totally restored to full energy and optimism due to such a hearty breakfast – oh no, wait a minute, still feeling like total and utter crap, I get up and decide to get dressed. Thank heavens for stretchy waistbands, as it means I can let the trousers dangle floor-wards whilst still holding the waist and lasso them onto the end of my foot, at which point some hard yanking and painful leg stretching means I just about manage to get them on. It sounds easy enough, but the entire process takes over twenty minutes. This is what it's like to be eighty, I muse, just without the accompanying smell of wee and poo (that I am aware of).

A midwife appears to do some checks. Her fingers are barely on the bay curtain before I ask: "Can I go home today?"

She checks her notes. "Well, you are not due out until tomorrow."

"Oh, but I am feeling SO much better!" I exclaim in my best Famous Five voice and gurn my face into a rictus grin. I even bounce on my toes for added zest, which nearly sends me into a relapse, but I think I may have got away with it, as she pauses for a second, then tells me it's a possibility. She leaves me and I punch the air in triumph, then quickly sit down on the edge of the bed as all that exertion has worn me right out.

Mike arrives and I tell him the plan; I will be hop, skipping and tra-la-laing my way round the ward until I get let out.

PILES? CALL THE AMBULANCE

A commotion across the room attracts our attention and Mike and I look on. There is something fascinating about other people's woes, and the Snorer is moaning and gnashing her teeth in pain. Not only does she have the world record in snoring, it appears she is Olympic Champion in moaning. The way she is bleating on about some pain she has, I am expecting the resuscitation team to arrive any minute and whisk her off to intensive care.

There is much consultation with the midwives and eventually one turns up wearing a dark blue uniform. Crikey, you know it's serious when Navy turns up.

"Yes, dear," she says to Snorer, "but if you take some pain killers you will feel better. I know piles are painful but they will improve."

Piles? Bloody piles? She has had four midwives fussing round her for over half an hour and warranted an appearance from Navy, all for piles? Good grief, she wants to try on my sliced-open tummy for size. My piles haven't had a look-in since the operation. I have to leave today. I am not sure both of us will survive another night.

SHOWERING, EN FAMILLE

I am informed that I have to shower this morning. I am wondering if that is standard procedure but the midwives probably had a conversation something like:

"She wants to go home today."

"Fine, she's been cluttering up the place long enough. Just don't let her out smelling like that, for god's sake."

As a C-Sectionner, showering is now in the high risk, adrenaline sport category for me and I am not allowed to go in alone. I am not sure why – maybe the water might dissolve my stitches and I will end up being washed down the plug hole, organ by organ, but rather than be accompanied by a midwife (holy shit, it might be Ginger McWitch – I'd never get out alive) I opt for Mike. Which means we have to wheel Ellis in too, as he can't be left alone on the ward.

So we have our first ever family outing. It pretty much sets the pattern for how I imagine a family day out to be. We talk about what we are going to do and formulate a plan of action, we spend an inordinate amount of time gathering all the required paraphernalia, double checking as we go, it takes us ages to get to our destination and when we do finally make it, there's a sodding great queue.

However, we do eventually get into the shower room and very slowly, with the aid of my ever helpful husband, I get undressed. I shuffle under the shower and it is absolute bliss. I stand there until there is a real risk of turning into a giant prune and then set about trying to wash. This is not such a blissful activity, involving far too much bending and stretching, so I decide that anything below my knees can do without a wash for now.

With the help of Mike I put on the largest pair of knickers in the world, which I'd had the foresight to pack in my hospital bag and are now indispensable, being the only pants I own whose waistband doesn't sit exactly where my scar is, by dint of the fact they practically reach my breasts. I would worry they are a passion killer, but after what Mike has witnessed over the last five days, those apple catchers are the least of my worries.

BATHING MADE EASY

We return to the bay to find Lovely waiting for us to check how we are getting on with the breastfeeding. I give Ellis a boob to chew on as she gives us some final tips and pointers. It seems impossible that I will ever get the hang of this, as Ellis slides off my nipple again, probably having fallen asleep with boredom whilst waiting for my milk to arrive. Lovely assures me I am doing fine and wishes us well.

I pack my bags up and get ready to leave, even though my departure has not been made official. More ward info-tainment is laid on, as an elderly lady in the palest blue uniform (in fact, almost Ocean White, I would say) wheels a mobile bath in and gives a demonstration on how to bath your baby. Mike and I watch intently, as this seems to us a highly risky venture without the attendance of a fully-trained scuba diver with first aid training. She makes it seem so easy, as she flips the Orgasm Lady's baby round in the water as if she was rinsing off a ready-to-roast chicken in the sink. Rather than give us confidence, her breezy competence makes us feel terrified of trying, but we agree that we will definitely bath Ellis tonight. Or at some point this week, at least.

Navy turns up with the appropriate forms; it is official, I have been paroled. I can hardly contain my excitement. She runs through the standard exit questions:

"What contraception have you got planned?" Now, I am all for making cheap gags at inappropriate moments, but I could see by the steely glint in her eyes that she will slap me if I make a comment about there being no need, given what I have just been through. I am guessing she has heard that one at least four times a day for the last twenty years and so it is probably wearing a tad thin.

"Have you been given painkillers to take home?" I was very disappointed when I was handed some innocuous looking tablets earlier in the day. I was hoping for some more of those yummy morphine syringes to take home and administer at my leisure, but it wasn't to be, so I just shake the bottle of tablets to show her I have the drugs.

She gives me a leaflet about the do's and don'ts of being a C-Sectionner. Do: take it easy, rest often and look after your scar (I fear they may have forgotten that I have a newborn baby to tend). Don't: walk up the stairs – so that's the downstairs bedroom for me then. Don't: drive for four weeks. Four weeks? I can probably manage two, as it will take me that long to master getting Ellis' car seat attached, but a whole month? Don't: do the Hoovering for four weeks. Ah, that's more like it. I might highlight that one and stick it on the fridge when I get home.

"Any questions?" she asks us.

"Yes," I reply, pointing to the reddish-brown patch on Ellis' head. "What is that, exactly?"

It turns out that it is leftover womb or vagina gunk, which has yet to be cleaned off. I am so glad I have been rubbing my mouth against it for two days. I make a mental note not to lick my lips until I have washed my face.

"Seeing as it is getting late in the day, do you want to stay for dinner?" enquires the midwife.

Stay for dinner? Stay for dinner, here? Voluntarily? I would rather eat my own placenta. Actually, given the state of the pork hotpot, I am still not convinced that I haven't been doing just that.

OUR ESCORT

We are not allowed to leave by ourselves – we have to wait for an escort to walk us to the door. I have no idea why. Maybe they are worried that parents might take a look at their baby and decide they could probably get a better looking one, so do a last minute swap before making a run for the car park. I can't say it's the most productive use of a midwife's time, as she walks at a snail's pace down the corridor with us. Now I am officially free, I stop the 'look at me, I feel great' act as, quite frankly, it is fucking knackering, and I resort to the slow-shoe-shuffle. Finally, we make it to the car park. Mike and I both look at Ellis, tiny in the huge padded shell of the car seat. Bloody hell, we actually have a baby.

Mike fastens the baby seat in place in the back seat, giving me enough time to discover half a sandwich from the local garage that Mike abandoned yesterday. I eat it without taking a breath, hoovering up every last dry, slightly stale crumb. God it tastes good, and there was never a point in my life that I thought I would say that about a foodstuff bought from a petrol station.

We drive home slowly, to avoid me yelping when we go over a bump, and reach home. Ah, home. I walk in and relief floods into every cell. Home. Our lovely, warm, friendly home. We place Ellis on the table, still in his car seat. He is asleep, unaware that he, too, has come home. Mike and I stare at him for a while.

Fucking hell. We've got a baby.

HANG ON, MY LIFE IS NOT WHERE I LEFT IT (WEEK 1)

The first week home is unsurprisingly strange. Ellis is sleeping a lot, which is something I hadn't quite realised would happen and we are both mightily thankful. Even when he cries, it is a more of a quiet mewling. Well, this is okay, I think. Almost manageable. Whilst he sleeps I potter around, doing a spot of housework (very, very occasionally) but mainly pointing to the bit in the C-Section leaflet about sitting down and taking it easy. I do exert myself at one point, standing at the bottom of the stairs and yelling to Mike about what clothes I would like bringing down from the bedroom upstairs to our makeshift one downstairs, and after six episodes of 'oh, sorry, I forgot, can you get my hair dryer too', 'bum, you'll have to go back upstairs again, there are no socks here,' and 'rats, you couldn't go up and fetch my other big pants, could you?" I have enough sartorial supplies within reach to last a month and Mike joins me in needing a sit down.

Ellis' world extends no further than about thirty centimetres from the end of his nose, according to the books, so there is a lot of nose-to-nose contact as we try and engage and entertain him in his waking moments. We take his spaced-out and slightly 'who the fuck are you two idiots' expression to be one of utter contentment on his part.

I feel remarkably not-too-bad all things considered, which I put mainly down to the sheer novelty of the situation I find myself in. I am convinced that if I had had this surgery without the end product of a child, I would be bed-bound, wailing with pain, wallowing in self pity and planning to stay there until I felt better... in about a month's time. As it is, there is so much to divert my brain from dwelling on me that hours go past without me thinking about it at all, and I only remember when I get up too quickly or accidentally pull my knickers up past my scar. Up and over, that is the key.

The only time I succumb is around seven 'o'clock, when the exertion of the day catches up with me and my body decides it is time for a shake. I usually crawl into bed at this point and curl up under the duvet, shuddering uncontrollably for a while and sometimes having a little cry, just to make myself feel better. It is not a particularly productive time as I can't sleep, but there is little point attempting anything constructive unless I want to vigorously mix up some milk formula.

THE POST-BIRTH POO (3 DAYS OLD)

Apparently, after giving birth, having a poo is off the agenda. It is de rigeur for mothers to be constipated and, not wanting to be left out, my bowels decide to pack up and go on holiday for a few days. I dare not cough too hard these days for fear of blowing my stitches, so any muscular encouragement from me is strictly off the agenda – for the second time, I am, I find, too posh (or too crap) to push.

So in its own sweet (probably not an appropriate adjective) time, my bowel action returns. I fairly skip from the bathroom having completed Mission Impossible, feeling a good two stone lighter, whooping with delight. I am chuffed and consider sending out a round robin email to share the good news, but luckily, Ellis starts crying and I get diverted from my task.

BITCH FROM HELL

The doorbell rings. Mike answers it and there stands a midwife. I am immediately annoyed that she has the presumption to turn up unannounced, but I suppose that on the second day of having our baby at home, where the fuck else would we be?

She sits down opposite me and rests her prodigious breasts on the edge of the table. Getting out her notes, Boobs enquires after Ellis, to which I reply that he is fine.

"What is your feeding routine?"

"Well, I do a mix. Mainly formula at the moment, with breastfeeding when I can." I smile, feeling a little smug.

She, however, looks horrified. "My. Girls. Do. Not. Do. Formula," she annunciates slowly and clearly, obviously having decided I am mentally impaired for mentioning bottle-feeding. She continues to glare at me and I suddenly feel like I want to cry. I thought I was doing okay, persevering with the breast, waiting for my milk to arrive (although I am beginning to think my boobs have called a wild-cat strike and are waiting for better pay and conditions), expressing regularly and making sure Ellis is getting all the nutrients he needs with the bottle milk in the meantime. But no. She scribbles something in her notebook, presumably 'Very Bad Mother'. And anyway, you supercilious old witch, since when am I one of 'your girls'?

I swallow back the tears as I really don't want to cry in front of her, and clench my fists under the table. I would really love to punch her right now.

Boobs blethers on for a bit about how I should be dropping the bottle and solely breastfeeding, and I watch her lips move, but in my head, I am shouting 'LA LA LA LA' very loudly to drown her out. I am sticking with Lovely's advice and Boobs can just fuck right off.

I exact a tiny bit of revenge by asking her to look at one of my bumper-sized post-birth sanitary towels to check that the discharge is normal – I am fairly sure it is, but you never know if what you are looking at is okay, or an essential part of your womb that really should still be inside you. I was hoping she would get so close that I could accidentally nudge it into her face with my elbow, but without even taking it out of the plastic bag she assures me it is fine.

I bring the visit to a close as soon as I can and see her out. I shut the door and lean my head onto it. Then I cry.

DRESSED FOR (UN)SUCCESS

Ellis is not a small baby, but not large either – an eight pounder. Every single item of clothing we dress him in, however, swamps him. Hands disappear regularly up sleeves, his feet are more often than not adorned with cloth flippers and his tiny little neck pokes out of the cavernous neck line like a cocktail stick from a sack. It looks disconcertingly like we have shrunk him in the wash.

BATH TIME

Mike and I obviously have a fit of bravery and decide to give Ellis a bath. We have been loaned what I can only describe as a bath sling – a wire frame over which is stretched some towelling material, which you place in the bath and the baby reclines onto, body submerged, head clear of the water.

Having undressed him ('ooh, don't break his leg,' and 'whoops, that popper seems to be caught up his nose') we gingerly place him on the sling. Cue manic screaming. We gently swish the water around to comfort him, or to petrify him further, we are not sure which. Further yelling ensures. We wet his hair and he turns puce with the exertion of all that full-pelt crying. We abort any further attempt at bathing, get him out, get him dry, get him dressed and all go for a lie down.

THE CRYING GAME (2 WEEKS OLD)

Wow, we have made it through a whole week. Unsurprisingly, I have not been tempted to break the rules and do some Hoovering, but more surprising is the amount that Ellis now cries.

We frantically riffle through all the baby books we have, trying to uncover the source of the problem. All paths seem to lead to colic. We read up on colic one evening.

"Right, I have read everything there is about it. And I still don't know what causes it," I say, snapping the book on the top of the pile shut.

"Nope, me neither," concurs Mike.

There is a long pause. It is an unusually silent one, as Ellis is actually asleep (for now).

"So...what actually is colic?" I venture.

"No idea."

I open the book again and re-read the colic entry. It tells me that most babies with colic will stop crying incessantly after about three months. Oh my god. Three months? I lay my head on top of the books. That's another two and a half months to go. Ellis may have stopped crying by then, but I am not sure I will.

WINING, NOT WHINING

What I hadn't previously realised is that, just because I have given birth, it doesn't mean I can return to my old drinking habits. Breastfeeding means that you give your baby a little bit of what you are ingesting – and a little bit of a lot of wine is not a good thing. Which is a complete downer, seeing as I have spent the last nine months counting down the days until I can indulge.

As each evening falls, I long for a little glass of the ruby nectar but feel I shouldn't. And then one evening, I do. I feel so much better, just so long as I don't focus on the guilt. It's not big or clever, but it is bloody lovely. Oh fuck it, just add it to the 'Bad Mother' list, I must be on page four by now.

Respite and sanity arrives in the shape of Super-Grandma, come to lend hands and support as Mike returns to work this week. Granted, she doesn't have a magic wand to stop Ellis crying, but it is almost magical to me that she rustles up delicious lunches whilst my back is turned, is there with a muslin cloth before I even know I need one and generally stops me going slightly insane. I wonder if I can persuade her to stay forever?

THE INAUGURAL NCT COFFEE AND CAKE

All the NCT girls have arranged to meet in a local coffee shop. None of us has quite thought through the logistics of eight women turning up with prams and changing bags, and even though there are actually only six of us in the end, it tests our pram-manoeuvring skills to the full, as well as the patience of the other customers. However, we manage it and launch into conversations about crying, bathing and feeding our babies. Only ten minutes in and I already feel saner, having realised that it is not just me who feels more than a little bit incompetent at this point in time or who has very little clue as to what the hell is going on. As there is one amongst us who has not yet given birth, we agree not to tell birth stories yet – no one wants to be searching for an industrial sized cork two days before they are due.

We all look at everyone else's babies, cooing and ahhing and secretly thinking that ours is by far the most beautiful, thank god, though it is difficult to make an accurate judgement as blankets are pulled up to chins and hats are pulled down to eyebrows in that new-mother 'they could freeze to death if I'm not careful' paranoia.

We chat away, all sneaking darting looks into our prams, praying to the god of sleeping babies for ours not to wake up. Dealing with a crying baby in the privacy of your own home is one thing, trying to do it in public? No thanks. I am certainly not ready to get my boob out for a spot of breastfeeding. The thought is enough to stop my milk production in its tracks.

DRESSED TO (UN)IMPRESS

Does Ellis really need to be dressed in a garment with arms and legs? It is still causing us no end of problems. Given that Ellis has the most attractive frog's legs, permanently bent at the knees with his heels almost together, along with flailing arms that never seem at rest, dressing him is an arduous task.

First off is the Vestathon. Almost immediately it gets caught around his ears as I try to get it over his head, meaning he spends several long, screaming seconds staring at the inside of his vest as the folds gather around his nose and his mouth and we both try not to panic. Finally he is in, with only one episode of uncontrollable crying (and this time it is Ellis, which makes a nice change).

Then to the Baby Grow. Trying to straighten aforementioned frog's legs for long enough to get them into a Baby Grow is a real skill yet to be mastered by us – they seem to spring back like an elastic band at every opportunity, leaving the Baby Grow either on the floor or dangling from my hand. I breathe deeply and try again. And again. Finally, the Baby Grow is almost filled with legs. Right, now to those arms. He suddenly goes into jazz hands mode, fingers spread wide. Unsurprisingly, his thumb gets caught in a hem (hem? Who allows hems on baby clothes? It is surely an incontrovertible health and safety issue, is it not?) and having freed that, I notice there are only three fingers and a thumb visible out of the other sleeve. Shit, I think I've snapped off his little finger. Thankfully, it is still there, and I gingerly pop it out of the cuff. Finally, when all limbs are in correct clothing holes and fingers can be seen through sleeves, I popper the suit from neck to toe, only to reach the bottom and find I have one half of a popper spare. Buggar. Buggar. Buggar

THINGS I THOUGHT I'D NEVER DO #1

Obviously, motherhood is one long string of activities that I thought I would never do. But some are more odd than others. I really could not have seen myself cheer and clap when someone burps, proclaiming them "very clever" and laughing with delight, but this is what I do with Ellis on a regular basis. I sit him on my lap or my shoulder to wind him, tapping and stroking away until he lets rip with a corker, at which point I eulogise about its merits. Actually, I may have done this prior to having Ellis, but alcohol-induced burp celebrations don't count.

ASSUME THE POSITION (3 WEEKS OLD)

I have quite a set-up going in the bedroom to facilitate breastfeeding. We find the perfect chair – not the chair that we purchased for the job, as that is still sitting unused in Ellis' nursery, but an old chair we have had forever that has high, wide, padded arms. Rather than the 'roll of carpet' hold that can get a little tiring after forty minutes (Ellis isn't one to rush his milk, in fact, I would say he is a downright dawdle-pants) I can lay Ellis on the arm of the chair, putting him at exact nipple height.

I start the breastfeeding routine as I mean to go on; I have the ipod and speakers to hand, pre-loaded with nursery rhymes and my favourite tunes, and in that first week, every breastfeed is a long jolly sing song, or if I'm not in the mood for singing, I'll tell him a story. Approximately a week into this, I come to my senses and get Mike to set up the tiny portable TV about a foot from the chair as all that half-a-pound-of-tuppenny-rice rubbish is starting to melt my brain and curdle what little milk I am producing.

So, increasingly, I find myself in the corner of the bedroom, ensconced in my chair, TV on and my top hitched up over one or other of my boobs. Ellis is on what the books describe as a 'growth spurt', which basically translates as an almost insatiable, fiendish appetite for milk. When I am not feeding him, I am noting down the minutes he has spent suckling in my breastfeeding book (I laminated my birth plan, it should come as no surprise that I have a breastfeeding note book), when I am not doing that, I am expressing, and when I am not expressing I am decanting breast milk into milk bags and freezing them. It is like painting the bloody Forth Bridge, but without the views and with more dripping nipples.

I have heard a midwife say that breastfeeding is a great way to bond with your child. I am not so sure about this. It is not as if I can gaze into Ellis' eyes due to the fact that his head is sideways on to me; I get a cracking view of his ear and some of the side of his face, but that is about it. I am never quite sure if he is actually taking on milk, or just having a little fondle of my nipple with his tongue and I am always alert to him falling asleep on the boob – if I am not, I can have got all the way through Cash in the Attic before I realise he has not been feeding for the last twenty minutes. The breastfeeding sessions are taking longer; ergo, the time I have in between them is getting shorter. I am afraid that osmosis is occurring between my bum and the breastfeeding chair and one day soon no one will be able to prise us apart.

WHO ASKED YOU, ANYWAY?

There is something about small babies that makes people (many of whom would normally elbow you out of the way to get to the shorter checkout queue) talk to you, or even worse, pass uninvited comment about your offspring. This mainly happens in Tesco, where I am dillying, dallying and generally fannying about trying to remember what I have forgotten to write on my list.

One woman stops me by the milk and starts up a conversation about Ellis. By the time I roll to a stop, she is right next to me, and as she talks she shuffles away slightly. God, did I forget my deodorant this morning? I wheel forward a little and she moves back. Crikey, maybe it's the slightly crusty stain on my shoulder that is putting her off. I advance once again, and she retreats - by which time we are in danger of leaving the milk section altogether and making a foray into juices and smoothies. It is only then that I realise she is moving back so that she can look at Ellis in the pram. I find this curious. Why would she want to do that? I mean, I think he's gorgeous, but I do realise that I wear a rather large pair of Mummy Glasses. (Mummy Glasses are bifocal, just to clarify – look down to your tee shirt and you don't notice the kaleidoscopic pattern of sick stains, milk dribbles and other fluids that once were inside your baby, look up and your baby appears to be amazingly, breathtakingly beautiful. They are a marvellous invention, there is no doubt about that). Never having been one to really see the point of small babies, other people's interest in mine does perturb me slightly. It seems a little like taking an active interest in tortoises.

Two days later, I am loitering in the nappy aisle when a middle aged woman stops and peers into the pram.

"Ahhhh," she says and looks up at me. "Never mind, he'll grow into it eventually," and off she walks. Grow into what exactly? I assume that she is talking about his winter all-in-one, which is a head-to-toe outfit stitched together from what seems to be left-over duvet and currently swamps Ellis. But then I start thinking: maybe that wasn't what she was referring to. Maybe she was being rude? Maybe she meant he would grow into his head? Or his ears? What a rude bitch, I think, and lean over toward Ellis. "Ignore her," I whisper, "She's probably menopausal."

GOODIE TWO SHOES ARRIVES

We have the first Health Visitor visit today. She appears to be about seventeen, with dimples and a bedside manner that veers from cloying to patronising with the merest flick of her perky little ponytail. She talks with a light, sing-song voice that seems to have been developed in an attempt to demonstrate empathy and kindness but actually makes me want to poke her in the eye.

Goodie weighs and measures Ellis and notes it all down in his red medical book – he has put on some weight, and all is fine. I breathe a sigh of relief – we must have been doing something right.

I ask about the fact that Ellis has been producing some alarmingly green poo and Goodie replies that green poo is a sign that he is being under-fed. Or over-fed. Right. Thank god she is here, I would be so confused without her indispensible advice.

Never mind, I think, maybe that was a bit technical, let's try another one. Why does Ellis cry so much? Shortly after she begins to answer, I realise that it isn't an answer at all. She gives a whole range of reasons, none of which I haven't already read in one of the books I have consulted, and is generally so vague that she is no help at all. It is a white noise of a response.

When she has gone, I sit down to take stock. I am over-feeding or under-feeding Ellis, and his crying is due to colic, or tummy pain, or constipation, or lack of sleep (surely, that's me, not Ellis?), or being in need of a cuddle (ditto), or hunger, or not being comfortable, or he is just crying because he can. Well, that's sorted that out then.

WE HAVE ROYALTY IN OUR MIDST

Every time we put Ellis in his Moses basket he cries, without fail. I like to think this is because he has the same aversion to wicker as I have, but I fear it may be something else. So Mike and I devise a number of strategies to mini-mise the crying, including making sausage-blankets that we tuck either side of him, wrapping the mattress in a cellular blanket, and warming the mattress and blanket slightly with a just-warm hot water bottle before he goes down. The lengths to which we are going in order to achieve a non-crying scenario are getting a little silly and I start to feel somewhat like a footman to some royal guest. At this rate it won't be long before we start ironing his newspaper and lightly fragrancing his nappies.

ZOMBIE (4 WEEKS OLD)

I am getting up approximately every four hours to feed Ellis. He has no concept of nighttime and I am, quite frankly, losing touch with it also. There are no words to describe how tired I am feeling. Well, I am sure there are plenty, but my brain is barely capable of getting me dressed without a calamitous error (showering all over using dandruff shampoo and putting tops on back to front are not uncommon in my world any more) let alone giving me a choice of vocabulary to peruse. So I will just repeat the only word I have at my disposal: tired, tired, tired, tired, tired...

ROUTINE, SCHMOUTINE

"Let's try and start a routine," I tell Mike one morning. We discuss the possible routine to adopt and I become excited about getting a bit of structure back into my life and feeling less like I am just at Ellis' beck and call.

However, our planning doesn't factor in Ellis, and that, quite frankly, is our fundamental error. Ellis, it turns out (despite me patiently explaining the plan to him in great detail) doesn't want a routine. He eats when I want him to sleep, sleeps when he should be eating and cries with gay abandon.

"Let's not try and start a routine again," I tell Mike the same evening, before lying down and putting a pillow over my head.

OH, IT'S WORRY 'O'CLOCK. AGAIN.

My grey hairs are multiplying. Worry has now joined its stable mate Fatigue and both have gatecrashed my life in the rudest way possible. I wouldn't have minded, but neither brought a bottle.

Ellis is a constant source of worry. One day he doesn't sleep at all during the day and I fret that he is ill, or has some condition that means he won't ever sleep again (oh my god, the terror induced by that thought). It is a real concern. The next day, he sleeps all morning. Then I worry he is ill, or has some condition that means he won't ever wake up again. I tiptoe into the room, holding my breath, trying to hear him breathe. Ah, there it is, phew. So I tiptoe out again. But should I wake him? Am I seriously considering waking a sleeping baby? I should be productively using this time to get some washing done, or do the dishes. But I am too worried, so I hover around, hoping that he'll wake up soon.

Then Ellis does wakes up and starts crying and I wish he was still asleep as, for some reason, I have not done any of the jobs I wanted to do whilst he was taking his nap. Damn.

GROWING

All this breastfeeding is having some effect – Ellis' toes now reach the end of his Baby Grows, something that seemed almost impossible to consider four weeks ago. He has also developed baby acne, which I thought was some kind of wind-up until I read it in the baby books. I wonder if babies are subject to any other adolescent ailments – maybe a distinct reluctance to get out of bed in the mornings? Hmm, chance would be a fine thing.

THE COLIC EPIDEMIC

The NCT girls gather for our weekly meeting in a local coffee shop. It is like a coven but with less facial warts and more Bugoboos. Tea, cake and empathy are all in full flow and it is, as always, a relief to share our nightmares – both literal and baby-shaped – and our challenges.

One of the mums mentions that her baby has colic. We all fervently agree. "Yes, my baby has colic too". "And mine, it's an absolute nightmare." "Yes, I think mine has too." We compare and contrast colic medicines, feeling a tad better that we are not alone in our suffering. Or our babies are not alone in their suffering, should I say. We eat more cake, drink more tea and feel, even for a couple of hours, like slightly less crap mums.

GROUNDHOG DAY (5 WEEKS OLD)

Ellis: feed, poo, cry, sleep, cry. Feed, poo, cry, sleep, cry. Feed, poo, cry, sleep, cry. Feed, poo, cry, sleep, cry. Feed, poo, cry, sleep, cry.

Repeat to fade...

THE NIGHTTIME HEEBIE JEEBIES

I open my eyes. It is pitch black in the bedroom and I freeze. I have fallen asleep with Ellis in the bed with us and now he's not there. Fuck. I sit bolt upright, eyelids peeled back into my skull, trying to make out shape and form in the grainy darkness. Fuck. I imagine him, tangled in duvet, slowly suffocating. Buggar. Oh, hang on, now I can see a bit...wait...he's over there, in his Moses basket, where I left him after the last feed. Oh, thank god for that, it was just another momentary lapse of sanity. I sink back down into my pillow, heart rattling in my chest, adrenaline coursing through me, cheeks flushed with fear.

I rarely get through a chunk of sleep these days without being visited by the heebie-jeebies. It is usually the same scenario – I wake up utterly convinced that I have fallen asleep in bed with Ellis and he is nowhere to be seen – which is ironic seeing as we have never brought Ellis into bed with us. Much duvet flinging and rolling over of Mike follows, as I frantically search for what I am now sure is going to be our dead baby in the crack of one of our bums. It is only after my panicked search that I tend to remember to check the Moses basket, where Ellis, without fail, always is.

One night there is a slight variation on a theme. I wake up (or maybe I don't, maybe I am still asleep and dreaming, I am the least person qualified to tell) and look over to where Ellis is. Except that the Moses basket stand is empty, and Ellis is in his basket, on the floor. I wonder why Mike has seen fit to do this, but lay back down to return to sleep, only to spend the next five minutes worrying that I shall wake up at the next feed time and accidentally step on him. So I sit up again, resolving to move Ellis back to his rightful stand. Only to find that he is already there. Why is my brain being so cruel? What have I ever done to it that it feels necessary to exact such terrible hallucinogenic revenge? I never thought I would say this, but bring back pillow flinging.

SCAR TROUBLE

Oh look, here I am, back at the GPs. Why I do not have a reserved parking space by now to go with my very own waiting room chair, I do not know. I wish there was some kind of Air Miles type scheme for your GP. Malady Miles. I would be racking them up like there was no tomorrow by now and planning a free trip to Sydney.

My scar is giving me some pain and whilst I can't see it (there is the small matter of a post-birth belly obscuring the view, which I fear is less to do with baby fat and more to do with Fruit Pastilles) a brief positioning of a complex series of mirrors shows me glimpses of some very angry looking flesh.

I study the view out of the GP's window with my trousers and pants round my ankles whilst the GP kneels in front of me to do her inspection. I'll give childbirth credit for one thing; I have so little dignity these days it would be embarrassing, if I actually gave a shit. The GP produces the longest cotton bud I have ever seen and swabs the scar.

"Yes, there is an infection there. I'll give you some antibiotics, and call back in a few days for the results – we'll know what the infection is then."

Great. I have some unknown interlopers in my scar.

"I advise you to wash it twice a day." I really want to try to do this, but deep down I kind of know that washing a scar comes some way down the list of pressing jobs to do whilst I am trying to care for a baby.

"And it would be useful to let it air as much as you can – lie down and let the air at it, that will help." She's starting to take the bloody piss now. Lie down? I barely have time to poo these days, let alone recline on the sofa and fan my nether regions.

THE CULT OF BREASTFEEDING

Gone are the days of topping up Ellis' feed with formula as my milk is on full throttle; I have delightfully dripping nipples and some smashing milk stains on my pyjamas from nocturnal leakage.

However, breastfeeding is still not without its problems. Ellis struggles to latch on, he fidgets and comes off the boob a lot and generally is not keeping up his side of the bargain. So on the advice of a midwife, I attend a breastfeeding clinic laid on by the NHS.

Let's be clear – I do not want to go. But I feel duty bound to go for Ellis' sake, so I trot off with him to the local hospital, back to the new wing and the stained chairs. I join a group of about twenty women with babies of varying ages, sitting in a large circle. In the centre of the circle are all the babies, lying or crawling on a patchwork of mats and blankets. Already I have the sense that I don't belong here. These women probably knitted all these blankets.

As the group settles I realise that it must be Halloween that evening, as some mothers have oh-so-hilariously dressed up their babies. There is one in an orange romper suit with a hat in the shape of a pumpkin, a little baby boy done up as Dracula and another, well, actually, I don't know what she was meant to be, it may have been just an unfortunate looking baby with poor dress sense.

I have very few hard and fast rules about being a parent, and those that I do have are slowly eroding away in the face of having to apply them in the real world, but here I draw the line. Babies should never, ever, be dressed up in a comedy fancy dress outfit. No. Never. Without exception. I do not want to see a baby dressed as a fucking Christmas pudding – it is not funny and they do not look cute. They look bloody ridiculous. And that goes for Santa costumes. Your baby looks like an idiot. And doubly for Halloween outfits. Do these women not have enough to do? A baby is not a doll. If you want to play fancy dress, buy yourself a bloody Tiny Tears. It would be a lot cheaper, less tiring and it wouldn't have to be inflicted on the general public.

So after all the other non-fancy dress mothers (bar one) eulogise over how gorgeous and totally funny Freddie looks in his black cape and gelled up hair and how they wish they'd thought of it (and I have stopped grinding my teeth), the meeting is brought to order.

The formula (granted, this is not a particularly apt description given the presence of the breast Nazi) for the meeting seems to have been taken from an AA meeting. In turn, each woman introduces herself and shares with the group a summary of her breastfeeding-related problem in a confessional, slightly pitying style.

The health visitor leading the group then gives her advice and everyone else is invited to chip in with their ill-informed opinions. There is one particular woman who insists on standing for the entire meeting with her baby balanced on her hip (it's the mothers version of a slightly supercilious 'hand on hip' posture, I think) dispensing advice to all and sundry. She has all the bloody answers this one, and not many people get a word in edgeways. Of course, breastfeeding is second nature to Gobby, she is at pains to point out, which begs the question of why she is still coming to the meetings. Oh that's right, to show off. At one point, after a woman has explained her distressing breastfeeding related problem, Gobby pipes up with the inimitable advice: "It does get better." Well, thank fuck for that insight, Miss Marple. Hands up who feels better now?

The room is tropically hot, which seems a pre-requisite for any room in which there might be a baby present (apart from the labour ward, which is trying to deep-freeze its occupants). I think the midwives are in competition with the GPs as to who can melt a patient first. Twenty babies are lying in front of me, a bristling tangle of flailing limbs. Many are starting to cry, which encourages others to do the same. The noise level is increasing, a discordant ensemble of wailing which we are forced to talk over in ever-louder voices. I suddenly realise I have stumbled into my idea of hell.

Then it is my turn. I do the required confessional, explaining that latching on is a problem, particularly when I have to breastfeed in public. I know lots of women who have no qualms about the whole boob-out-in-public thing, and more power to their nipples. Me? Not my bag. I think the root of the issue is that holding Ellis under my arm to feed and finding a comfortable position without my trusty high-armed chair is problematic, and this causes all sorts of knock-on problems of latching on, staying on and exposing myself in an unsightly way to a room full of strangers who have no more desire to see my boob than I have to show them. Not to mention that Ellis takes so long to feed, the staff are sweeping up around me and ostentatiously clearing their throats and checking their watches before we are even halfway through.

The health visitor tells me that latching on can be easier if I stand up and do it. Righty ho. So having just explained that I don't feel comfortable breastfeeding in public, she is making me stand up and do it? I can imagine being on display in my local coffee shop. 'Yes, you at the back there, I don't think you can see my breast well enough, shall I just stand here a bit longer? Or maybe do a pirouette just before you tuck into your iced bun?'

Gobby, of course, has something to say on the matter but I don't listen, I am too pissed off about the ludicrous advice I have just been given. I want my money back. Okay, so the meeting was free, but still, I think some compensation is in order.

I tune back into the meeting just in time to hear a woman tell the group that she loves breastfeeding so much she is already dreading giving it up as she wants the exclusive bond with her baby to last forever – she hates the thought of sharing him with anyone. Holy shit. This one has graduated from boiling bunnies – she must be onto at least horses by now. Please can I leave soon?

Then we have a general chat about other baby-related challenges we are facing. Someone says that their baby screams every time they put them in their Moses basket, so I tell them that I warm the blankets with a lukewarm hot water bottle for Ellis, as I think it is sometimes the sudden cold that provokes the outburst. The health visitor nearly chokes on her herbal tea. She jumps up and, in a high-pitched voice, tries to tell the group that hot water bottles and babies don't mix. She is practically spasming with fear-induced apoplexy that everyone will now try and put their babies on top of a scorching hot water bottle. I don't know what it is about health professionals, they universally think that every member of the public, particularly the ones who have just given birth, are total fuckwits. I know, I know, some are - but quite frankly it is getting right on my tits. On the infrequent occasions that Ellis hasn't got there first, of course. I am hoping she is going to forcibly eject me from the group, but no such luck, I have to endure another twenty minutes of inane baby chat before the tea break, at which point I whip a biscuit from the plate (call it compensation) and make a quick exit.

CLUTTER, CLUTTER, EVERYWHERE

There is no direction I can look that doesn't have a view of a variety of baby paraphernalia. Every room seems to be populated by an outbreak of stuff. A baby swing takes up a large corner of the dining room, an essential piece of kit in the 'getting Ellis to sleep' process, but a constant source of stubbed toes. The kitchen surfaces are peppered with bottles, standing with their curved bellies like flocks of translucent penguins; those that need washing, those that need sterilising, those that we are not sure if we have sterilised or not. Muslin cloths hang from every available chair and hook so I sometimes feel we are living in a Chinese laundry. Scrunched-up Baby Grows huddle, waiting to be transported to the washing machine whilst a variety of plastic toys lie in wait on the floor to trip us up. This shit gets everywhere. We have the occasional tidy up, which pushes back the tide momentarily, but you can't fight the entropic force of baby crap. At least not without a flame thrower, an industrial-strength Hoover and a skip.

BABY ON LOAN

I have a feeling. Not the one coming from my scar, which is curiously numb yet often painful. No, it comes from much deeper within. It is one of those nagging, never-not-there kind of feelings. The sort that seems to hang around in your mind's peripheral vision, so that when you try and focus on it, it dissipates too quickly to really work out its form. And then one day I see what it is. It is the feeling that Ellis is out on loan to us – that we don't actually have a baby - don't be silly - we're just looking after one. And any day now, the doorbell will ring, someone will turn up to claim him, and we shall have to hand him back. The thought of letting Ellis go is terrifying, and then the next thought makes itself known: ooh, just think, you can actually have a full night's sleep. Once I let this 'baby on loan' thought form, I do start to twitch every time the doorbell goes. Whether it is borne from a sense that we shouldn't really be parents, with our fumblings, second guessings, and make-it-up-as-we-go approach to parenthood, or if it is just my mind fucking with me once again, I have no idea. But he is not a library book, a hire car or a hedge cutter. He is ours, forever, and for that I shall be eternally thrilled. A full night's sleep would be rather nice, though.

JUST DON'T USE THE R WORD
(6 WEEKS OLD)

True to textbook form, Ellis seems to be having a growth spurt. It's not that I can hear his bones creaking as his toes burst through his baby grow, but boy oh boy, is he keen on his milk at the moment. A two and a half hour breastfeeding session ensues. I run the gamut of almost the entire afternoon's televisual entertainment: Cash in the Attic, Worthless Old Crap in the Attic, Flog It, Flog your Granny, Granny in the Attic. As my milk finally slows to a dribble, my brain does too.

We are having some modicum of success with a routine – perhaps – sometimes, if the wind is in the right direction. The key thing Ellis has taught me in his six, fun-packed, milk-sodden weeks of life is that it is sheer folly to state anything categorically. Always, always, hedge your bets, add several caveats and entertain the thought that you are most probably wrong.

"Oh, I know that face, Ellis, you've just had a poo, haven't you, poppet?" I check for poo: nothing. "Oh. I knew that, really."

"He'll sleep for a good hour now, he always does." "Are you sure you only want twenty minutes sleep, Ellis? I can re-warm your sheets if you like?"

He is usually (sometimes, perhaps) getting a morning sleep with a shorter afternoon nap, although on the days that I have really, really urgent things to attend to, Ellis will renew his subscription to the Wide Awake Club and make sure I don't have a moment to myself.

There is an antidote to Ellis' occasional wakefulness - a vigorous walk in the pram. Foolishly, I try to combine this extreme walking with doing something vaguely useful, like buying some food to eat or popping into the chemist for some other piece of urgent baby paraphernalia that I didn't know I needed until someone I met knew someone whose sister said she found it indispensible. There is a flaw to this walk-with-a-purpose thing – the moment the pram stops, Ellis' eyelids ping open and he starts to cry. What is needed here is a New Mum Phone Ahead Service: "Yes, hello Boots, it's me. Put a pack of nappies, a pram rattle (blue, not pink for chrissake) and a pack of baby wipes together, I'm coming through in ten minutes." I swoop in, right change at the ready, head to the counter, dump the money, grab the carrier and with a squeal of pram wheels, I am out of there before Ellis can say "Waaaaaaaaaaaaaaaaaaaa."

It doesn't quite work like that in reality. Inevitably, I ask for something taxing like baby skin cream that they keep behind the counter for some ridiculous reason – just in case someone buys five tubes of it and snorts it all in one go, maybe. I watch the shop assistant trundle off, my eyes flicking twixt pram and receding assistant. My arm pumps the pram back and forth as I urge her to get a bloody move on. I silently will her to go straight to the bottom drawer where I know it is, but what with the time it takes her to bend her arthritic bones over and open four other drawers on the way down, Ellis is starting to stir. I pump faster, adding a sideways swivel to make it feel like he is navigating the pedestrians on the High Street. She comes back, slowly, and rings up my goods with the nonchalance of someone obviously not versed in the paramount importance of keeping a baby asleep. Finally, I punch in my pin number as Ellis starts to whimper. Fuck, I have to go. "Here's a five pound skincare voucher for..." Too late, the front wheel of the pram is already spinning out of the shop door and I am marching forth, planning a route through Tesco aisles to allow me to grab all the ingredients for tonight's meal without actually stopping.

THINGS I THOUGHT I'D NEVER DO #2

Our house is a poo-fest. Mike, who pre-Ellis, was a fully paid up member of the Poo-Haters' Club and couldn't even bear to talk about the stuff, let alone come face to face with it, has had some kind of Colon-to-Damascus conversion and is as fascinated as I am with the product of Ellis' bowels. Many of our conversations revolve around the output of Ellis' bottom: what shade of green it might be, what's made it appear a little granulated, what the heck those flecky-bits are, or it seems a little runny, or a tad dark, or a smidge beige.

We are often to be found bent over a nappy, inspecting, discussing, comparing and contrasting. Poo is an excellent barometer of baby wellbeing, so it is such a shame that, for all our poo-pontificating, we have limited excrement expertise. A few books give us some handy photos, and we have the trusty NCT handout (which quite frankly I should have laminated given its close proximity to the sticky stuff) but we lack a little insight.

"Ooh, it looks a little like he's been eating grass, there's green bits in it."

"Has he been eating grass?"

"Nope."

"Probably isn't grass then."

"No, probably not. But why is his poo so weird?"

"Dunno."

"No. Me neither."

It is amateur parenting at its finest, but our lack of knowledge doesn't stop us frequently talking poo. I can't tell you the time I had lunch, but much to my own amazement I can tell you, to a tolerance of a few minutes, when I last inspected a poo-laden nappy and what precise shade of brown it was.

ONE IN THE EYE

We are currently running a sweepstake on who gets peed on the most when changing Ellis' nappy. Crack open that nappy without due care and attention and there is a distinct possibility that I will get a spray of wee up the front of my jumper, or over my hands, or across the change mat and on the odd occasion when Ellis is really trying hard, across the floor as well. I think he saves it up, knowing that a nappy change is near, holding back until he hears the unmistakable ripping of the nappy tabs.

We develop the fold-over technique, where several sheets of toilet paper are folded over to create a thick wad and, holding this in readiness, I open the nappy and place the wad over his willy, so that it absorbs the stream should he decide that this is the perfect moment to relieve himself. And although I am getting to know the tell-tale signs of when he is locked, loaded and ready to fire (his little chap gets bigger and points less southwards) there have been times when I am left with a sodden, dripping lump of toilet paper in one hand, a pooey nappy in the other and a line of pee up my tee shirt for good measure. Note to self: appropriate attire for nappy changing is a cagoule and waterproof balaclava.

One day I forget the toilet paper and open the nappy. Sure enough, Ellis starts to pee. How he manages it I do not know, but this time, he pees right in his own eye. Now, as a mother, I am imagining the appropriate response here would be to act concerned, jump to his aid and wipe his eye. Which I did do... eventually. After I have laughed so hard a little bit of wee comes out of me too.

ONE HAND CLAPPING
(OR MAKING LUNCH)

Six weeks into motherhood and I am becoming an expert in at least one thing: doing stuff one-handed. Eating is the first task to be mastered using only my left hand, as Ellis firmly ensconced in the other – quite simple, just so long as Mike is around to pre-chop everything into bite-sized pieces. The eating dinner with one hand thing is often accomplished standing, jigging Ellis up and down on my hip as he refuses to sleep. Well, at least I get to use up the remainder of my bumper pack of Rennies, which would otherwise have gone to waste.

Making a cup of tea is next, which is fine, if I ignore the sense of 'accident waiting to happen' as I pick up the kettle and bring it only feet away from Ellis who is on my other shoulder. Making myself some lunch is a tad more problematic – toast is off the menu as it gets as far as exiting the toaster, then stalls at the buttering stage. I just cannot get enough purchase to spread the butter and simply end up dragging the toast off the plate. I consider getting my rather handy dad to rustle up a toast-buttering jig that can be held with a judiciously placed hip against the side of the kitchen surface, but discover soup-in-a-pouch just in time. One snip at the corner, a couple of minutes in the microwave: job done. Delicious. If a little lacking in the toast department.

With a small baby, it is amazing how quickly my achievements have been scaled down. Where once I was churning out documents for clients in forty minutes, or getting a week's washing done in a morning, I take my slightly smaller triumphs where I can find them these days. Hurrah! Get me! Super Mum! I have just made a cup of tea and only had to re-boil the kettle three times due to Ellis-shaped interruptions! Call the local paper, I have managed to get the washing basket downstairs! Stop press! I am dressed and it's not even noon!

I loathe being in pyjamas when not in bed. Slothophobia, I believe it is not called. Prior to Ellis, I can remember, maybe twice in the last ten years, still being in my nightwear as the morning draws to a close (excluding illness, of course, where the triumvirate of pyjamas, duvet and sofa are medically proven to ease suffering and hasten recovery). With Ellis, every day is a pyjama morning and I hate it. It is part of the new-mum essential morning look, though, and I have to begrudgingly accept it. Along with the PJs, which are inevitably spotted with dried-on stains of milk, milky sick or coffee splashes (you try drinking coffee whilst simultaneously singing a nursery rhyme, jigging your baby from side to side and wiping a dribble of snot from his nose) I sport fetching bed-hair, slightly puffy 'it-can't-be-time-to-wake-up-yet-can-it?' eyes, a mostly dirty muslin trailing from my waistband and a pair of sloppy slippers, also embellished with the must-have stains of the season.

One morning I am breastfeeding Ellis and the doorbell goes. In a daze

I pop Ellis off my boob and hasten to the door. As I start to open it, I feel a breeze in a place where breezes don't usually get felt. Shit, I've still got my left boob hanging out. Just in the nick of time I spare the postman a full frontal of my milky breast by strategically holding Ellis over the offending body part. God, I might have to put a Post-It on the inside of the front door from now on: 'Remember: put your boob away before answering'.

Mike is not as fortunate as our postie. I wander into the kitchen having just completed breastfeeding (for now).

"Christ, what's that thing hanging between Ellis' legs?" he asks, staring slightly agog and looking rather alarmed.

As Ellis is rather comfortably nestled round my neck, I feel between his legs, wondering if he has had some kind of silent prolapse of his internal organs.

"Ah, yes, that's my breast," I reply.

Who says a baby kills the romance between a couple?

THE PUNCH BOOB

Ellis has a new habit, and whilst pretty much everything your baby does is lovely, exciting and fascinating, this is one habit I am hoping he will grow out of pretty damn soon. When he is breastfeeding, he will punch my breast hard with his balled up fist. Repeatedly. Now he has always been a bit of a flailer on the boob, but this is different – he has a highly accurate sense of target, for a start, and it is not without a modicum of pain. It reminds me of someone at a vending machine; they have duly put in their coin, out comes a cup but only a dribble of liquid refreshment is dispensed. So they bang the machine, which elicits another dribble, then they bang again. After much banging with clenched fist they take their quarter cup of cold coffee and leave in a huff. I have a sense that this is what's going on here – for Ellis, my boob is the slightly old, faulty vending machine and I think he would rather like an upgrade.

But once I realise that this is what's happening, I am less annoyed about being repeatedly punched (well, just slightly) and simply swap Ellis to the other boob, or give him a top up of formula or a bite of my Mars Bar. Okay, I made that last bit up. He can get his own bloody Mars Bar.

GP CHECK UP

I am back with Doctor Scatty for my six-week check up. We get some way into a question and answer-based conversation about my wellbeing before I mention my scar. She looks puzzled and glances down at her notes.

"Oh, you had a C-Section!" she exclaims with surprise. I take a deep breath and nod. How does this woman manage to make her own bloody breakfast of a morning?

"So, what do I need to ask you now you are a C-Sectionner...?" she muses, mostly to herself but I am sure she would not have minded contributions from the floor. She looks a little puzzled and turns to her computer screen, pauses, then types something. I swear she is typing 'things to ask a C-Sectionner on 6wk check up' into Google.

THE ENIGMA CODE

My large A4 feeding book is my bible. I use it religiously, and often refer back to it to glean any truths hidden within its pages. In only a month and a half it has become dog-eared, crumpled and milk-stained. Each feed is logged with the start time, how many minutes of sucking occur (Ellis does so much – excuse the phrase – titting around on the breast he can be there for forty minutes and only have drunk milk for ten of those, so I feel his quaffing quota is a key piece of data to collect), and the finish time. My quest? To discover the secret to Ellis' feeding, to decipher the logic of why some days it takes two hours to get through a feed, and on others it takes forty minutes. There are already pages and pages of numbers, totals circled, minutes totted up. If I can find the code, I can surely make this feeding malarkey a whole lot simpler.

Goodie, the Health Visitor comes for a visit. She evades all my questions over a cup of tea and we start to talk about breastfeeding. I show her my book.

Goodie clears her throat. "Well, yes. Some mums can find it a little..." there is a long pause "...obsessive to note down the feed times."

Good grief, Goodie has actually said something that could be construed as an opinion. Whilst I am slightly annoyed that she is as casting aspersions on my grip of sanity, I am totally heartened by her newfound ability to stick her neck out.

I have half a mind to tell her about a gadget that one of the NCT girls has: an 'It's Been'. It is a portable little device that has a number of digital displays on it – each one showing you, in minutes, how long It's Been since your baby's last feed, or their last sleep. It is an anal retentive's digital wet dream quite frankly - and I was horrified. And secretly a little bit jealous. But I think the It's Been does have the potential for another digital display, showing you how long It's Been since you last had a normal life. Mind you, they would probably have to rename it Has Been. Or Just Stop Fucking Counting, You'll never Get It Back.

Goodie shrugs. "Although of course, some mums find that sort of recording of breastfeeding really useful."

Oh bollocks, there she goes again.

I find much more helpful advice when I speak to another midwife (not Boobs, I will never speak to her for as long as I live). She tells me that it can be helpful to eat a piece of cake or some biscuits to boost... To be honest, I never did find out what it was supposed to boost, as I was so excited by this news I jumped straight on the phone to text friends the amazing news. "Gr8t news! Eat cake + bikkies. Good for the boobs. Midwfe sez. Yip-e!"

BREAST SHELLS

It is time to crack open the box of breast shells as I feel those drips of milk soaking into breast pads, or my pyjamas, or onto my foot if I am getting dressed, are just too precious to waste. I pop one into my bra, but it refuses to stay put – it must be the maternity bra, which provides about as much support as a scaffolding pole made of liquorice. Damn these shells. But I have bought them; ergo I am bloody well going to use them. But how to keep them in? A brainwave strikes, and after much rootling around in the kitchen drawer I find my solution: Sellotape. Not a conventional solution, granted, but it works very well. I go about my household business, humming a merry tune (that would be Twinkle Twinkle, then), smug in the knowledge that I am racking up little puddles of the albino nectar for my son. It is all going so well, until I absentmindedly bend down to pick up a discarded muslin and the contents of the shells fall out and dribble onto the floor. Oh crap. I tear off the shells and toss them in the bin. I must learn how to differentiate between a brainwave and a brain malfunction. Breast shells. What kind of a shit invention is that?

REVELATION (7 WEEKS OLD)

As usual, at around 8pm, the bewitching hour begins. I give Ellis a feed and he is his typical punching, flailing self. We put him down but he screams until we fear for his eyeballs not being able to stay in his skull, so pick him up and walk him round. And round. And round. I do a figure of eight around the kitchen table, into the lounge, round the sofa (not forgetting to step over the trailing cable, a temporary feature of our TV set up that has somehow become permanent) and back into the kitchen for another lap of the table. All the while singing nursery rhymes, trying not to think about how much my legs and arms ache and hoping beyond hope that Ellis falls asleep before I wear my feet out into raw, round stumps. But still he cries.

Mike and I do relays with him, perfecting the handover into a seamless transition of which even Ellis is not aware. Back and forth, round and round, for hours.

As I am contemplating joining Ellis in his uncontrollable screaming, Mike says to me: "Do you think he might still be hungry?"

"I only fed him an hour and a half ago," I reply, secretly affronted that aspersions are being cast on the milk-giving performance of my boobs.

"True, but..."

At this juncture, anything is worth a try and we hastily defrost a bottle of breast milk from the freezer and offer it to Ellis. I expect him to take a few sips, maybe an ounce at the most. We watch him drink the milk and not stop drinking until the telltale sound of a squeaking teat and a satisfied burp from Ellis tells us that six ounces is now none. He has drained the lot.

Mike and I look at each other. Holy shit. All these evenings, in purgatory, listening to Ellis cry, and all along he was hungry. We put Ellis in his Moses basket and he immediately falls into a sound, sated sleep.

"Whoops," I say. This doesn't quite cover it, really, the fact that we have been starving our son on a nightly basis, but there is not a lot else we can say about being rather rubbish parents, and I a rubbish mother, with rubbish boobs.

SAY CHEESE

Seven weeks. Forty-nine days. One thousand, one hundred and seventy-six hours, give or take a few. Now those hours have not been without joy. Having Ellis on my shoulder, feeling his compact body radiating warmth against my skin is a feeling to keep for a rainy day. Stroking his hair. Singing him songs and seeing him look back at me with interest (although this could, of course, be fear). Watching him sleep, his little nostrils flaring almost imperceptibly as he exhales, his crinkled hands either scrunched up by his ears or with fingers fanned across the top of the blanket. It is a marvel, this thing before me. Curious and unfathomable, delightful and surprising. And fucking hard work. I am so tired (did I already mention that?). This in itself is manageable, except that tiredness never travels alone. Oh no, he insists on bringing all his sodding mates – short temperedness, frustration and over-emotionalism - along for the journey. Which makes me feel even more rubbish and tired.

I haven't reached the end of my tether, but I can see it in the distance, and I have to admit, it is looking a little frayed. Forty-nine nights of broken (actually, not just broken, smashed to smithereens) sleep and I am feeling it. And just when I think I can take it no more and wonder about chucking Ellis out the window, he looks up at me and smiles. Not a half-cocked, could-be-wind, excuse for a smile but a broad, beaming grin. Blimey, that changes everything. Who cares if I am tired, that alone is worth the entry price. He is not just a boob-sucking, poo-producing, crying machine – he is a person, with the ability to light up my day with a smile. Suddenly, being a mother takes on a whole new dimension, and the end of my tether is suddenly nowhere to be seen (for now).

THE EATATHON

We are getting on quite well with Ellis' routine, so it is about time he threw a spanner in the works. Ellis embarks on an eatathon, mainly my boobs but with able help from the freezer's stash of breast milk too. My god, we should have got him sponsored, we would have raised a fortune for charity. The feeding routine is suspended while he takes on enough milk to drown a small herd of cows.

READING MATTER

Despite me seemingly spending most of my days feeding Ellis, I keep on with the post-3am feed expressing. I sit at the kitchen table, fixed up to the breast pump, the rest of the house in darkness. I usually use the time to read the paper, or a magazine. But tonight I forget to gather some appropriate reading material before I start and only when the milk is splashing against the inside wall of the bottle do I realise that I have nothing to read. There is no way I am stopping the expressing – it is too much of a faff, and leads to precious milk being spilt. Which I do cry over, because I am tired and slightly over-wrought.

So I read the only things to hand – a leaflet that fell out of the paper earlier about car insurance, right the way down to the copious small print – and what a fascinating read it is too - then I graduate to a scrunched up Tesco receipt. I read it thoroughly, which still leaves plenty of time to count the number of words, check they haven't made an adding-up mistake (I give up on this quickly, as I can't carry the nine without losing my place), see if I can make an anagram out of any of the food stuffs I bought that day (answer: no) and then study the repeated message on the back for grammatical errors (annoyingly, none). I engross myself with that three inch long piece of paper for over twenty minutes, by which time my boob is an empty husk and I have a full bottle of milk. I wonder briefly if this is normal behaviour, to get quite so interested in a shopping receipt, but quickly decide that at this point in time I am probably the least-qualified person to answer that question.

BABY MASSAGE

One of the NCT girls has arranged for a baby massage lady to come to her house to give us a short course. It is a great idea and we each arrive with a baby, strapped into its car seat, swinging from the crook of one arm, and a rolled-up towel under the other. I imagine a soothing, relaxing half hour, rubbing oil into Ellis' skin and generally having a very chilled out time. I should have known better.

Of the eight of us, at least two are standing up and jigging babies around at any given time, trying to stop them crying, one is having to leave the massaging altogether to feed their baby and another is having to do an impromptu nappy change as their baby has just shit herself. It is not so much relaxing as a tag-team relay of tending your baby. At one point I sit on the sofa feeding Ellis, watching the others massaging and wonder why I have spent £8 to feed Ellis in someone else's house. And then the group has to sing 'This little Piggy' whilst twiddling our offspring's toes and I am kind of glad I am sitting this one out. Communal singing and massaging? I obviously didn't read the small print carefully enough when I signed up for this course, as I am sure I would have spotted that. The tea and cake are very nice though.

GROWING, GROWING, GONE TO THE LOFT

I have a wobbly tower of Baby Grows and vests that Ellis no longer fits into. It is amazing, in seven weeks, just how much he has grown, but not so incredulous when I think of all the milk he has troughed. We start a 'pack away in the loft' pile, which starts off at the bottom of the stairs and over the course of the week gets shoved halfway up, then to the top of the stairs, then onto the landing chair and finally into a box and into the loft. It's an indisputable fact now; Ellis is growing and there is no stopping him.

THE GP CHECK (8 WEEKS OLD)

I take Ellis to see the GP for his eight-week check. I don't get to see Dr Scatty, which is a real shame because I could do with a laugh, but instead get Scowlie. She is obviously not having a good day – well, at least I hope that is the reason for her face.

I get Ellis undressed and lay him on the couch. As soon as Scowlie is within close proximity, Ellis lets out a rather impressive stream of pee, angling his willy just right so that she gets a good drenching. I have to stop myself from bursting into spontaneous applause, because, not only is it hilarious, it is also gleeful to know that a medical professional can make such a fundamental schoolgirl error as to not employ the use of a willy shield of some sort.

Having mopped herself down, Scowlie proceeds to hold him mid-air on his tummy, leaving head, arms and legs flailing in space. "Oh, he's a strong boy," she comments and I wonder if that is GP code for "less milk for you, fatty". Ellis then gets weighed in at 12lb 7, an increase of 9 ounces in a week. Blimey, I shall need a forklift truck to get him out of his Moses basket at this rate. Finally, she lays Ellis down on his back and pulls him up by his hands. But rather than sit up, which is the object of the exercise, Ellis goes the whole hog and stands up on his feet. I am not sure who is more surprised, me or the GP, and then I look at Ellis and realise that he is the one who is most surprised of all. The look on his face clearly says: "Cripes, I didn't know those two things at the end of my legs were for standing on."

SLEEP

I think I am a little obsessed. I think about sleep a lot. I don't do it much, which probably accounts for the thinking about it. It's a bit like when I try and eat healthily. I can go for days on end, when I am not on a diet, not thinking about (or eating) biscuits. The moment I decide to diet, that's all I think about. "I must sweep the biscuit, er, I mean floor today." "Answer the cake will you? Did I say cake? I meant door." At least now I do feel that I am used to having precious little sleep, which is a step on from the dearth of slumber being a total, horrifying, mind-numbing shock. In the early weeks of Ellis, I felt like I could sleep standing on one leg in a saucepan of boiling water, I was that tired, but since I have been getting the luxury of four whole hours of unbroken sleep between feeds I feel as if I can survive (just so long as I don't look in the mirror).

Just to spice up the sleep that I do get, my mind is still up to its old tricks. One night I get into bed, frazzled after a particularly trying bout of getting Ellis to sleep in his Moses basket. It is the dead of night (why is it called that? Because if you have the misfortune to be awake to witness it, you feel bloody dead, that's why) and as I lay down, staring up to the murky heights of the ceiling, I look at the clock – 1am. I sigh heavily. Ellis starts crying again. I have fed him, I have changed him, I really don't know what else to do.

A slight pause, then Ellis cries again. I sit up and repeat to the sleeping mound of duvet next to me "I have fed him, I have changed him, I really don't know what else to do."

Mike stirs – I don't know how he hears me, I am barely shouting.

"What?"

I reiterate my despair and Mike looks puzzled.

"But he's only just woken up," he says.

I look at the clock. It is nearly 4am. I put him down three hours ago, laid my head on the pillow and I could have sworn blind that he started crying immediately my eyes had closed. Yet three hours had passed, during which time I got some sleep.... allegedly.

It's certainly a curious place I am living in at the moment. Time warps and bends out of all recognition, my brain doesn't know what it is doing or where it is from one moment to the next and I am not sure when it is all going to end. Once upon a time I used to pay good money for a night out like that.

THE BASKET TOSS

The advice is clear on putting your baby to sleep; don't put the baby in the bed whilst he is asleep, make sure he is awake but drowsy. I think the concept behind this is that the baby will be alert enough to be aware of his surroundings and being put into bed so if he wakes later, he will know where he is and what has happened, rather than waking up and screaming: "Help! Someone's left me in an over-grown picnic basket! And I bloody hate wicker!"

However, like most pieces of advice, they only pertain to other people's situations. Mine is totally different. If I put Ellis in the Moses basket whilst awake, he remains awake for an inordinate amount of time, passing a few hours with crying and whinging. So for many weeks I rock, hum and pace him to sleep in my arms before gingerly, and with baited breath, lowering him into the basket, sliding my hands out from underneath him a millimetre at a time and backing out of the room with uncharacteristic stealth and crossed fingers, only exhaling when I am safely back in the kitchen.

However, like all things baby, time proves my technique redundant and now I am nonchalantly tossing Ellis into the basket, humming an upbeat tune and giving him a cheerful "night night" before skipping from the room. Kind of.

THIS BABY IS SPONSORED BY... MUSLIN CLOTHS

A 'mussie' (let's get with the parental lingo) hangs from every available surface. I can stand at any point in the house, stretch out my arm, and grab one. Over the back of every dining room chair, nestling with the tea towels on the kitchen hooks, scrunched into each corner of the sofa, under bed pillows and over bathroom towels. There seems to be no baby-related emergency that won't be made better by a mussie. Sticky slugs of snot creeping mercilessly toward top lips: gone in a second. Pools of milk vomit in your lap: absorbed in an instant. Globules of spittle dangling from mouths: wiped away before they break free. Mussies are the uncomplaining, unflinching worker-bees of baby-related products. And they even have their own signal so you know when to wash them – stretch the mussie out by the corners and if it 'crunches' and 'crackles' you know it is time to bung it in the washing machine. Genius.

DUVET SLAMMING

It may not be clear at this juncture, so I will reiterate: I am not that partial to getting up in the middle of the night. It could even be said that I am not at my very best at this point on the clock – aesthetically, most definitely not, as at this time I am already working the morning look but with extra crumples and a scattering of those attractive skin creases across my face I get when I lie on the seam of a pillow for a while. Some may go so far as to say I don't get up with good grace. Some people might say it, but they do it bloody well out of earshot if they know what's good for them. I admit it. I am Bitch Incarnate on those night feeds, perfecting the art of motherly cooing at Ellis and a few rounds of Twinkle Twinkle, all delivered through gritted teeth.

When I wake up to the sound of Ellis crying (and let's dispel another myth right now: as a mother I did not automatically become attuned to my baby's cry – I can sleep for a good ten minutes before his cries become so ferocious I am stirred from my slumbers) I pray he will stop. Funnily enough, as a strategy, this is total crap. So I heave my weary self from the warmth of the duvet, leaving Mike to snore to his lungs' content. Now, I have never laboured under the illusion that I am particularly caring; when I was told to go and queue up for a nice big dollop of caring, I accidentally stood in the line for a great big double-scoop of cynicism with a flake of scepticism thrown in for good measure. So getting out of bed night after night to breastfeed Ellis seems more than a little unfair to me. And whilst the nice part of my brain thinks it is a good thing that Mike is sleeping as he has work in the morning, the other (probably larger) part of my brain thinks 'hang on a fucking minute, this is not fair'.

So I develop the art of duvet slamming. I get out of bed, hold the duvet up behind me as I exit, and hurl it back down to the mattress as hard as I possibly can. It lands with a soft 'whumpfh'. This isn't quite the desired effect - I would prefer something more along the lines of extreme door slamming where walls and windows tremble with the aftershock – but as silent nighttime protests go, it's a winner for me.

THE POSTNATAL DEPRESSION CHECK

It is time for the postnatal depression check. Goodie the health visitor arrives armed with a multiple choice questionnaire designed by the best brains in the business to spot those often subtle signs of postnatal depression. To summarise, it goes something like this:

Are you depressed?
a) Yes
b) No

I am guessing that most people would just say no – it's not the sort of thing that one readily admits to, is it? Mental health is a thorny topic at the best of times, and there is such an overwhelming urban (and rural – in fact I would go so far as to say nationwide) myth that mothering is natural, that the 'mother's instinct' is within us all and that if you can't cope you are not only not really a mother, you are a pretty shabby excuse for a human too. I still search for my mothering instinct on a daily basis and have come to the conclusion it was surgically removed by accident when they did my C-Section. So unless they receive a form back on which a mother has scrawled 'I hate you I hate you I want to die' in her own blood, I am guessing this particular questionnaire has not winkled out many psychological problems.

Okay, I am being a tad disingenuous – there is more than one question, after all. But they are so obvious, so banal, that even circling one letter every few inches seems like a criminal waste of ink.

Think of a frying pan. Do you:
a) Use it to cook breakfast in
b) Use it as a means to stop your baby crying
c) Use it as part of your tap dance routine when you sing songs every morning because you are so happy.

Do you find you cry:
a) Only when you stub your toe really, really hard
b) All the time, even in your sleep
c) Never. Crying is a sign of weakness and you are a strong and perfect mother

These might not be an accurate representation of the questions, but in spirit they are close. There is one question, however, that sticks in my mind.

Can you still see the funny side of things as much as you used to?
a) Yes

b) No

c) What does funny mean, again? (Okay, this last bit wasn't there)

Of course, the truth of the matter is b) but obviously I ticked a) as I knew too many b)s would set alarm bells ringing in Goodie's head (there is plenty of room for them, let's face it). What a fucking question. Can I still see the funny side? Well, let's think. I have not slept properly for two months after a week in hospital eating shit and not sleeping, I have no idea what I am doing, I leak a bit of wee if I cough hard, dribble milk from my nipples if I cross my arms and some idiot with a ponytail comes round my house and keeps asking me stupid questions. Do I look like I am fucking laughing?

Goodie sits down to tot up my score. "You haven't got postnatal depression!" she chirps as I fight the urge to stick her pencil up her left nostril. At least that would mean she wouldn't be able to lodge it in her ponytail for safe keeping, which I find very strange. Perhaps she keeps her purse and gerbil in there as well. Oh, and her personality.

"Any more questions?"

Stupidly, I do ask a question. It's a fairly simple one, not too taxing, so I am hoping that she will actually respond with an answer.

"What is best for Ellis' skin – Vaseline or aqueous cream?" There you go. A) Vaseline or b) aqueous cream. Multiple choice – I am speaking her language.

"Apply it in the direction of the hairs," she replies. What? That is an answer, granted, but it's an answer to a sodding question that I didn't bloody well ask. Why can she not give me a straight answer to anything? Does she think I will sue her if she says the wrong thing? That if she says Vaseline I might take her to court for making my baby too slippery? Has the world gone stark, raving mad? Have I gone stark, raving mad? Give me that bloody form back, I think I am depressed.

STILL DON'T MENTION THE R WORD

The Holy Grail of getting Ellis to sleep longer at night continues. Everything we try seems to have the opposite effect at the moment. When I am finally roused from my sleep by the sound of Ellis crying, I have a second of sleep-deprived optimism that the clock will read six or seven 'o'clock in the morning. It has yet to happen. The first night we try a feeding routine specifically designed to help him sleep longer, Ellis wakes up extra-specially early, at 2.30am. Oh, the joy. And then just in case we are labouring under any illusion that we have even one iota of a clue as to what we are doing, he throws in an extra night feed two hours later. Bless him.

LEFT JAB, RIGHT JAB (9 WEEKS OLD)

Mike and I take Ellis to be immunised against a string of diseases, ill-nesses, syndromes and ailments, none of which I seem to be able to commit to memory. He gets one in each leg, the lucky boy, so just when he thinks it's all over, he gets the same pain all over again in the other thigh. I get the job of holding him still, which immediately makes me want to twitch uncontrollably and I fear that I shall be responsible for having the first baby ever immunised via his eyeball. Luckily, however, the nurse has a good aim. The scream of pain that Ellis produces is a new one on us – we exchange an 'ooooh, so that's what a pain scream sounds like' but after about thirty seconds of crying and a rather erroneous promise to Ellis of a large helping of ice cream from me (which almost prompts the nurse to reach for her multiple choice question-naire 'Are you fit to be a mother?') he is smiling again.

It turns out that this is the easy part of the immunisation process. For the remainder of the day, Ellis whimpers, dribbles and clings in strict rotation and after a few hours of this, I break another cardinal parenting rule that I had arbitrarily set and we decamp to the lounge for a spot of TV watching. He lies on my stomach, vaguely interested in that large rectangle of noise and sound for a while, then falls asleep. The relief is welcome but temporary, as by half seven in the evening Ellis is running a temperature and refuses all but the most cursory suck of milk. When the eating machine turns away from the breast, I know all is not right in his world.

Mike hot-foots it to Tesco to bag a bottle of Calpol, which we stupidly did not have the foresight to buy previously in ten gallon barrels. He arrives back breathless but triumphant, having snatched the last bottle from the clutches of a desperate mother holding her weeping child. Well, sort of.

Not long after we administer a spoonful of that strawberry nectar, Ellis cheers up markedly and decides he is peckish after all, drinks his own body weight in milk and falls fast asleep. And we become the latest in a long line of harassed, worried parents to discover the miracle that is Calpol.

THE EXPRESS TRAIN TO FREEZERVILLE

Still I express at some ungodly hour of the night / morning. It is a revela-tion to me how much a barometer of wellbeing my breasts really are. If I am feeling a little under par (relative to my state of uber-fatigue, of course) my milk dwindles to a few drops and after a good hard twenty minutes expressing I have mustered barely enough to worry a teaspoon. Conversely, if I top the 100ml mark, I am on top form and am doing a little jig of triumph as I sashay to the freezer to deposit my night's work. Where once there were exotic cheese-cakes and juicy cuts of meat in the freezer drawers, there is now row upon row of small bags, solid with my pale milk. Those bags represent a good few hours missed sleep where I have been expressing rather than sleeping and I feel being milked on a daily basis is starting to take its toll. Not to mention all those breastfeeding sessions, with their guesswork, and frustrations and antiques programmes. I make a decision: I will breastfeed Ellis until his is three months, then stop. I suddenly feel bloody great. The end is in sight. I can see the light at the end of the tunnel and it's formula shaped. Hallelujah.

The following night I express and it seems a little less like drudgery now I have an end goal in mind – to build the freezer stocks of milk. Ellis can still have breast milk, but out of a bottle, via the freezer. It's the best plan I've had for months. I try to set each breast up in competition with each other. 'Come on Leftie, Rightie was on fire last night, we pulled a solid ninety'. 'Okay, Rightie, now's your chance to show Leftie who's boss; you may be a tad smaller but just consider yourself compact and bijoux.' I appreciate this is not particularly a sane thing to think. In fact, I may soon make myself take the multiple choice questionnaire entitled 'Are you bonkers?'.

READY, AIM, FIRE

At 4am, Ellis is making it clear that he is hungry, so I settle him on my boob and he partakes with gusto. Eight minutes later he comes off, so I pick him up, anticipating a quick wind and then straight back to bed for the pair of us. He seems unusually restless and I wonder if he wants some more milk. It is at about this point I feel an instant warmth spread over my shoulder with an accompanying sound effect of fast-moving liquid hitting upholstery. Ellis has projectile-vomited onto my left shoulder, spraying the chair for good measure. I quickly move Ellis to my lap to begin the mop-up operation, where he promptly repeats the exercise and covers the clock, my bottle of water, my watch and various other items put out of harm's way on the bedside table. I am drenched in milky sick; it is dripping down my pyjamas and I can feel a small rivulet of vomit trickling down my shoulder blade. I look at Ellis – there is not a speck of sick on him. How the hell does he do that?

LET'S ASSUME IT'S FRIENDLY BACTERIA

When Ellis first arrived, Mike and I were fastidious about sterilising every-thing and anything that came into contact with his mouth, and anything that may have been compromised was sent straight back into our sterilising dome to have the life nuked out of it in the microwave. Drop a teat on the floor and it was straight back in the dome. Leave a bottle out on the kitchen table for a while and back in it went. It was germ warfare: we had pulled out the big sterilising guns and were victorious at every turn.

But as the weeks pass, so does our zealousness. A teat that drops to the floor gets the five second count – if you pick it up before you reach five, we consider it germ-free. The left-out bottle is put to use, just so long as it has not been left out in darkness (working on the premise that the nastiest germs are no doubt nocturnal). The expressing bottle and trumpet get put back in the fridge for use later, as we have assumed that at five degrees centigrade, the germs will be too bloody cold to be bothered to do anything apart from knit themselves scarves. After all, there is much talk these days about friendly bacteria. It seems that unfriendly bacteria live under the rim of the toilet and want to kill you, whilst jolly, amicable bacteria live in yoghurt drinks and tummies and just want a chat about the weather, and so who would deny them a home?

My whole 'germs just get a bad press' approach is based upon the fact that Ellis has my nipples in his mouth several times a day, and they don't get put in the dome for a few rotations of boiling sterilisation, so I think there is a point (usually at the intersection of laziness, fatigue and being too busy) whereby common sense must prevail. I don't check this with the health visitor though; for fear that I will be told I should dangle my boobs in Milton fluid for five minutes before each breastfeed.

PAINTING THE TOWN RED
(OR AT LEAST PALE PINK)

How utterly, inordinately exciting. It is the NCT girls' night out, and my first night out since Ellis was born. Not since the age of nine has a trip to the local pizza restaurant been quite so exciting or eagerly anticipated. I actu-ally put on mascara, something I haven't done for some considerable while, and change my clothes for reasons other than that the ones I am wearing are covered in sick.

There is much talk of babies around the dinner table, as we are still very much in New Mum territory – a disorientating place with no maps, very few sign posts and a landscape that can shift from hour to hour – but we do manage a foray into other topics. Much wine is drunk, interspersed with everyone muttering 'I really shouldn't, but go on, just one more' as we all try not to consider the night feed that by 10.30pm is fast looming up at us.

I thought I would worry about Ellis, but as he is safe in Mike's hands and as Mike will do his usual evening bottle feed, I can simply revel in being on my own. It is the strangest feeling, and more than once I think I have forgotten something before I remember that I have come out without my son. If I squint really hard, I can almost see my old social life, but it disappears before I get a chance to have a proper look. Mind you, all that red wine might be affecting my eyesight.

A VISIT TO THE NURSERY

We are off to nursery, to look round. We are not sure when Ellis is going to start (ask me some days, I say tomorrow) but as with everything education-related, it seems that you are leaving it too late these days if their name is not down by the time your foetus is the size of an orange pip.

I am sporting some smashing looking eye-bags and a slight hangover from my night out, but I try and look vaguely compos mentis and not breathe wine fumes on anyone in case they vet the parents as part of the admissions policy.

We are asked to put on plastic shoe covers, but the dispenser is empty, so we are offered some from the bin. I feel this is less about hygiene and more about giving the kids a laugh at the twats with blue condoms on their feet. We are shown into the baby room where Ellis will be. It is noisy and full of babies (which I know should come as no surprise, but somehow does) and I feel a little nauseous. The sandpit has spilled some of its contents onto the floor, there are Play-Doh crumbs on the table, that child in the dungarees looks like he hasn't had his hair brushed this morning and that one over there has a huge bogey dangling from her nostril. Either that or some Play-Doh. Oh god, I really do feel sick, this is horrible.

I realise that I am woefully under-prepared for our visit. In my head, we were going to have a look around, ooh and ah at the marvellously talented finger-painted pictures that look alarmingly like dirty cell protests and leave. I hadn't quite factored in that I would have to contemplate leaving Ellis in the hands of strangers sometime in the not-too-distant future. I feel distinctly emotional as we are shown around.

We have a chat with the slightly over-earnest manager, a tiny woman with sharp features and excessively curly hair. She is obviously a fan of the theory of childcare, and enthusiastically regales us with the approach that the nursery takes.

"We don't use the 'n' word here, though." She says at one point. I look up at Curly, wondering if I have heard correctly. The 'n' word? I should bloody well hope not. Racist terms like that have no place in a nursery, for god's sake.

She continues to talk and then I realise that she means 'naughty'. Apparently, 'naughty' is too...naughty... a word and may give children issues with self-esteem, or their behaviour, or something. I have to admit, my incredulity does stop me fully listening at that point. I appreciate that, theoretically, the approach may be sound; if your child is not the brightest button in the box, it may be a little damaging to refer to them as "Thickie" – to their face, at least. But if they shove their toast in the DVD player, what are you supposed to say? "Please don't be so contextually inappropriate with your breakfast materials"? But apparently, this is not the only linguistic evolution there has been since I was last naughty. They don't do drawing at nursery – they do 'mark making'. I ask you. I can only think that 'drawing' is far too suggestive of the requirement of a modicum of talent, whereas mark making? Any idiot with a crayon clenched in his fist can make a mark. In fact, scrub the crayon. He can shuffle around the floor without a nappy on and he'll be making marks before too long. I feel my hangover getting worse.

The staff are friendly and attentive and rush around tidying away Play-Doh crumbs and sweeping up sand. All the babies look marvellously happy and there is an impromptu sing-song happening in the corner. But I hate it. I think I would like to lie down on my bed and have a little cry. I blame the hangover.

YOU ARE FEELING SLEEPY...
NO I'M BLOODY NOT

The quest for Ellis to sleep longer at night goes on. It is a quest in the true sense of the word; a long, arduous journey, with two brave souls battling against the odds and with much potential peril to themselves in order to reach the Holy Grail. The only difference is that there isn't a dragon. Oh, yes there is, that'll be me. I get wind through the NCT grapevine that a couple of the girls have tried a particular type of formula milk for the last evening feed that claims to be for hungry babies – and reportedly they got a straight six hours slumber from their offspring as a result.

I barely stop to get my shoes on as I race to Boots to pick up a few cartons of the stuff. Six hours sleep? Just imagine it... Mike duly administers the formula and I practically skip to bed with anticipation of getting all that rest. There is, therefore, some mild annoyance on my part (this may be a gross understatement) when Ellis starts to exercise his lungs even earlier than usual, at ten to three in the morning. Holy shit. One grumpy breastfeed later and he is back in his basket, but only until six am, when he decides that the day should begin.

Twenty-four hours later and the whole process repeats itself, with the supposed hungry baby formula proving to be more of a stimulant than a sleep aid. Maybe I should inject some Ready Brek into the milk - that would surely have the required effect. But maybe breakfast porridge wouldn't quite do the trick – perhaps I should go straight for a three-course Sunday roast.

HALF A POUND OF... LASAGNE AND
RICE, HALF A POUND OF TREACLE...

It has become quite apparent after just over two months of parenting that my repertoire of nursery rhymes is shameful. I confidently launch into one, having summoned the first few words of the initial line, only to find there is a gaping great hole in my memory where the rest of the lyrics used to be. There is a copious amount of ad-libbing:

Half a pound of...lasagne and rice
Half a pound of treacle.
Mix it up ...and sick it all out.
Pop! Goes the weasel.

Little Bo Peep has lost her sheep
And doesn't know...where to sign on.
Leave her alone

And... she'll get stoned
Watching the TV 'til midnight.

Eventually, I Google some rhymes so that I have at least a handful that I can sing properly. Boy, are some of them vicious. Sheep's tails getting lopped off and hung on trees in some kind of Mafia-style warning to livestock everywhere. Babies put in cradles in tree branches that are then blown to the ground – where are social services when they are needed? Someone sneezing during playtime and that's it, the whole lot of them, dead on the floor. A rabid blackbird pecking off the nose of a maid, no doubt getting blood and mucus all over those clean sheets she was hanging out. It's not right.

I sing Sing a Song of Sixpence to Ellis a lot, and he seems to like it (well, he doesn't scream all the way through it, which I take as tacit approval). But it is not long before we are both bored of the two verses I know, so I make some more up in the spirit of the original but with what I like to think are useful bits of advice for my son, including a page boy who falls into a fire (moral: don't warm your bum too near an open flame), a Prince who plays with bricks whilst a pauper plays with sticks (moral: get yourself a good job or failing that, marry into royalty), a gardener in the tavern, propping up the bar (moral: keep an eye on your staff, they're bound to be slacking off) and a poacher who is wanted on three counts of theft (forests make good hiding places).

VISITORS (10 WEEKS OLD)

We operate a fairly strict lock-down policy in the early weeks of having Ellis to give us a chance to get back toward some semblance of normality before opening our doors. However, it becomes clear that there is no point waiting another fifteen years, so we invite friends to visit if they wish.

Visitors are not without their challenges. A cup of tea can be a test, given that it requires clean mugs, milk in the fridge, tea bags and often one-handed kettle operation. I also feel slightly duty bound to at least attempt some clearing up before they arrive, which these days is mainly about hiding soiled muslin cloths under sofa cushions and kicking errant toys out of main thoroughfares.

We have two visits in quick succession that make us question our new open-door policy: the first involves a small child (not ours) falling over and splitting their head open, covering the floor in blood and causing much panic; and the second, which involves a full bottle of formula powder (not ours) being accidentally thrown all over the dining room (unfortunately, this is ours). I thought it was Ellis that was supposed to make all the mess?

However, redemption comes in the shape of a friend, who arrives one day with a Marks and Spencer carrier bag bulging at the seams, full to the brim with delicious readymade meals and scrummy delights. She proceeds to put them all away, cook one of them for our lunch and tidies up afterwards. As she stoops over the dishwasher I take a quick peek up the back of her jumper to see if she is hiding a pair of wings, but no. She is a bloody angel in my book, though; a vision of loveliness bearing lime green carrier bags.

DON'T LOOK A GIFT HORSE IN THE MOUTH (UNLESS THE RECEIPT'S IN THERE)

I find the area of baby presents somewhat tricky. It is not without effort to muster a sincere gasp of delight as I unwrap the thirteenth set of hat and mittens and reassure the giver that no, they are the first to have thought of such a marvellous gift and I am sure Ellis will wear them all the time. Maybe. We are being deluged with 'cuddly' (I use the term advisedly, as some of them are just pig-ugly) toys and are starting our own European Stuffed Animal mountain. I would like to rip their heads off (the toys, not the people who have spent their hard earned cash on them - even I am not that ill-tempered) and throw them in the bin, they irritate me that much.

And the clothes, bloody hell, the clothes. I admit that I am fussy. I don't like anything with ears on, or anything that is overly fluffy or furry. I know what clothes like this are trying to do, they are trying to make your baby seem like a pet. And whilst Ellis may sleep in a basket and need toilet training, that is where the similarity ends. I don't like garments with "cute" animals on, because they are invariably not cute and more often than not involve a disgusting palette of pastel colours. I am positively allergic to any item of clothing that implores you to demonstrate love for the unfortunate wearer ('Cuddle me!' 'Hugs please!'). And I can barely bring myself to even think about those hilarious slogans that deface otherwise quite wearable tops that make an oh-so-witty remark about its owner: 'Look out, I'm trouble!' 'Cheeky Monkey!' 'I'm momma's little hellraiser'. No you're not, you are just a baby with a parent whose friends have no taste in presents. 'I'm so cute!' No, you are not so cute, you are so un-cute your parents felt it a necessity to put you in that ridiculous tee shirt to make themselves feel better about their ugly baby. We did receive one item of clothing as a present that nearly achieved Awful Present Bingo full house: a furry jumper, with ears and a cutsie-wutsie embroidered teddy bear on the front. In pastel blue. It nearly brought me out in hives just unwrapping it, so I opened the bottom drawer of Ellis' tall boy with my foot, dropped the heinous jumper in and sealed the drawer with crime scene tape.

I think it is about time that someone starts the tradition of the Birth List (I appreciate there is something askew with the idea of a tradition being started rather than evolved, but once this begins I swear it will take off like bloody Concorde). Everyone is happy to deal with a wedding list – a list of presents, both practical and whimsical, that the soon-to-be-wed couple have chosen, because – and here is the genius bit – because they like them. Just to reiterate that: they like them. They have chosen the items themselves, will appreciate them and will want them under their roof. Compare that to the hideous rag-tag line up of soft toys and puke-inducing outfits that you have thrust upon you when you have had a baby. It could all be done online – www.dontbuymybabyshitpresents.co.uk - the entire transaction over in a couple of minutes and the parents actually end up with what is required. A set of nail clippers might not be the most glamorous of gifts, but a darn sight more useful and wanted than some baby wristbands with bees and butterflies on, which seem primarily designed to freak the baby out ('eek, every time I lift my hand there's a sodding great bee sitting on it...wahhhhhhh!').

THIS BABY IS SPONSORED BY... VANISH SPRAY

I am developing trigger finger. I use my Vanish spray on a ridiculously regular basis due to our unfailing inability to get the nappy on right, meaning that we often have poo spills on the inside of Ellis' Baby Grows. Vanish makes short work, not only of the orange poo stains, but the brown and the black as well. I have no idea what is in that stuff, but my god, it really does do what it says on the tin. There is only one name in the entire world that would be more appropriate for this product: Shit-Out. I am guessing they dismissed it on the grounds of it not translating well into German or something.

HOW ARE YOU?

Mike is out for the evening and so I am on last feed duty, after which I put Ellis in his basket (I do hate saying that, it sounds like he is my pet Chihuahua). I immediately get into bed and start to drift off, half listening to Ellis gurgle away in a milky haze. I am teetering on the edge of sleep as I send a quick wish out to the fairy godmother of tired mothers for Ellis to sleep until at least 4am when I am vaguely aware that unusually, he is making quite a lot of vowel-type sounds – lots of 'oooo's and 'arrrr's. Maybe he is thinking of becoming a farmer.

I drift, ever sleepier, toward slumber. Then I hear it. As clear as a bell, as loud as if it were said right next to my ear and moreover annunciated absolutely precisely: Ellis asks "How are you?" There is a definite emphasis on the middle word, as he is clearly concerned for my welfare. This is not a nonchalant opening conversational gambit, this is a genuine enquiry as to my health. I freeze. I have just heard my ten-week-old son ask me how I am.

I will clarify at this point that I am not one of those mums who claims their baby is a virtuoso pianist just because he accidentally hits two harmonious notes on the piano with his fist, or is going to be a Premiership footballer (heaven forbid) just because he toe-poked a sponge ball during a nappy change. But in my half-asleep, sleep-deprived brain, I hear him ask that question, in a little baby voice. And I am petrified. I actually dare not lift my head off my pillow to look at Ellis. I am not entirely sure why, but I think having been an aural witness to something so strange, I am not convinced that I won't see him reclining insouciantly in his basket, flicking through the Financial Times with a small glass of port in his hand. Instead, I simply lay back, heart racing, sadly contemplating the demise of my sanity.

THE ONE-STOP STRATEGY
(11 WEEKS OLD)

Ellis has now been waking only once in the night for a few weeks, but on the occasions that he reverts to his former two-stop refuelling strategy, it is awful.

When Ellis' ear splitting screams eventually rouse me from my slumbers, I open an eye and see how I feel; if it seems that I fell asleep only a few moments ago, it must be 3am. If I feel normally tired, it is 4am. Only one hour apart, yet a world of difference – a 3am wake up means that I will spend the following day feeling like crap warmed up in a rusty frying pan and Ellis will want another feed at about 6am, whilst a 4am wake up means we will both sleep through until 7am.

As I open my eyes I know it is only 3am. Buggar buggar buggar. As I sit on the side of the bed and fish around with my feet for my slippers I know there is only one thing that will make me feel even the remotest bit better – a good, hard duvet slam.

SILENT BUT VIOLENT

Pooing is less frequent at the moment, perhaps only one or two a day, but that is no cause for celebration. We moved up a nappy size a week ago, fed up with the gravity-defying back leaks that kept occurring, where, even with his willy poked well and truly downwards, Ellis would pee and somehow manage to do so with enough force that it would travel up his nappy, probably encouraged by some weird capillary action caused by his bum crack, and all over his back. A full change of clothes was not an uncommon state of affairs at least twice a day.

Whilst the bigger nappy seems more effective at retaining the liquid onslaught, I doubt any nappy or hermetically sealed bum device can be victorious in the Battle of Exploding Poo. Ellis lets these landslides of shit out in absolute silence - we have no idea how he does it. There must be so much G-Force at work when it exits it is amazing it is not accompanied by the whistle of displaced air or, at the very least, his bum cheeks rattling. The first we usually know about it is when one of us touches his leg and it is warm and squelchy to the touch. It has been known for the poo to reach the kneecap of one leg.

I think that there is a definite gap in the market for a nappy that alerts you to the fact that it has just been covered in shit. Sometimes, if Ellis is in his bouncy chair and I am washing up, or picking up mussies from the floor, or scraping poo from his vest, it can be some time before I realise he has filled his nappy due to the skill he has of releasing it without making a sound. If the nappy could warn me, it would save Ellis sitting in his poo, fidgeting and generally spreading it to every corner of the nappy, and averting plenty of the poo-overboard disasters. A nappy that has a little sound chip, for instance, that shouts "Shit alert! Shit alert!" would be most useful. Or one that lets off a recording of a great big blow off. Or perhaps one that just says "uh-oh, pass the Vanish".

And then there is the accompanying problem of getting Ellis' clothes off without spreading the poo everywhere. Initial efforts culminate in poo between toes as well as on the back of his head, which is lovely for everyone involved. We are now perfecting the 'fold and pull', whereby the vest or Baby Grow is folded into the offending poo, thus covering it before it is pulled clear. Unravelling those cotton parcels later is a real treat, I can tell you.

OH, THOSE RULES ARE SO LAST WEEK

Suddenly, Ellis is changing the rules yet again. His morning sleep, usually a good two hours, comes in at sixty minutes, almost to the second. Hang on a minute, I am only halfway through my chores, having carefully planned my two-hour slot in advance – this just isn't fair.

I get him up and lay him on the play mat to pass some time – sorry, I mean to stimulate him in active play. Ellis stares at the animals dangling in his face and looks pretty unimpressed. I check the clock and now it is my turn to look unimpressed. How am I supposed to keep him entertained until the next feed in an hour and a half's time with only the aid of a giraffe, a monkey and a pair of butterflies?

I lie down next to Ellis and manage to pass half an hour, which includes quite a lengthy monologue by the orange monkey (who inexplicably has a Birmingham twang by way of Wales – I was never much cop at accents), an existential discussion about whether Barbara the butterfly is chasing Bill the butterfly or vice versa and we lay on our backs, staring up at orange monkey whilst I sing a few rounds of London's Burning.

I find it incredibly hard to keep an almost-three month-old entertained. We go from the play mat, to songs, to the sofa to have a 'lift and fly', to the window to look at birds, back to some songs, to some tickling and to rolling a ball to him via some concerted raspberry blowing and another stint on the play mat. I am fucking exhausted. Ellis looks at me with a 'is that all you've got?' look on his face. I have never really seen the point of babies. Don't get me wrong, I understand from a genetic perspective that they are quite handy in terms of perpetuating the human race – this much I get. It's just that on a smaller scale, they are just ...pointless. They don't do anything. Well, they eat, and shit, and if you are lucky, sleep. Oh, and burp and vomit. And after a while, they do smile, and that is great, admittedly. But in terms of redeeming features, it's not headline-grabbing is it? I would like a baby to come with a few more features, maybe. "Look, mine has this wicked little extra arm that you can open a bottle of wine with", "oh, mine has a Sudoku that appears on his tummy every morning". "Ooh, nice, fancy a swap?"

Finally it is milk time and I warm up six ounces of breast milk, confident that Ellis will slug down four of them, then, depending on the position of the sun, the stars and his mouth, he may or may not snack leisurely on a further ounce for dessert. However, this rule seems to be out the window too, as he drains the entire bottle and looks up at me expectantly, as if to say: "okay, nice starter. Where's the mains?"

I suddenly realise that he is entering another growth spurt. The rule book has been doused in milk and tossed aside with contempt and without any prior warning. Help.

END OF BABY MASSAGE

Our baby massage lessons have finished and I can't say I am wholly disappointed. I am not sure that Ellis actually made it through any of the sessions in their entirety, due to either hunger, boredom or general irritation that I had stripped him off in the middle of the day and made him lie on a towel whilst I rubbed his limbs.

All in all, I am pretty relieved that I will no longer have to wiggle his fingers whilst singing about 'Peter Pointer' (which is surely a euphemism for a penis?) and 'Ruby Ring' (let's not even go there).

IT'S CHRISTMAS TIME (THERE'S ALWAYS A NEED TO BE AFRAID) (12 WEEKS OLD)

Christmas day. Does it make us bad parents that we haven't bought Ellis anything for Christmas? Probably. But in our defence, he did get mountains of stuff from friends and family, some of which is cool enough for us to definitely be claiming that we bought it for him if he ever asks.

Christmas with a baby takes on a different style to previous years. No more weeks of cooking in advance, preparing everything from bread sauce to apple pie from scratch. This year, it is packet sauces and frozen puddings – and long may it continue. There is nothing quite like a twelve-week-old baby (no, really, there is nothing like a twelve-week-old baby) to shed light on the most productive use of your time, and poring over a Ramsey tome, wondering why his apples are golden brown whilst you have cooked yours for three times as long yet they still have the anaemic glow of feta cheese, no longer qualifies.

We are taking Ellis on the road after the Yuletide festivities to visit an assortment of cousins, aunts and uncles. The journey from Essex to Sheffield is planned somewhat more strategically than previously, with journey legs being meticulously designed around a complex matrix of variables, namely sleep patterns, feeding times and service stations. The times these coincide are a thing of rare joy.

Preparing for the trip comprises the longest list of items to pack that I have ever seen, compared to the list I quickly scribble for the belongings I am going to take, which could have been written on the back of Ellis' hand. I admit I may be packing for Worst Case Scenario: 'so, if Ellis has a shit landslide after breakfast, then is slightly sick mid-morning, then his nappy leaks wee just before lunch, that makes at least four body suits and vests per day: making a total of...sixteen of each.' Thirty-two items of clothing? Will we need to hire a trailer?

Packing the car is like one of those infuriating puzzles where a cube is deconstructed into a variety of odd-shaped bricks and you have to fit all the pieces back into the original shape. I did try one of those puzzles once, and the only way I managed it was to accidentally lose half the pieces down the back of the sofa and claim that a cube can have wobbly edges. There is a logic involved in packing a car boot with baby paraphernalia that would tax a rocket scientist. Not only do you have to be able to fit it all in, and then be able to shut the boot and all the doors once it's packed (preferably without the help of three grown men), ideally it all needs to be packed in the reverse order to which it will be required. I can imagine little fun to be had from having to remove twenty-eight items of baby crap from the boot of the car in a service station car park to retrieve a bib that somehow ended up right at the back, whilst a howling wind threatens to freeze Ellis' ears clean off.

As our first trip gets underway, I am slightly nervous and have that nagging feeling that I have forgotten something crucial. As we pull away from the house, car axles groaning, I check that we have actually remembered Ellis. Twice. He is still there the second time I look.

Feeding Ellis at the first service station is a breeze, accomplished while we have a restorative coffee. Changing him, however, is a different story. The changing cubicle doubles up as a disabled toilet. I find this a curious, somewhat disturbing alliance of customer functions.

"Okay, so we have the restaurants, slot machines, toilets and dis-abled toilets. Crap, I've not left any room for baby changing facilities."
"Can't we build a shed in the car park?"
"Hmmm, I like your thinking, but I'm not sure the mothers would really go for that. And you know how much they can nag."
"Right. What about using the water hose in the garage forecourt?"
"You don't have children, do you?"
"No...ooh, what about using the disabled loo? You'll never get a cripple and a baby needing the toilet at the same time, will you?"
"I take back everything I said about you being a fucking imbecile, that's a genius idea."
"You called me an imbecile?"

Personally, I would have preferred a shed in the car park, but there you go. I arrive at the disabled loo just behind an elderly woman who had obvi-ously set out from her car a week last Thursday and is just arriving at the toilet door, walking sticks flailing slightly out of control. She disappears into the cubicle in slow motion and I jig Ellis around a bit whilst we wait. And then wait a bit more. Ellis starts out in good humour, eyes wide open as he stares agog at the goings on around him, seemingly astonished by the fact that the universe actually consists of more than ten people. But it quickly becomes old news, and Ellis looks at me as if to say 'yeah, right, I get it. People every-where. So show me something new please.' I jig him around a bit more, not wanting to stray too far from the cubicle lest someone else takes my place. I pray that a disabled mother doesn't turn up, as that would win hands down in a game of Disabled and Changing Toilet Top Trumps and I would have to relinquish my place. I start to cast around for other likely places I can do a nappy change and seriously start to consider the nearby fruit machine, but eventually discount it due to the large joystick that could really make Ellis' eyes water if I wasn't careful. I am bored, Ellis is bored, and I am sure Mike thinks we have been abducted by aliens. And then Ellis starts to cry. I don't blame him, I feel a bit like blubbing having waited with a not feather-light baby in my arms for over twenty minutes. What if she's bloody died in there? She may have over-exerted herself on the straining front, causing her teeth to pop out, and as she leans forward to retrieve them – whoops – she slips on the floor, bangs her head and that's it, death by constipation. Should I knock? Quite frankly, if there is a dead body in the disabled loo, I can't see that I am going to get in there to change Ellis any time soon – I fear it would not be good form to step over a still-warm corpse to unlatch the changing table from the wall.

After a long, torturous wait of over twenty-five minutes, I hear the lock being jiggled. Christ, either than woman needs a serious bowl of bran or she took twelve minutes to walk from the door to the loo, one minute to have a pee and twelve minutes to creep back again. Twenty-five whole minutes. It's thrown our schedule way off, that is for sure. She totters out without so much as a word, but frowns at the squealing Ellis. A thought involving walking sticks and bum holes springs to mind, but I let it pass as I rush into the loo.

THE FIRST LANDMARK

"It gets better after week six, don't worry." This was the advice of several friends with babies (the same ones who didn't breathe a word about what having a baby was actually like until I was in the same situation). Having passed through that momentous time, I have to say I wasn't particularly convinced. Week seven felt pretty much the same as week six, and week six was pretty crappy all in all.

"It gets better after twelve weeks," they would also say. Yeah, whatever. I am beginning to think my friends are all lying toads. But by Jove, I think they might just be right. Ellis is three months old and I really do think I am sort of enjoying it...mostly. I feel (say it quietly, for fear of invoking the wrath of Grumpius, the Greek god of sleepless mothers) a little less tired. Ellis is smiling a lot, which is about as comprehensive a system of feedback that I can expect from a three-month-old human being, and doing things like nappy changes and getting him dressed does not often involve tears, swearing, poo under the fingernails, bending his limbs into unnatural positions or forty-odd minutes of my life.

And I love him beyond anything and everything I thought humanly possible. When Ellis finally popped out and blew that bubble at me, I didn't love him. At that particular point in time, I am not sure I had enough energy left to love anyone, apart from the anaesthetist, of course. Should I have loved him from the outset? (Ellis, that is, not the anaesthetist). Who knows. The myth of Motherhood states that you love your baby the moment you set eyes on it, that 'mother love' is within us all. Hmmm. I think this may be utter bollocks and comes from the same camp that claims a mother can tell her child's cry from forty paces in a room full of children. Which is also rubbish as far as I am concerned – I have trouble recognising his cry when I know for a fact that there is only me and him in the house. But then I was never a 'love at first sight' kind of girl, unless you were talking cheesecake. I don't think I have ever 'fallen' in love, hurtling at a thousand miles an hour, free-falling through a chasm of emotion, heart racing. I'm not sure I like the thought of falling in love like this, it suggests grazed knees and muddy palms (which, come to think about it, is probably more likely to occur in the lust phase). I think I perhaps pootled in, thoroughly enjoying the stroll and hoping perhaps I might end up somewhere lovely, but oops, mind that puddle now, what a lovely day and why not check the map? (laminated, of course). The destination is no less breath-taking and exciting to experience, but the route is a little more considered perhaps. So I am growing to love Ellis more every day, as he gradually becomes a real, interacting, interesting, curious and baffling person and less like a pooing, crying, milk-sucking robot.

Either that or I am just feeling remarkably chipper due to the fact that I have given up daytime breastfeeding.

A BIT OF A BASKET CASE (13 WEEKS OLD)

Our return from the trip away seems like the ideal time to get Ellis out of his Moses basket and our room and into his cot, which has been lying dormant in his bedroom for months. We are thrilled at the prospect of getting our room back, as it means we can get undressed without the fear that the soft crumpling noise of our garments hitting the carpet will wake up the sleeping Ellis, and moreover we can actually put on the light to get our pyjamas on, rather than grope uselessly around the duvet and the surrounding floor in a desperate attempt to locate them. Mind you, I have learned the art of stubbing my toe without yelping, which is a useful trick to have in the armoury.

We assume that the transition to the cot will not be too hard, as during our stay away, Ellis has been happy to sleep in a variety of strange rooms without seeming to mind in the slightest – wherever we lay his basket was his home.

We do our usual pre-bed routine involving bath and a feed, with some soothing lullabies thrown in for good measure. Giving him a final kiss, I lower him gently into his new cot.

For one second, Ellis is perfectly silent. I look down at him, with his froggy legs and clenched fists, adrift in a sea of mattress and looking suddenly tiny after the giant he had become in the cramped confines of the basket. Then Ellis decides he is definitely Not Happy and starts to scream like his lungs depend upon it.

After some futile comforting and a short chat about the importance of being behaviourably flexible enough to embrace change, I tell him that he will have to get used to it and then immediately relent in the face of a rather large tear that rolls down his scarlet face. We are not willing to capitulate totally, however, and decide on a cunning compromise. We pick him up, place him in the Moses basket and place the Moses basket in the cot in some kind of Russian doll arrangement. Hah. What a ruse. And sure enough, this set up works well enough to satisfy both parties so we retreat from the bedroom backwards and on tiptoes before Ellis reneges on his part of the deal.

We discuss the problematic issue of basket-to-cot transition over breakfast and decide that what is required are cot bolsters – large, long, sausage-shaped cushions that lie down either side of the cot to give Ellis the illusion that he is not three miles from the edges and is in fact snug as a baby in a wicker basket. We clock up many miles (both actual and virtual) in our search, but to no avail. As bedtime looms, true to the adage that a desperate mother is the necessity of cobbled-together invention, we improvise with two tightly rolled cot blankets tied to the cot bars, with my U-shaped feeding cushion providing a bolster at the foot.

"Do you think this is safe?" Mike asks.

"Well, I don't think he'll notice if he bumps his head on the blankets," I reply.

"What about cot death? What causes it?"

"Errr..." I start to reach for the ties holding the blankets to the cot sides. Death by blanket-sausage is not something I want on my conscience, thank you very much.

"I know you are not supposed to sleep them on their tummies," I add, worried that I am sounding as useful as a health visitor at this point.

"Or share a bed with them," Mike adds.

"Or smoke near them." This final contribution has exhausted our knowledge of the causes of cot death and we stare at the cot for a while before coming to the unspoken conclusion that, in the absence of knowing what the fuck we are doing, we'd better just get on with it.

After milk and lullabies, I place Ellis gingerly in the cot, holding my breath. He instinctively stretches out his limbs and settles quickly into position; one hand touching the left hand blanket, the opposite foot resting on the cushion – perfect reassurance that he is once again in an Ellis-sized space.

DIAGNOSIS LOTTERY

I think babies have a sixth sense. They identify the first iota of parental confidence as it tentatively blossoms and use their special powers to obliterate it. Ellis' routine has become vaguely (almost) predictable and whilst we would never be so bold as to claim competency with the parenting malarkey, we could go so far as to admit we might actually look a little bit like we know what we are doing.

And then we don't. We put Ellis down as usual at seven 'o'clock and settle into our evening. But as our knives and forks come together across our empty plates the baby monitor springs into life, all lights blazing. Ellis is absolutely yelling his head off. Two months ago, we would have thought nothing of this, simply rolled our eyes, sighed and gone to tend him. But now, it's almost shocking. I am somewhat indignant that Ellis is breaking our agreement that he sleeps from 7pm to 11pm. A baby's gurgle should be his bond, and he definitely gurgled as I outlined the schedule that he was to follow.

I go to him and try my limited repertoire of Getting Baby Back to Sleep tricks, including humming, shushing (though if I were Ellis, being shushed would just prompt my to ratchet up the decibels significantly), rocking, jigging, stroking, singing, pacing, then finally standing still - this is less of a trick, more of a strategy to preserve a little energy. Nothing is working. As the last refuge of the desperate, I feed him and we eventually manage to get him back to sleep.

But by half ten Ellis is awake again. I listen carefully to his cry, mindful that all the books say that by now, a mother can distinguish the type of cry of their baby. Bollocks to that. I can safely say with confidence that yes, my baby is definitely crying. After that, I am on very shaky ground. I check for poo: none. I check for sick on the mattress: none. I peek in his vest for a rash: none. I may not be able to read a cry, but there are no flies on me when it comes to looking for things.

We take it in turns to pace the anguished Ellis around his room, but to no avail.

"Maybe he just had a bad dream," I say.

"What, that he woke up and his crappy parents didn't know what was wrong with him?"

Hmmm, point taken.

"God, I wish he would stop crying."

"What do you think is wrong?"

We pause to look again at our puce-faced baby, screaming as if his life depended on it (which, for all we know, it does) then back at each other.

"Don't know."

"No, me neither." Another long pause.

"Do you think it could be teething pains?"

"What, this early?"

"It's half past bloody ten."

"No, not early in the day, in his life."

"Oh. Well. Maybe. His cheeks are very red."

"So would yours be if you'd been screaming your head off for as long as he has."

Another silence ensues.

"Oh, it could be wind pain; he hasn't pooed since this morning."

"Sounds very plausible. You're probably right."

"Yes, wind pain."

"Mmm, wind pain, poor thing."

"Probably explains why he's knees are drawn up to his tummy."

"Oh, are they?"

"Well, they were a minute ago. He'll do it again in a second, I'm sure."

"Mind you, at least now we know what is wrong with him. It's horrible not knowing why he's crying."

"Wind pain. Tsk."

This episode, and many others like it that we have experienced as novice parents, teaches me something. That is doesn't actually matter what you decide is wrong with your baby, nor how medically inaccurate that diagnosis might be. It is just important that we pick something, post-rationalise the life out of it and stick with it. It is amazing how doing this immediately makes the whole situation that little bit more bearable.

WHO ASKED YOU ANYWAY...AGAIN

Having weathered the flurry of strangers' comments in the first few weeks of taking Ellis out and about ("oh look, a little baby!" "Yes, well done you, now back on the sunshine coach please.") the comments pretty much stopped, much to my relief.

However, as I am standing in a queue at Tesco, the man in front of me turns and looks at the pram. As it has been pouring with rain, I still have the rain cover down.

"It's surprising that he doesn't suffocate in there," the man says.

It is not the most promising of conversational openers. I look up to see a sixty-something-year-old man and quickly realise, given his luridly patterned jumper that stops a good three inches above his waistband, an open anorak with sleeves that really don't trouble his wrists in the slightest and hair that wouldn't look out of place on a yeti, that he is a bit of a basket case. Or given the supermarket context, off his trolley.

I give a non-committal half-smile, hoping that he will turn round, but instead he proceeds to stand in front of the pram and wave to Ellis, who simply stares into space. The exuberant waving continues for some time and I look away, willing the queue to move or for the man to have a sudden heart attack. When I look back, he has expanded his repertoire of salutational miming to include hopping wildly from foot to foot. I pull the pram back into me as far as it will go, wondering if this loony is going to give Ellis nightmares.

"He's waving back, he's waving back, he's waving back!" exclaims the man excitedly. Such is the outlandish nature of the claim, I can't stop myself from peering into the pram to check. I see Ellis' forefinger is twitching slightly. Not quite a full-blown wave then. More likely Ellis is wishing he had a shotgun right now. I know I do.

Having finally escaped the nutter, I walk back toward home. It strikes me that what I really need are some James Bond style pram accessories. A hidden water pistol that senses strangers getting their faces (or any other part of their anatomy) too close to the pram and shoots a stream of high-pressure water in their face. Even better if it could be boiling water, but imagine what the midwife would say about carrying a modified tea urn that close to a baby. A rusty set of sharpened keys that pop out of the side of the pram frame to teach all those twats a lesson who park their cars way too far onto the pavement. And maybe a set of parking sensors on the front wheels to stop me crashing into the back of people's ankles when I am not paying attention. Oh, and perhaps a pram that is designed so that I don't break four nails every time I try to manoeuvre it into the car boot. Stop it now, that's just fucking ridiculous.

SHOE-GAZING

Ellis has discovered his feet. He props them up on the bar of his reclining chair and stares at them for ridiculously long periods of time. He often startles himself when one of them twitches or moves, and I can add to the general sense of wonderment by putting a sock on one, or tweaking his little toe. I think it might be fun to cover one of his feet with a mussie, but Ellis nearly shits himself when he witnesses his right foot suddenly disappearing, so after that I leave him to his own staring devices.

FSS SYNDROME (14 WEEKS OLD)

Oh, the pure unadulterated joy. Ellis has "slept through" from the eleven 'o'clock feed to 6am. For the first time, it feels like a pleasure to wake up at this previously ungodly hour of the morning, accompanied as it is by a slightly weird feeling that I soon realise is the result of getting over eight hours straight sleep.

This happens two nights in a row, but I am no fool. I resolutely do not get my hopes up that it will happen again, for therein lies the path to madness. I call this FSS Syndome: the False Sense of Security Syndrome. Little known in medical circles, but widely recognised amongst new parents, it is a danger-ous ailment that can strike parents at any time. It is not life threatening, but leaves you with a lingering sense of foolishness and irritation.

"Have you noticed that little Freddie doesn't pee now when you take his nappy off? He must be learning to pee only in his nappy...Ugh.."

"What's the matter?"

"Freddie's just bloody well peed in my eye."

So I am definitely not thinking that Ellis will now sleep from eleven til six on a regular basis and sure enough, the following night he awakes at 4am. I accept this with stoical resignation – well, perhaps with much grinding of teeth, a couple of overly-dramatic sighs and one large duvet slam, but seeing as only Ellis can bear witness, let's go with graceful stoicism. However, the next night, Ellis sleeps through again. Oh my god, he really has cracked this sleeping, I think with barely contained glee. It is at this point that FSS Syndrome strikes, for as soon as I have allowed that thought into my head, Ellis does not sleep through again for many, many, many weeks.

WOMB WITH A VIEW

During my pregnancy I came to the realisation that I was not the centre of my world any more. Unsurprising and unnervingly egotisical as that might sound, I think there is something natural about standing at the very hub of your own life. Your experiences surround you, your past, present and future contain you and whilst other people are most definitely standing on that central spot with you, close by and an integral part of your landscape, you are the one with your big toe right on that spot. The spot around which everything else rotates. And then your womb fills with foetus and the gravitational field gets warped. I found myself orbiting my womb, metaphorically speaking. (If that had actually happened, I am sure it would have made the papers. Think of the damage I would have caused). I went from a woman, to a womb with a view. I was there simply to communicate the wants, desires and well-being of the resident in my womb.

On entering the GP's surgery for check ups, the first question was always "How's baby?"

Friends quickly became a lot less interested in me, but were routinely fascinated by womb talk. Conversations at home and outside revolved around Prawn. And even in my own head, I played a poor second to the foetus in my belly. It wasn't altogether unpleasant, this shifting of importance – no one was more fascinated with the whole thing than me. It was just such a wholesale change.

I thought perhaps that I would revert to being me, inhabitant of the centre spot, once the baby was born. Errr, no. Now I am a mummy. Which is not like being a person at all. The same friends who wanted womb talk now ask firstly about Ellis. Kisses that I think are headed for my cheek are diverted to the small bundle resting on my shoulder. The doctors and midwives fuss and pour their medical attention onto my offspring, and I am there simply as a way to transport said baby to and from the surgery and to report back on feeding routines. I am now an empty womb with a view. With a nice line in scars.

This is how it should be, of course. Mummys are probably genetically programmed to think first about the baby before everything else, otherwise there would be far more scenarios involving mothers at the supermarket throwing their basket down in horror and running for the car, realising that they have forgotten to bring the baby with them.

THINGS OF THE PAST

I don't know who these people are that say their lives have not changed since they have had children. They are either pathological liars, or so stinking rich that they have twenty-four hour nanny cover. I only found out recently that there was such as thing as a night nanny. Someone who arrives at bedtime and looks after your offspring all night should they wake, leaving you to have a full night's sleep and awake refreshed and full of energy. I nearly clawed the bags under my eyes off my face with jealousy.

There are lots of things that are now 'things of the past'.

Reading. I have not read a book since Ellis was born. I will dip into the baby books, glance at the newspaper headlines, but that is about the sum total of my reading activity. If I do actually open a book when I'm in bed, I invariably say to myself, 'I will just read a couple of pag...zzzzzzzzzzzzzzz'.

My social life. Don't get me wrong, before Ellis was born I wasn't out partying every night or holding elegant dinner parties with witty and erudite guests who nibbled their way through their poussin with superlative table manners. But going out is such a tricky proposition these days. It entails finding clothes without dried sick or snot on them, trying to persuade friends that eating at 6pm is a great idea so that I can get back and still get to bed on time, and not drinking too much as the idea of a drunken breastfeed at 4am is too much to bear. It just takes so much...energy. I think about it, with every will to organise it, then fall asleep.

Clean shoulders. Most of the clothes I own now sport some kind of shoulder stain. Even those fresh out the washing machine seem to have the memory of a stain if you catch them in the right light.

Lie-ins. I can't bear to talk about this, it's too upsetting.

HOT CHEEKS (15 WEEKS OLD)

I take Ellis to the drop-in clinic run by the health visitors. I had never previously been to the clinic, having had quite enough of Goodie's prevaricating and issue-avoidance tactics to last me Ellis' lifetime, but as a quick check on our scales at home reveal he may have topped the stone mark, I feel I should get an official weigh-in to mark the occasion.

I am called from the waiting area into the health visitor's room and get Ellis undressed. The room is boiling hot and Ellis and I are both simmering nicely against each other as we wait to be seen. I sport an attractive sheen of sweat on my forehead, Ellis a pair of comedy bright red cheeks.

Goodie approaches. "Oh, look at those teething cheeks," she exclaims, looking at Ellis. I express my doubt and point out the tropical temperature of her room, but she is having none of it. Bloody typical. She gets a sudden attack of Confident Diagnosis and all Ellis has is hot cheeks.

Spurred on by Goodie's sudden assuredness, I ask her whether the small dry rash on Ellis' forehead could be eczema.

"Let's see...yes, it could be, possibly. Or just a dry rash. Or a reaction to his shampoo?"

Ahhh. Normal service has been resumed.

TAKE A BREAK FROM THE OLD ROUTINE

Oh, for the confidence of week 14, when Ellis was in his routine (I have blanked the three 'sleep though' nights of that week from my memory, it's too distressing). This week, he has woken up at 3.15am, then 2.45am the following night. It is truly a double whammy of pain. Not only does the opportunity of a six-hour block of sleep evaporate into the air, the possibility of a second night feed yet again looms large. And the feeds are not inconsequential – it is not a quick pit stop for a top-up, more of a service including full boob drain followed by some breast-in-a-bottle action.

Getting up once in the night at 4am is surprisingly okay (now, there's a sentence I never thought I'd utter) but getting up twice? It's too reminiscent of the first six weeks to be anything other than a terrifying prospect, not to mention it guarantees that I will feel like utter crap the next day.

When Ellis cries at this time of night, I lie in bed trying not to listen to the monitor, hoping the hope of the futile that he will somehow realise his mistake at waking so early and go back to sleep. Funnily enough, he never does, provoking much duvet slamming and expletives uttered in a shouty whisper. Where did that lovely routine go? It puts me in mind of that old adage 'one step forward, forty-three back', which is only rivalled in usage-frequency in our house by 'pass the cloth, I have sick on my jumper'.

GETTING TO GRIPS WITH THINGS

Ellis is now starting to grasp objects – well, when he can be bothered. Many times the whole 'getting an object into the hand' thing is purely accidental, I am sure – he flexes his fingers and a toy, the mussie or my collar just happens to get in the way as he closes his fingers and – hey presto – suddenly he is holding on. Other times, there is definitely a purpose to the action. However, there seems to be one drawback to this new trick; he has yet to master the art of letting go. So he will get hold of the activity toy and then get distracted by something else (such as the light, or his toes, or breathing) and totally forget the matter in hand. A short while later, he'll raise his hand and stare in utter disbelief at the toy he finds there. How the hell did that get there? And more to the point, what is it? He will then often wave the object around a bit, perhaps to see if it is a newly-grown arm extension or something else. Occasionally, an opportune sneeze will open his hand and the toy is released, or more often finger fatigue sets in and it plummets to the floor.

THE KILLER DUCK STARE

It is bath time and Ellis is having a gentle splash round in his bucket. We mastered the art of a no-tears bath time when my sister gave me a baby bath which, by any other name is a bucket, but in this instance is called a Tummy Tub. Which alliterative sophistication means it costs approximately five times as much as a regular bucket, but this bucket-reinvention is genius – Ellis feels snug and upright, not supine and adrift in the vastness of the bath. Suddenly, half way through a rendition of Twinkle Twinkle, he goes absolutely rigid and wide-eyed. Good grief, what is going on here? I follow his unblinking, petrified gaze to a pair of small blue rubber ducks sitting on the bath edge, facing him. I look back at Ellis. Yep, he is definitely staring at them. I turn the ducks round so that they face the wall and Ellis immediately relaxes and smiles again. Well, no one likes to find themselves in a no-win staring competition with a duck, let alone with two.

WHAT'S YOURS IS MINE

I never quite realised, prior to becoming a mum, just how often you end up accidentally imbibing your offspring's bodily fluids.

I am holding Ellis in my arms, singing to him. I am just reaching the end note, which I sustain on a distinctly amateur wavering vibrato for dramatic effect, when Ellis lets out an almighty sneeze right into my open mouth from point blank range. I can practically hear the nose mucus splatter against my front teeth and feel the sensation of the bogey droplets hitting my tongue. If someone else had sneezed in my mouth, I would right about now be squirming on the floor in disgust, scraping my tongue fervently with a potato peeler. As it is my son, I wipe my tongue over my front teeth, swallow, and give a breezy "whoopsie-daisy" before wiping his nose and striking up a cheerful rendition of Old MacDonald.

This incident is closely followed by another. I am playing flying aeroplanes with Ellis (as opposed to non-flying aeroplanes, which is when I put Ellis on top of me and try to persuade him to lie still whilst I gather some energy – he is not so keen on that one for some reason). I am lying on the sofa and Ellis is on his sixth fly-by. My mouth is open from the exertion of repeated baby-lifting and Ellis' mouth is open from a mixture of exhilaration and fear. A very large dollop of dribble is collecting on his bottom lip and at the precise moment that his mouth is perfectly aligned over mine, the huge globe of spit falls and lands directly on the back of my throat. I instinctively sit up and feel the cold dribble slide down my throat. Smashing.

WRONG, WRONG, WRONG AGAIN (16 WEEKS OLD)

Ellis has an infinite capacity for proving me wrong – including his particular favourite; letting rip with a series of nappy-shaking farts that lead me to whisk him straight to the bathroom for a nappy change, only to find not so much as a skid mark.

Then there are the public instances, just in case there is anyone left who is labouring under the erroneous belief that I have a clue what I am doing. On arriving to meet the NCT girls for a coffee, I tell them all that Ellis is in a real grump and warn them that I might have to abort if he doesn't cheer up. I get him out of the pram and onto my lap where he immediately starts to beam smiles at them all, throwing in a couple of endearing giggles for good measure. He is practically wetting himself with happiness. The girls look at me as if I have been making the whole grumpy thing up and I look at Ellis. He smiles back, as if to say 'Grumpy? Me? I think you are very much mistaken. Again.'

A NAIL BITING EXPERIENCE

The thought of having to cut Ellis' fingernails strikes fear into our hearts. Those tiny, fragile fingers, those sharp blades – I cannot believe that this is not a job for a highly trained medical professional. Perhaps I could book an appointment to see the GP, and casually ask at the end, "Oh, while we're here, you couldn't just give Ellis' nails a little trim?" Hmm, maybe not.

Up until now, Ellis seems to have had quite an advanced system of self-trimming nails – as they get too long, they have been peeling off of their own accord, leaving me to pluck the loose slither of nail from its corner attachment. Easy. I have been laughing in the face of others' tales of nail-cutting mishaps – until now.

Ellis' nails have obviously hardened and no longer cut themselves. How inconsiderate. Instead, they have become razor sharp instruments of torture capable of inflicting very nasty scratches, over my face, my neck and after a night's sleep, over his as well.

"We must cut Ellis' nails today," I say to Mike, waving the nail clippers around.

"Yep," Mike replies.

"We must cut Ellis' nails today," I say to Mike the next day, waving the clippers and doing a mid-air 'snip snip' just to clarify.

"Yep," Mike replies.

"We must cut Ellis' nails today," I say to Mike the day after that, pointing to Ellis, who has woken up looking like he's had a midnight scrap with the cat next door and lost.

There is silent acquiescence from Mike. We both know today is the day, but neither of us really want to be the one wielding the nail clippers in such close proximity to our son.

"So...I'll do it then..." I say begrudgingly.

"Brilliant idea."

I sit Ellis on my lap. The sage advice of the health visitor comes back to me – instead of cutting, she told me to file his nails, preferably when he is asleep. Right. Should I moisturise his bloody cuticles as I am giving him this baby manicure? The thought of filing his nails is too ludicrous to pursue, so I take a deep breath and, holding his thumb between my fingers, I advance with the clippers. Then retreat. Not ready. I go in again, then back off for a second time.

Rather than witness the inevitable, it seems Mike has decided to make himself scarce, probably readying himself with a jumbo box of plasters in the next room. A wise man.

Right, this time I am just going to do it - I'm not removing a sodding tumour, I am trimming his nails. What is the worst that can happen? I then imagine the worst that can happen, which involves one or more of Ellis' fingertips rolling around on the floor. Okay, just don't think about it. Ugh, imagine the blood. Stop it now, think nice calm things. Would a fingertip grow back? La la la la, just cut the fucking nail.

Snip.

Oh, I've done it. And no blood. Not even slight chafing. This is easy – what the hell was I worrying about?

JUNGLE FEVER

The play gym is a central feature of Ellis' day – I put him there when I want him to have a bit of sensory stimulation, when I need to make a cup of tea or whenever I run out of other ways to entertain a three-month-old. It is designed on a jungle theme, replete with a giraffe, an elephant, a parrot, a monkey and a tiger. Now I am no wildlife expert, but I have a sneaking suspicion that not all these species actually do co-habit, but let's not get picky. 'Gym' is an appropriate name for it, as Ellis gets a great workout. His routine is a little limited, consisting mainly of kicking the giraffe repeatedly in the face and punching the monkey until it is hanging on to its branch for dear life. Each blow landed is greeted with a cheer by me, as I am choosing to ignore the fact that any punch or kick is an accidental collision of wildly flailing limbs and a low-dangling object.

My angel with the lime green carrier bags comes over to see us again. In an attempt to tire Ellis out and encourage him to take his long-overdue nap, we put the play gym on the table, place Ellis on the mat and sit either side of him. (I can almost hear the health visitor turning in her polyester slacks: 'You put baby on the play gym... ON THE TABLE? That's it, I'm calling social services'.) To be fair, Ellis would have had to master the art of a full body rotation, a triple roll and a dive in order to make it off the table top, not to mention avoiding two humans that are sitting in the way – but hey, he can grip an object now so who knows?

We sit there chatting, one either side of Ellis, who gets to work beating the shit out of the giraffe. Well, if you are going for jungle dominance, go straight for the big guy, it's the only way to alpha-male dominance. It is only after about quarter of an hour that I realise we are conducting our conversation with uncomfortably craned necks through several bright green felt leaves, two large silky butterflies and the arse of an inconveniently placed orange monkey. It's a strange world that a mother inhabits sometimes.

NO NAKED FLAMES
NEAR THE BABY, PLEASE

I book a doctor's appointment for Ellis as the scabby rash on his forehead is getting worse and the Health Visitor's exceptional display of fence-sitting means I need to get it looked at by someone who knows what they are doing.

As soon as my bum hits the waiting room chair, Ellis starts to scream. The three-year-old magazines on offer often make me want to do the same, but he is really going for it. I jig him up and down, walk him around (thus spreading the decibel-laden misery to all occupants of the waiting room), shake toys in front of him, hum to him, whisper 'please shut up' in his ear through gritted teeth – nothing has even the slightest effect. I am getting a whole bucket load of nasty stares from the other patients with a few rolled-eyes for good measure. It's no good, I really want to be 'oh, fuck you all' about it, but instead I feel bad – bad that I am disrupting everyone's peace, bad that I have no techniques at my disposal to quieten Ellis down and simply bad as a mother.

I take him through to the room next door - a sort of waiting room for kids. I pick up a procession of half-chewed, semi-broken, germ-laden toys and attempt to distract him out of his paddy, but all are met with the same tear-stained, screaming indifference. I am sweating with the stress and exertion of trying to stop Ellis crying and Ellis is turning redder by the second. At which point, the receptionist appears, having left her post at the other side of the waiting room. Looking at her face, I assume she has just sucked several lemons in a row.

"Which doctor are you seeing?" she asks in a dramatically loud voice, as if having to speak over a jackhammer.

I don't know, Lemon Bitch, you're the one who books the appointments, you tell me. "Err, not sure," I actually reply. She looks at Ellis as if I am cradling an armful of dog shit.

With a withering glance, she pivots on her cloven hoof and leaves the room, making a point of shutting the door on me. I watch her trot back to her desk and pick up the phone. She is way out of earshot - particularly as I have a screaming baby in close proximity - but I am guessing her conversation consists of something along the lines of:

"Hi Doctor, there is one of those bloody awful things in reception to see you."

"Errr, what's that then?"

"Oh you know, the smelly things...ridiculously noisy, always screaming... disgusting creatures."

"Um...you don't mean a baby, do you?"

"Yes, that's it, a baby" (shudders involuntarily). "Come and get it, will you, it's with a wholly incompetent mother and quite frankly, I don't get paid enough to deal with this."

"Right-o."

In a matter of seconds, a doctor comes to get me. On seeing Ellis and confirming eczema, he prescribes E45 cream, which quite frankly I am a little disappointed about as I could have got that without having to wait two days to see a GP, but no amount of asking about steroid cream will budge him.

As he hands over the prescription, he states solemnly: "the cream contains paraffin." Now, I am sure in GP-World this fact has pertinence and meaning. But not in my world. It has about as much resonance as if he had said "The sun looks 1600 times fainter from Pluto than it does from Earth".

So how exactly to reply to this fascinating fact about paraffin?

"Oh, so no naked flames near his forehead then?" I quip.

The GP looks up from his notes, absolute horror across his face. "Oh my god, no!" he exclaims. I try to assure him that I am joking, but I fear he may have left his sense of humour on the train that morning by mistake.

"Do you smoke?" he then asks, seeming very concerned. I can see he now has visions of me with a fag dangling from the corner of my mouth, eye squinted shut against the plume of smoke, repeatedly sparking up my Zippo lighter near Ellis' face for a laugh and using the hood of his baby suit as an astray.

"No," I reply and make a quick exit before he can conjure up any further child-abuse scenarios that he thinks might be appropriate. Fucking hell, it was only a joke.

THE END OF THE BREAST (17 WEEKS OLD)

I have been pondering how long I should keep up my one remaining nighttime breastfeed. Fighting in the 'Keep On' corner is the toxic residue of all that midwife and health visitor brainwashing about giving your child the best start in life, along with a certain convenience of not having to keep your breasts in a fridge, sterilise them or wash them after every use. But coming out strong from the 'Ditch It' corner is the fact that I don't think Ellis gets as much milk as he wants from my beleaguered breasts and breastfeeding is.. well, just a pain in the arse, to mix body-part metaphors.

On a 5.30am wake up, Ellis takes one look at the boob on offer and, with the merest touch of his lips, furiously starts to punch the remaining life out of it. I swap him to the other side, but this only provokes another barrage of flailing fists - I am guessing he is none too happy with the menu on offer tonight. So I hastily organise some breast milk in a bottle which he glugs with much satisfaction. And so by 5.35am, I have effectively reclaimed my breasts as my own. It can be reported that both parties are mightily relieved.

SCAREDY CAT

We've always suspected that Ellis may be a little on the scaredy-cat side; any bangs, clatters or crashes have him jumping out of his Baby-Grow in abject terror. This is usually met with a rousing, if a little unsympathetic chorus of "Custard!" (as in cowardly custard, not apple crumble and custard – random pudding insults have not caught on round our way) from Mike and I. But it is with great excitement that we fill a brand new bubble machine up for him at bath time. After all, every baby loves bubbles. those feather-light, shiny spheres of fun. I turn on the machine, which whirrs into action. Ellis looks startled and stares fixedly at the contraption on the side of the bath, as bubbles start to float towards him. As the first one reaches the rim of his bath bucket, he starts to cry. Not a little, hesitant, 'not sure' kind of cry, a proper 'I'm shitting myself in here mummy' kind of cry. We persevere for a few more seconds, thinking that any moment now, the crying will transform into gleeful giggling at this most entertaining and curious of spectacles. Errr, no. We make a tactical retreat, furiously pop every remaining bubble in its prime and put the bubble machine out of sight - at which point Ellis promptly stops crying. For the rest of his bath time, he keeps glancing over his shoulder to where the machine previously sat, checking that the instrument of torture that we inflicted upon him hasn't suddenly made a sneaky return. Bubbles: every baby's favourite. Not quite. More like bubbles: those evil orbs of malicious transparent torment.

TRIPLE JABS

It seems only a few days ago that we were last having our son jabbed in the legs with needles, but we are back again – this time, for three. Ellis is all smiles with the nurse when we arrive until she subjects him to the triple-whammy stabbing.

I give him a cuddle and his tears start to subside. He stares, leaden-faced, at the perpetrator of such pain.

"Ooh, dearie me, look at Mr Grumpy-poos," coos the nurse.

Hmmm, I think after sticking him in the legs three times with big needles, Ellis is justified not to be hysterical with laughter and gaiety.

"Give me a little smiley-whilely," she says and gurns at Ellis.

'Or, you can just fucky-wucky off," I want to reply on Ellis' behalf.

No amount of cajoling, ridiculous baby talk or tickling can make Ellis crack his thunderous face, perhaps proving that the ability to bear a grudge is, indeed, genetic.

THE ECZEMA-FACTOR

The small patch of eczema that Ellis was sporting on his forehead has been responding to the E45 cream – by laughing in its weedy, ineffective, paraffin-laden face and spreading like wildfire. A huge, scaly, thick scab covers his forehead, and drops down the sides of his face, creating a rather fetching facial accompaniment of scabby side-burns. He looks like a burns victim. It is of course, at this precise nadir of attractiveness that we attend a friend's daughter's christening.

People see Ellis from a distance, say their hellos and 'ooh, he's gorgeous' type remarks, only to get within ten feet of him before their faces fall and they wince and say "Oh. Oh dear. Whatever has happened?" I just about resist the temptation to regale them with a story about an unfortunate incident involving an electric cheese grater and Ellis' forehead, but only just.

What I also overlooked until we arrived is that I gambled with the Baby Stains Devil that morning when I got dressed and wore a black top. Unfortunately, it quickly becomes apparent that I am holding a losing hand. Or a scabby head, at least. Ellis relieves his itching by vigorously rubbing his face against my shoulder and chest, meaning that I spend the day with a heavy covering of eczema crumbs down my front. It looks like I either have the worst case of dandruff known to man, or I have been having a sneaky trough at the buffet. Either of which could be true, but in this instance, is not.

Mind you, the sartorial cleanliness level is set early on. Within a minute of entering the church, Ellis opens his mouth and projectile vomits, catching Mike's scarf and coat and my jacket. My first thought is that perhaps Ellis is allergic to organised religion, but maybe he is just keen to mark us out as still-new parents by making us spend the rest of the day smelling of Eau de Baby Sick.

IT'S ALL IN THE GENES

It is said that a baby is a product of its parental genes with a bit of new stuff thrown in for good measure. Well, I am not sure anyone has ever actually said this, and if they did it certainly isn't someone with any medical training. Oh, it could have been a health visitor, I suppose. But anyway, I think it probably sums up the situation well enough.

So witnessing the traits displayed by Ellis is a bit like a genetic who-dunnit – trying to fathom where that particular bit of behaviour came from. It has to be said, we are dealing with a pretty limited repertoire – his personality is not yet sufficiently developed that his friends will stop and exclaim 'oh, that Ellis, he's a real bon viveur,' or 'bloody hell, the way he runs is just like his mother' (god help him if this turns out to be true).

The fact that he has a propensity to either wake up from his naps brimming with the joys of spring or exuding the cold depths of winter is a good example. On waking, there are a few seconds where we wait with baited breath to see which one it will be. If his legs go in the air and he waves his toes around expectantly for a tickle, then happy days. If his face screws up and his fists clench, then we can expect a good quarter of an hour of Herculean effort on our part, trying to cheer him up and distract him from his uber-grump.

One day, Mike and I are discussing this, and he rolls his eyes.

"Waking up super-grumpy - well, we know where he gets that from, don't we?"

"Errr..." I hesitate, wondering how I can wriggle out of this one. "...your grandmother?" It is a feeble attempt and a pair of eyebrows are raised in my direction to tell me in no uncertain terms that I should be looking a little closer to home for the culprit.

"Well, you gave him his prodigious ability to pass wind," I retort.

"That may be so, but you gave him the ability to find it so bloody funny - all that smiling he does after letting one go."

That's what I like about the parenting experience. It makes one so mature.

THE ECZEMA FACTOR - PART 2
(18 WEEKS OLD)

Here I am, back at the doctor's surgery. I park the car and notice that we are a little early for the appointment due to my calculations that I need to attempt to leave the house with Ellis a good twenty minutes earlier than usual: extracting one adult and a baby from anywhere seems to involve much faffing around, several 'hang on, I've not got the mussie / nappy bag / car keys' type comments and at least five minutes to secure the car seat onto the back seat. I decide to hop in the back with Ellis as he seems quite happy in the car seat and so I join him for a little tickle and a song. It is only when I attempt to get out that I realise with a droplet of panic plopping into my stomach that the back of my car has child proof locks, meaning that children can't open the doors from the inside. Children and mummys, that is. I try the door a few times, as I can't quite believe that I have been such a moron, and any second now, it will spring open. But no. I consider climbing into the front seat, but a quick recce of the space between the front seats versus the width of my arse and that is quickly discounted as an option. There is nothing else to do, I have to expose my idiocy to the world at large and flag down a passer-by. I only have to wait a few minutes until a woman approaches. I knock on the window and make some lunatic mime involving keys and doors and she opens the door for me. I thank her and she does me the courtesy of not laughing out loud. I can just imagine her that evening. "Oh, Frank, you should have seen this bloody idiot in the car park today..."

Here we are again. I am still dreaming of my own seat in the doctor's waiting room, complete with brass plaque. 'Here sits Ellis and his mum (most days)'. I have now lost count of the number of lotions and potions that the medical profession have advised me to try with Ellis' eczema but each and every one of them has been as useful as applying a Mr Bump sticking plaster to a leg fracture. Whereas Ellis was looking somewhat like a burns victim, he now resembles a burns victim who has been thrown back into the blaze for a second go.

I finally get into the GPs room and am ready, all verbal guns blazing, to insist on steroid cream. I have done extensive research (my sister and my brother-in-law) and there is conclusive evidence that what is needed is steroid cream. I am not being fobbed off with rubbish creams that do nothing, paraffin or no paraffin. The GP takes one look at Ellis and tells me that he needs steroid cream right away. I could have kissed him on the nose, but then I see it has a rather off-putting cluster of thick black hairs sprouting out of it, so I just thank him instead. He scribbles out the prescription and empathises with me over the ludicrousness of the E45 advice, so maybe I could have put up with the nose hair, after all.

MILESTONES (OR INCHSTONES)

There is nothing we like doing more than having a look in a variety of those 'your baby in its first year' type books which purport to be a useful encyclopaedia of facts about your child's development, but are really just exploiting a parent's desire to have a normal child. They all have friendly, instructive titles ('From Birth to Birthday'... 'All you need to know about your baby and a lot you don't'...) but they should all be a bit more honest and up front about it and simply be called 'Is your baby a retard?'

There is no baby function too small or insignificant not to warrant being put against a key developmental milestone – anything from the first smile, the ability to follow your finger, babbling... essentially, everything a baby does can be listed and ticked off as you go.

When Ellis is developing on schedule, these key steps are a wonderful way of keeping track of his growth. Smiling a day before the book states it should happen obviously means we have an emotionally astute child on our hands, wise beyond his weeks. But the moment Ellis lags behind, these same milestones are obviously not worth the paper they are printed on.

One book states that a baby should be able to roll over from back to tummy by the time it is four months old. Now I have seen Ellis almost do this the grand total of once, and I fear it was the result of some rather over-exuberant leg waving that tipped him accidentally onto his side. More frantic leg waving, no doubt induced by sheer panic on Ellis' part that he could no longer see the ceiling, meant that he accidentally righted himself. But two weeks on and Ellis shows not the slightest bit of inclination to repeat the manoeuvre. I think that he has come to the conclusion that, having experienced the roll once, there is very little need to expend all that energy by repeating it. And besides, the world looks rather scary side-ways on.

Mind you, I am not overly surprised that he hasn't got the roll onto side or tummy off to a fine art as yet. Everyone tells me the importance of tummy time, which is when you place the baby on its tummy to encourage muscle strength and movement. I have not been what you might call diligent in the observance of tummy time with Ellis. I don't think he enjoys it very much – he assumes a face-down-in-the-padded-mat position whenever he is placed on his tummy and only reluctantly lifts his head for the briefest of moments in order to take in some much-needed oxygen. I place a toy a few inches in front of him to entice him to look up or, if I am really being overly-optimistic, to move toward it, but he resolutely refuses to even acknowledge its existence. So I shake it in front of him, but still his head does not budge a millimetre. He would rather inhale play mat than endorse tummy time with his involvement. There are rare – very rare – occasions when Ellis does attempt to move, mostly involving a short period of furious but futile limb waving, none of which even threaten to make contact with the floor to provide traction. He just looks like a clockwork bath toy out of water, with the accompaniment of much grunting.

And it always seems the wrong time for it. Too close to having just fed him and it all ends up with a large pool of vomit on the play gym mat, whereas too close to a nap, and Ellis is ratty and it all ends in tears. So really, there is a three minute window that is equidistant between food and nap that we can successfully attempt tummy time without sick or tears and oops, look at the time, we've missed it again.

BRAIN CHANGE

Many things seem to have happened to my brain over the last year. It has been through what is referred to as 'mummy brain'. Or 'nappy brain'. Or 'baby brain'. Or a thousand other ways to say you are acting like a buffoon. I say *been though* – this is perhaps not quite accurate. I think I am still going through it. There has been some talk in the medical world about proving that there is or is not such a thing as mummy brain – which seems to encompass everything from putting the milk in the cupboard and the dried up cups in the fridge, to forgetting your own name. Let me clarify this point and stop any more money being wasted on research (and how do they conduct this research, anyway – stick a mum in a room and watch how many times she turns to do something before completely forgetting what is was?). There *is* such a thing as mummy brain and I have it. It's not that my brain has changed, it is more that it is the same brain, but with barely any sleep to nourish it. I am quite used to the things that I do under the effects of mummy brain but it is a little bit more disconcerting for others when I inadvertently refer to Ellis as 'she' or go to leave the house without putting my shoes on.

My thought patterns have changed as well. Apart from those 'fuck I am knackered' thoughts, my first thoughts are always about Ellis. 'Ooh, I need a poo,' is immediately followed by 'when's the best time for Ellis that I can take a poo?'. 'Oh, that's a nice tee shirt,' is swiftly coupled with 'which colour is more Ellis proof?' I look at the time. 'What do I need to do for Ellis next?' It happens so naturally, yet is so strange that he has vacated my womb and immediately taken up permanent residence in my head. And he's not just a tenant – he's the bloody landlord.

But scariest of all is the huge, scratchy, black cloud of thought that inveigles its way into my consciousness when I am off-guard, seeping through my synapses, leaving an icy sting in its wake: a marrow-chilling, crushing sense of mortality. From the moment I saw Ellis, I thought about his seeming fragility and his loose grip on this world (after all, he has not really mastered the art of using his opposable thumbs yet). The myriad of things that could befall him made the three-month-old mark an almost impossible destination. But he arrived, fighting fit.

Yet the thought did not subside. Instead, it spread its tentacles further, and now those terrible thoughts of mortality extend to those others that I hold most precious in my life. Perhaps it is witnessing a new life that makes everyone else seem... well, that much older - and closer to stumbling off the end of this moving walkway that we endearingly refer to as life. Perhaps it is the fragility of that new life that makes me suddenly realise that, as much as I may wear my pants over my trousers (there goes the mummy brain again) I am not invincible – and nor are the people around me. Or maybe it is contemplating the possibilities of the life that Ellis has before him, whilst perhaps almost half of mine is already behind me.

These questions prick my brain and freeze my rationality in its tracks. I can feel the thoughts swelling, the abjectly terrifying scenarios of doom and death flashing unbidden into my head, causing my skin to go cold and my insides to contract in fear. In my mind, I run the gamut of terrifying outcomes for all and sundry, from cot death and car crash to heart attack. But my brain is the master of demise: there is no fatal outcome too outlandish to take up residence in my grey matter. Can a piece of unlined paper cause baby death? Can a short walk to the shops by Mike end in catastrophe? Does my mum pushing a supermarket trolley invite disaster? And faced with these moments, there is only one thing that I can say to myself that helps: "LA LA LA LA LA LA LA LA LA..."

ANOTHER FALSE DAWN (19 WEEKS OLD)

With the eczema just a distant memory save a few dry patches on his face thanks to the miracle of steroid cream, Ellis picks up the sleeping script again and sleeps through for four consecutive nights. Oh the joy. I am starting to look a little less like a panda and am less likely to nod off in my wine, er... I mean blackcurrant juice... of an evening. I am starting to feel – I may just whisper this – normal.

Which is why, of course, Ellis then wakes up at 4am the next night, yelling his head off for no good reason. What would be a good reason? His cot being on fire. Or a Rottweiler has just entered the room. Other than that, there really isn't one. So I settle him back down, only to be woken again at 5am. I repeat the process with less grace and tolerance and a touch more duvet slamming than before and crawl back to bed. One hour later, Ellis is awake and telling us, in no uncertain terms, that 6am is precisely the right time to start the day in earnest. Fuck. I spend the day like a zombie, with my panda eyes back on full form and a dread that tonight will be the same.

That night, Ellis sleeps through until 6am. How my life has changed. Pre-Ellis, to be woken at 6am by someone screaming in my ears would have been unthinkable and it would have taken a week of early nights to recover. Now, it is a total triumph. I still look like shit though.

THE START OF WEANING

Having threatened to wean from week 16 (mainly to annoy the health visitor but also in the search for the secret of Ellis sleeping consistently through the night) I decide that it is now time for Ellis to understand that there are other gastronomic delights available to him other than milk.

I mix up an ambitious quantity of baby rice and start Ellis off with a few ounces of milk. I then proffer up a small spoonful of rice to his lips. Obligingly, he immediately opens his mouth but then an impasse occurs; I am not sure if he should approach the spoon or if I should advance. But it becomes apparent after several stationary seconds that taking food from a spoon is a learned technique that – well, Ellis has not yet learned. So I employ a sort of 'insert spoon and scrape on upper lip' manoeuvre which at least gets most of the rice to remain in his mouth. Ellis takes a few spoonfuls, getting remarkably little of it down his front, in his hair or behind his ear. I think I am letting all those baby adverts of those 'cheeky little scamps' sending their parents into eye-rolling faux-exasperated cloud my perception. Why should he get it everywhere? I am holding the spoon for god's sake – Ellis can't even hold his own breath yet let alone cutlery. Overall, having swallowed the baby rice, Ellis seems highly unimpressed. I take a taste of the rice myself and immediately agree with him. The stuff tastes like wallpaper paste. I'd throw it on the walls if I were him.

MORNINGS ARE BROKEN

Ellis has now decided that 6am is the time he will start his day – every day. He is very much alone in this. As the monitor by our bed kicks into life I check the clock radio in the desperate hope that it is nearly seven 'o'clock. Nope. It is always around six. Worse still is when those luminous digits start with a five. Even 5.59 is depressing. Nothing any good ever comes from waking up when the time starts with a five.

We lay under the duvet, pretending to be asleep, listening to our son chatting, burbling and occasionally yelling.

"Read a bloody book, or knit yourself a boob, will you," I implore the monitor but Ellis just keeps making noise. What is an acceptable amount of time to ignore your offspring in these situations? I am guessing that the answer is not an hour and a half, so at about 6.15 one of us reluctantly hauls ourselves out of bed to retrieve him. When it is my turn, I stumble into his bedroom with my usual 240-volt inspired bed hair and crumpled face, and bless him, he makes a good show of seeming pleased to see me. Back in our bedroom, Ellis gets put between us on our bed and we try and gradually slide into the day with some singing, toe-tickling or pillow-peekaboo. It's a strange old life being a parent.

WEANING: PICKING UP THE PACE (20 WEEKS OLD)

I quickly ditch the wallpaper paste in favour of actual foodstuffs. I start with carrot – I have no idea why, as I don't like them, and Ellis accepts them with a distinct air of indifference. Maybe my wrinkled up nose and barely disguised grimace is putting him off.

So then I graduate onto apple, mixed with a little milk to tone it down. Oh, the sweet, mushy zing of apple. His first mouthful threatens to pop the eyeballs straight out of his head, such is the taste sensation that seems to be occurring on his tongue. Apple is a real hit.

I then get adventurous with a small bowl of sweet potato mash and Ellis polishes it off with gusto. Well, his approach to eating is a little more considered than perhaps that suggests. He seems to chew each mouthful approximately fifty times before swallowing. Chew is perhaps not entirely accurate, as this would suggest the presence of teeth, but he squashes it between his gums for minutes at a time. Six spoons of sweet potato take a good half an hour, but neither of us mind. It is fascinating to watch him master the art of eating, even if it is stone-cold sweet potato.

I am starting to get rather confident about this weaning malarkey. Okay, there has been a couple of minor vomiting instances, but nothing that a cheery 'whoopsie daisy' and a vigorous wipe with a mussie couldn't fix. One day I decide to try Ellis with some potato. I mash it up like my life depends on it, add some milk and then, in the pursuit of lump-free, silky smooth mash I sieve it. Twice. We settle at the table to eat. I offer up a spoonful of the most delicious mashed potato I have made. Ellis takes a small spoonful and holds it in his mouth for a while, with a kind of 'hang on, she's feeding me new stuff again...let me see if I like it...oh, that's okay, at least it doesn't taste like carrot' attitude. He then proceeds to swallow. I am not sure how far along this process he gets, but at some point the potato seems to have plugged his throat with an immovable, starchy tuber-based ball. He starts to cough and his eyes water profusely as I tap him on the back.

"Whoopsie daisy," I exclaim with a smile. (Which, incidentally, is one of the many things I find myself doing as a mother that is inexplicable. Why have I suddenly started saying this, always in an over-enthusiastic manner? I had never uttered those words prior to Ellis arriving, now it's peppering my sentences like I am some kind of 1950's nanny. I hate it and it makes me sound ridiculous. Right: a resolution. I will no longer say it.)

Ellis ignores my attempt to make light of what is turning into a Serious Choking Incident and turns a darker shade of red. I feel a small wave of panic rise up and prickle my neck. I tap his back harder, then a bit harder still. He is still coughing, and still unable to breathe. I quickly stand up with him, holding him over my shoulder, slapping him on the back very hard indeed. I glance over at the phone. Should I be dialling 999? If I can remember how to make my legs work, I will get the phone and do just that.

Then I hear a gasp, and some fast breathing. The potato blockage has gone and calm returns to proceedings shortly after.

"Whoopsie daisy!" I repeat again to Ellis, who is sitting on my lap looking rather alarmed and a tad bewildered.

We both look at the bowl of mashed potato in front of us for a few seconds. I push it away.

"Fancy some apple, poppet?"

NOW YOU TELL ME

I am regaling a friend with my potato-choking incident over a coffee. She recounts a similar story involving another foodstuff and her daughter turning blue. For every story you have as a parent, another parent will have a similar, if not even more alarming story to counter it with. The reassuring thing about this is that you quickly learn that there are very few things as a parent that other parents before you have not had to deal with, so it makes you feel that incidents like near-death choking don't necessarily mean you are a terrible parent. On the down side, it makes it bloody hard to wow a group of friends with amazing parental frontline reports and tales of derring-do. Every fucker has been there, done that, called the ambulance, got the vomit-spattered tee shirt.

As we round up the choking-themed chat, she says: "Well, if it happens again, it is best not to hold them on your shoulder to try and dislodge the blockage. You should lie them on your knee across-ways..." she mimes the position on her lap, "... and tap their backs there."

I look at her somewhat agog. How did I not know this? Why is this not taught as a matter of course to every pregnant mother? Forget parading a knitted boob around in front of us or getting us to ponder which of our myriad of fascinating hobbies may have to take a back seat once we have a baby – we should have been taught this on day one. I can't be the only buffoon who has almost choked their offspring whilst weaning.

So, I have now learnt two salutary lessons from this episode.

Don't put them on your shoulder; put them across your knee if they are choking.

Don't ever, ever, give Ellis any potato again. Ever.

I AM A PUREE MACHINE

It seems that all I do is peel, chop, steam, puree, pot up, label and freeze these days. Rather than try and prepare food for Ellis on the go (one attempt at peeling a butternut squash whilst holding a baby, and a half-try at switching on the food processor without making Ellis cry was enough to convince me to abort) I undertake my first puree marathon one evening.

There is the three-tier steamer on the go, with another make-shift steamer next to it. A conveyor belt of raw fruit and vegetables go from chopping board into steamer, then out into bowls to cool. I am rapidly running out of work surface. Bowls of apple balance somewhat precariously on top of the radio, a plate of steaming sweet potato is nudged begrudgingly onto the window-sill. Then it all gets pureed in the processor and put back into bowls. I lay out a sea of tiny little freezable pots. Who knew Tupperware came in such ridiculously small sizes? When all this baby food is just a distant memory, I will be able to save the sum total of three baked beans in the fridge safe in the knowledge that they are in an airtight container. Teaspoons of puree are plopped into each pot, some being a heady cocktail of more than one foodstuff. Apples and pears. Sweet potato with a dash of butternut squash. Butternut squash with a blob of apple. Mango and nectarine. Let's go crazy: mango, apple and pear. And let's not forget the prunes. Prunes go with everything - carrot and prune being a particular favourite - and they have the added bonus of keeping Ellis regular, so everyone wins with prunes. On go the lids, and then to the onerous task of labelling. I find tiny round labels to fit on my tiny pots and hunch over the surface, scribbling tiny words onto a string of thirty labels. It is at this point, when I am utterly sick of the sight of fruit and vegetables, my back aches and I have a mountain of washing-up piled up in the sink that I seriously wonder why I am not feeding Ellis out of a bloody jar, which involves a quick trip to the supermarket and about three hours less hard labour. I have no answer to this. There is some vague notion of the nutritional value of making everything from fresh produce, but all I keep thinking is: open jar, stick spoon in, feed baby: done.

I complete the labels and stick them on the pots but the admin is not done yet, oh no. A woman who laminates her birth plan is not the sort of woman who throws thirty pots of puree into the freezer without some kind of stock-take system in place. So I write a list of all the pots I have just made and stick it on the wall next to the fridge. At a glance I can then see what I have in stock to feed Ellis at any given time, tick off the ones I have used, and know when I am running low on any given puree. It just seems a sensible thing to do (mind you, I have been suffering sleep deprivation for four months, so perhaps my idea of what constitutes sensible is a little askew).

Finally, I wash up before collapsing in a chair. I been doing this since Ellis went to sleep and I am knackered. I look at the clock. Oh, time for bed then.

A BLOODY GOOD LIST (21 WEEKS OLD)

The NCT girls are gathered at my house for our weekly tea and cake chat-fest. We talk about weaning in fascinating detail ('ooh, I never thought of adding apricot', 'isn't it a nightmare mashing bananas that aren't quite ripe?' and 'I have a carroty poo stain on my trousers that just won't bloody shift'). Still, our get-togethers are an amazing source of information, empathy and relief. I pick up tips on how to do stuff differently, lots of sympathy when I am at the end of my baby tether (otherwise known as the umbilical cord) and feel better when I know I am not the only mother who is stumbling around the darkened room called 'parenthood', stubbing toes, bumping into things, trying to find the light switch and, on the odd occasion, willing to trade my soul for an exit. When Mike and I have a question about Ellis, our first reaction is: "Ask the girls." No one actually has the definitive answers but that is not the point. Most of our responses start with, "I have no idea, but what I do is..."

We are gathered in the kitchen as the kettle is boiling. One of the girls spots my freezer menu on the wall and asks me what it is. I take her through the stock-take system. There is silence in the kitchen for a few seconds, before all that can be heard is laughter. I didn't realise that my freezer list held so much comic potential.

"Well, how else can I know whether I have any apple, carrot and prune puree left?" I ask, but no one responds, seemingly all too busy trying not to let a bit of wee escape due to prolonged and enthusiastic laughter. Now there's a thing: pelvic floor exercises. Everyone tells you that you should do them regularly in pregnancy and when you have a small child. No one does. I think if they said that you bring a whole new meaning to the phrase 'wetting your knickers with laughter' if you don't do them, they might have better success with the uptake.

The hilarity finally subsides. "Actually," one of the girls says, "It's a rather good idea."

You see, there's nothing like a bloody good list to flush out the obsessive compulsives amongst us.

OH CHRIST, NOT THE BLOODY HOSPITAL AGAIN

Like some recurring nightmare, I am back at the GPs yet again. I console myself with the fact that I am at least getting good value from my taxes these days. In fact, all I need is to start using the bus, have a fire extinguished by the fire service and get an abandoned vehicle removed, and I would consider myself to be getting jolly good value indeed.

I have been prompted to attend the doctors after experiencing heart palpitations last night. We were sitting on the sofa and I felt my heart skip a beat, then do a little two-step to catch up with itself before returning to normal. I thought it may be the shock of actually sitting down and relaxing, but it happened a few times.

'Ooh, that doesn't feel good,' I thought, and mentioned it to Mike.

His immediate response was that I should get to the doctors the next day. I hate it when I hear irrefutably sensible advice like that – there is just no room for disagreement. I would much prefer something along the lines of 'why don't you stand on your head, see if that helps'. Patently ridiculous and something to really get your teeth into.

So, here I am, waiting for an 'emergency' appointment. I use the term advisedly. I hope I am not an actually medical emergency, as Ellis and I have been waiting for almost an hour. There is only so much jiggling of the toys I have brought that Ellis will tolerate before filling the waiting room with screeching decibels.

Finally, I get to see a doctor. I explain the issue and she checks my blood pressure. Just the sight of that poo-brown cuff makes my heart go like the clappers and by the time it has squeezed the life out of my arm, I am not at all surprised that the reading is high.

"Right, I want to refer you to the consultant at the hospital, you will need to go to A&E as soon as possible."

Oh bloody bollocking bollocks.

"Oh," she adds nonchalantly, "you can't drive."

For a moment I'm not sure if she had seen me reverse the car into the tight parking space in the surgery car park. Well, 'reverse' makes it sound like the manoeuvre was completed in one attempt, which wasn't strictly the case.

Then I realise she means that she is not going to allow me to drive.

"Err...I am going to have to," I reply, nodding at Ellis in the car seat.

"Can't you walk?" she replies.

Oh yes, what a spectacular idea. I shall walk the mile home with Ellis slung into the crook of my arm like he's a wicker fucking picnic basket, pick up some essentials then walk the seven miles to the hospital. In fact, why don't I skip the whole way? She has obviously never lifted a car seat. Just looking at mine gives me a hernia.

"No," I reply bluntly.

I think she sees the look in my eyes and decides that she probably doesn't care enough whether I faint at the wheel or have a heart attack en route to pick this particular battle.

So I head home armed with a referral letter and an ever-deepening sense of dread. I decide to wait for Mike to return before facing A&E – the thought of doing it single-handedly with Ellis is enough to bring on a relapse, even though I don't know what I am relapsing into – and after many calls to track him down, Mike comes home.

We head to the hospital – another exciting family outing to commit to memory - and take a seat in the waiting room. It soon becomes very apparent that I am not getting out any time soon, let alone being seen, so I bid a nervous and resigned farewell to Mike and Ellis and they return home to start the bath and bed routine.

I am finally taken through to A&E and put in a cubicle, which seems to be tucked away from absolutely everyone else. Even the lights have not been switched on above me, giving the whole place a slightly overcast feel. How very apt, I think grimly. I am hooked up with a spaghetti of wires to an ECG machine and left to bleep to my heart's content. Or my heart's malcontent, perhaps. Just as I am beginning to wonder if I have been forgotten, a woman turns up who gives herself a title that I instantly forget, but it seems she is the consultant's monkey. Monkey-girl produces a stack of paper from behind her clipboard. Oh goodie, a form. She starts to ask me questions – I am slightly disappointed that it is not multiple choice – and it soon becomes clear that this is the longest questionnaire in the history of the NHS. Just as I start to lose the will to live, she leaves, to be replaced by a nurse, who takes a blood sample. I think I should have a tap installed in the crook of my arm, it would save everyone a lot of time and effort.

And so I wait. And wait. And wait a bit more. Thank god for the games on my mobile, or I think I would start to rock silently and scribble messages of hate over the cubicle wall in my own blood.

Just as I am about to crack my high score on Word Mole, a consultant turns up. We are over an hour and a half into my visit and I am keen to know what is wrong with me. I am hoping for the diagnosis to be indigestion, but a little voice in my head keeps running through alternative options including two weeks to live, an incurable disease or something that necessitates having all my limbs amputated. I don't know who it is, this voice, but I am guessing it is no medical expert.

The consultant checks all the readings from the machines I am hooked up to, looks at his notes, makes me hold my hands out to see if they are shaking (perhaps he thinks I am drunk. I know I wish I was) and says nothing. Then he leaves.

I am starting to get a little peeved by the lack of communication and as time slides by my own diagnosis gets graver and graver. With the emphasis on the grave.

Two hours ago, I was alone in this bank of cubicles, but as we tip into early evening it is filling up nicely. I gather my next door neighbour is an old lady as I hear her wavering voice and shuffling feet and her elderly status is confirmed as a middle-aged couple walk past my cubicle and greet her as 'mum'. They leave her shortly and come and stand outside my cubicle, for reasons not clear. Maybe the old dear has just farted. I would really love to shut my curtain, but the staff here were obviously all born in a barn and leave it open every time they leave.

The woman is mightily pissed off about being here, judging by the thunderous look on her face. They converse in terse whispers spat over the distance they are standing apart. I strain to hear what they are saying, just to relieve the boredom of counting ceiling tiles, but can't quite make it out. The woman then steps into my cubicle and goes over to the basin, preening her hair in the mirror. Well, don't bloody mind me, love, I am just waiting to hear whether my heart is going to the knackers yard or not. She continues to faff with her hair.

"You fucking vain bitch," snarls her husband.

Blimey, I know doing your hair when your mother-in-law is lying in bed three feet away suffering from an unspecified ailment is probably not what the Gentleman's Guide to Hospital Etiquette recommends, but his reaction is perhaps a tad strong. Though I agree with him on the vain bit. She is trespassing in MY cubicle, after all.

"Piss off, wanker," she retorts and smoothes her hair down again, tipping her head forward slightly to what I can only assume she thinks is the most flattering angle to view herself from. I would say from the roof might be better, but each to their own.

I feel a bit more chipper all of a sudden as I realise that I have my very own sweary soap opera unfolding before my eyes.

"You piss off," comes the startlingly original reply. Damn, surely they can't be running out of profanities already? I thought this was going to be entertaining.

"No, you piss off."

"No, you piss off."

Oh god, someone shoot these people please.

A nurse appears by my bed. "As you have been in hospital within the last six months, I need to take a few swabs."

Oh good, I was getting bored. Having the longest cotton bud stuck up my nose and down my pants (using different ends for each insertion, I hasten to add) is just what I need to pass the time. If I am found to have a super-bug, does that mean I get a room to myself? Or perhaps hosed down by a man in a full-body suit and gas mask?

I hear a nurse go into the old woman's cubicle and tell her that she has to have a catheter inserted so should try to relax. It's a bit like telling someone that they are about to be poked in the eye with a shitty stick, but should try to keep their eye open and not blink. Almost immediately, a tremulous wailing starts from the old lady.

"Noooooo..." she moans repeatedly. "Stop iiiiit..."

"Just relax please," reiterates the nurse, sounding very much like she is gritting her teeth. Maybe it's the exertion of the insertion.

The howling continues and despite the platitudes of the nurse that it will soon be over and if she only relaxed a little it wouldn't hurt so much, it seems little progress is being made.

There is a brief hiatus in proceedings. "Okay, I will just use a little more lubricant," says the nurse. I am hoping she has come with a party pack of Vaseline, because by the sounds of it, she'll be there some time. This woman obviously has a vagina like a Venus Catheter Trap.

Then the son pipes up. "Come on mum, you can do it." I am sure she is thrilled that her son is witness to a nurse trying to shove a tube up her dry and shrivelled private parts. Well, it's something to tell the grandchildren.

Some time later, after many texts to Mike to pass the time and to get some crucial updates on bath time and which stories were read at bedtime, another consultant arrives. He is very upbeat and relaxed about my fate, so at least someone in the cubicle is. He reviews my notes, looks at the bleeping machines and nods.

"Well, it's nothing to worry about."

I exhale loudly, not realising that I had been holding my breath. Relief floods over me and I smile.

"It seems you have –" and then he uses a medical term that seems to be lacking in vowels and overcompensating with six too many syllables "- which basically means that sometimes your heart gives out an irregular rhythm. It is very common."

Thank god for that. I'm all for a touch of the common when it comes to my afflictions.

"Can I go home then?" I plead.

"Just waiting for the blood results to come back, then yes, you can go."

I could have got up and done a jig, I am that happy, but I am somewhat held back by the monitors still attached to me.

I lie back once the consultant has gone, texting Mike the good news and relishing the thought of my imminent exit. But an hour trudges by and no one comes to release me. Eventually a nurse arrives.

"What's the hold up?" I ask.

She tells me they are still awaiting the test results and on further pressing, reveals they are checking that I don't have a thyroid problem. "Oh, that sounds nasty," I say, but she reassures me that it just means taking some tablets to stabilise it and further monitoring. Five minutes later, the initial consultant arrives back and starts to ask me further questions and check all my readings again.

Hang on a blinking minute, I was on the verge of going home less than an hour ago, now he seems to be starting the examination process all over again.

"Just want to be sure," he says, somewhat dismissively. What he fails to clarify is: sure about what? Sure that I can go home? Sure that I have been misdiagnosed? Sure that he didn't leave his pen in here? Sure that I need a heart transplant? He leaves and I try not to cry as I text Mike a warning not to pour the tea just yet.

Another nurse arrives and informs me that I have to be moved as I have used up my allotted four hours in A&E. Well pardon me, I would have taken out a week's rent if I had known I would still be here at nine 'o' fucking clock in the evening. She unhooks me from the monitors and I stand up.

"Sorry, we have to wheel you to the ward on the trolley," she says, gesturing to the bed.

"No, I'm fine thanks, I'll walk."

"No, you are not allowed, I have to push you." Holy shit. I cannot believe I am not allowed to walk. I suddenly feel twice as ill as I did two minutes ago and five times as pissed off. I am wheeled to what they call a 'halfway' ward, which as far as I can tell, is so named due to it being halfway between hell and a living nightmare. The elderly man opposite me seems to be coming round from an operation and is moaning, making repeated grabbing motions in the thin air in front of his face with his gnarled hands. Two women in the beds next to him seem to be playing some kind of medical Top Trumps.

"Oh, I had the most terrible varicose veins. Ended up with ulcers. Oozing, they were, oozing."

"Ooh, I know. I got an infection..." she mouths something in an exaggerated fashion and nods knowingly. The other woman winces in sympathy. "Deary me, you should have smelt it," she laughs abruptly, tutting and shaking her head. I am suddenly glad that I haven't eaten since lunchtime.

Luckily, I am diverted from this fascinating insight into stinking infections by a nurse who comes to hook me back up to a monitor.

"My hands are so sore," she says, apropos absolutely nothing. I am not sure how to respond to this. Maybe she is the nurse who was trying to catheterise the old lady and the procedure has taken its toll.

"All this hand washing, plays havoc with my skin."

Right. She is complaining about having to keep washing her hands. Firstly, washing hands seems a fairly fundamental part of germ control and moaning about it seems a little churlish. Secondly, I am the patient and she is the nurse. Ergo, I moan, she listens, not the other way round, surely? Thirdly, if I was her, it wouldn't be what my hands look like that would be causing me the most angst. And fourthly, shut up will you, I just want to get the fuck out of here please.

I lie back in despair. A&E seemed so temporary – whilst there, it always seemed a viable possibility that I could go at any moment. But here, in this shithole of a ward, I feel my chances of escape dribbling away by the second. I miss Ellis. I think it is the most time I have ever spent away from him, and it is strange and not pleasant. I miss having Mike here. Before Ellis, any situation like this would be handled in tandem, with Mike providing his superlative support by saying just the right thing, doing just the right thing, and having just the right confectionary embezzled in to cheer me up. But now I am here, facing – well, I am not quite sure any more – whatever problem I have, alone. It's not the most fun I have had whilst reclined on a bed.

Then the Monkey-Girl turns up again to explain that the blood test is back and I have an over-active thyroid, which is causing the palpitations. Blimey, I am not sure any part of me has ever been described as 'over active', but I am sure this is not a good thing. I had my thyroid tested prior to being pregnant, and it was fine. But now it's not. That pregnancy has a lot to answer for.

"So we need to start you on some medication."

"Right," I sigh.

"But we haven't got any, so I will give you a prescription to get tomorrow." I am partly annoyed that they have run out of tablets, but simultaneously heartened – if I can wait until tomorrow to start, I think there is no danger I am going to keel over in the next twenty-four hours.

"We are going to keep you in overnight," she says, smiling.

I, however, am not smiling. Not in the least.

"No, I can't stay," I blurt out in a panic. The thought of spending the night here, in the hospital where not long ago I was incarcerated for a week, in this ward full of deranged post-operative OAPs, is enough to make my heart give out all over again.

"Why not?" she asks, a little startled by my vociferous response.

"Because..." Oh bollocks. Why can't I? I am not sure 'because I hate it' or 'it smells of wee and the bed is hard' will be reason enough. Quick, think. She looks at me expectantly. Buggar, buggar. Oh, wait. I have it.

"Because I am breastfeeding."

It is the golden key that unlocks the door. No medical professional operating in the NHS today could possibly stand between a mother's breast and her baby: it is sacrosanct. It is the irrefutable law that breastfeeding comes before everything, because no one would have it on their conscience that their decision to keep me in would mean that my child would be fed (make sign of the cross repeatedly) formula milk. It is written in the stars. And the nursing handbook. It is also a whopping great big milky lie, but she doesn't know that. I have just played my Get Out of Jail Free card and by the look on her face I know I am shortly to be skipping out of this shithole.

"Right, I will get you discharged." Bingo.

POOLOGY

Weaning brings a whole new dimension to Ellis' poos. For a start, they are more solid, which I see can only be a good thing as it lessens the chances that I will be spending the evenings scraping liquid poo off the inside of his dungarees. A weaning nappy reveals a fascinating strata effect of poo – different colours and densities depending on what Ellis has eaten and when. It could almost be a science – a sort of geological approach could time the poos. Not carbon dating, more like carrot dating. Poology, if you will.

Given that the consistency of the poo these days is a little more dense, Ellis is more vocal about passing them. Each poo is delivered with a remarkably throaty 'grrrr' and slightly flushed cheeks, often at the dinner table. I suppose there is a logic to this – faced with a bowl of sweet potato, he has to get rid of the stewed apple first – a sort of a 'one in, one out' policy. By four 'o'clock one afternoon, I am amazed as Ellis has his fourth poo of the day. Surely, that must be it, I think, as I put another nappy on him. But no. There is one more lurking in there. And henceforth we refer to our son as Ellis Five Poos.

AITCHOO (22 WEEKS OLD)

Ellis has caught a cold. Nothing serious, just a cold. A loud sneeze precedes the appearance of a pale green, glistening slug of mucus that slowly creeps towards Ellis' mouth. Bloody hell, baby mucus has to be the stickiest substance known to man. What is in this stuff? If a tissue is not to hand, I swiftly remove the slug with a mussie, folding the cloth over as I go. Ten minutes later I can hardly prise the fabric apart – the mucus has set hard and formed an impermeable bond. Forget superglue, three teaspoons of this gunk and you could stick a man wearing a boiler suit, his wife and his dog to the ceiling.

It is the silent sneezes that are the worst – I have no idea that Ellis has sneezed, as he reclines in his chair and I busy myself with a household chore. I look over at him at some point, and he has his mouth open, an oscillating length of snot bridging the gap between his top and bottom lip. He knows there is something there, he knows it is not altogether pleasant but has no idea what to do next. It is a race against the seconds to reach him with a tissue before the mucus flops into his mouth to provide a tasty afternoon treat.

I discarded the 'over the shoulder' mussie weeks ago as Ellis was not really dribbling milky vomit onto me any more, and after a rather unfortunate incident where I absentmindedly put my jacket on over the aforementioned mussie, only to reveal it again when I arrived at the local cafe, I ditched it. However, the mussie is now firmly reinstalled as there is nothing Ellis likes to do more than save up all his snot until I am giving him a carry, then wipe it all over my shoulder with some deft left-to-right head manoeuvres. It is not a pleasant feeling to take your top off at the end of the day and have a large, rigid, slightly crusty patch of bogies scrape against your face.

I RECOGNISE THOSE, DON'T I?

I am drying myself after my morning shower, singing to Ellis who is sitting in his chair on the bed. This particular morning, he stares fixedly at my boobs. His gaze is intense and unwavering and he has a strange look on his face. It's almost a look that says 'ahhh... they used to be mine.... those were the days.' Swiftly followed by, 'are they supposed to be that close to your knees, mummy?'

THE SEARCH FOR THE INNER BITCH

It is common knowledge that pregnancy does funny things to your head. I have been tired, emotional, elated, scared, fascinated, scared a bit more, excited and over wrought. Which is fine, apart from the fact that, most days, I have often not yet finished my Shreddies before experiencing the whole gamut of these emotions. I have become much more prone to tears, some of them justified (and usually prompted by either a medical predicament or a medical practitioner) but often just because I feel like it.

I had assumed that I would be back to my old self once I had actually given birth and the hormones had got back into the old routine. Just add that to the ever-growing list entitled 'Things I was totally fucking wrong about'. (Right next to the list entitled 'Things I was totally sure about and now am not'.) Now Ellis is here I am a blubbing machine. And I hate it. Pretty much anything can set me off, from a sad article in the newspaper to some crappy TV drama. Even if I am not reduced to tears, I have reactions to things now that I never had before. I hear a news report on the radio about the death of a small child. Before I was pregnant, I would have carried on wiping the dishes and humming without a care in the world. Now I react in exactly the same way as my mum reacts on hearing such things: with a wince, a heart-felt 'oh,' and a pained expression as the cold enormity of the scenario momentarily freezes your insides. Where has all this fucking empathy come from? I find it a little nauseating and more than a tad irritating. And more to the point, where has my inner bitch gone? I thought she was taking a sabbatical whilst Prawn was in residence, but it seems she has found a nicer place to stay and has little intention of returning. Maybe I can entice her back with the promise of some fresh kitten hearts.

TAKE COVER (23 WEEKS OLD)

I fall ill with some kind of tummy bug and am laid out for a day. I can barely lift Ellis and the smell of his fruit puree has me staggering to the toilet. Mike steps in to the child care breach and I sweat it out under a duvet. I get a day off from baby duties only to spend most of it staring into the white depths of a toilet bowl. Bloody typical.

Twenty-four hours later, however, and I am back on duty feeling almost fine and can look a bowl of puree in the eye without wanting to vomit. Ellis turns his nose up at his dinner, but as I had sneaked in some stealth corn (having previously refused corn served solo, I am trying to introduce the flavour without him noticing. I have no idea why) I assume he has sniffed it out and is playing hardball. So I crack open an emergency pouch of puree, which seems to please Ellis no end. 'No more of your homemade crap, mummy... mmm, some processed stuff instead, top notch'. He finishes it off but refuses pudding. Which should have set alarm bells ringing, but I am happy that he has at least eaten something and pass him over to Mike whilst I clear up.

Suddenly, I hear a shout from Mike. Not one known for raising his voice, I swiftly turn to see what has happened. I look just in time to see Ellis' mouth closing and an extraordinary amount of sick dripping off Mike. A shiny layer of vomit slides down his jumper, rivulets run lumpily down the creases in his jeans, a myriad of sick particles spatter his arms and face. Ellis has the good manners to at least look shocked, but not as shocked as Mike. Initially, I am taken aback by the sheer volume of vomit on display. It is said that, at this age, a baby's stomach is about the size of their fist. Well they are bloody wrong – there is no way on earth that this amount of sick would fit into something the size a large eggcup. A medium-sized bucket, maybe. Either that or Ellis has two extra stomachs that he keeps in his thighs as some kind of gastric back-up for vomiting emergencies. My shock soon dissipates into barely controllable mirth, which I divert from becoming howls of laughter by focusing on getting Mike cleaned up. I have half a mind to ask him to step into the garden so that I can just hose him down, but instead opt for a combination of sick-scraping with a spatula and puke-wiping, to at least stop him dripping on the floor. I wipe a couple of small drops of sick from Ellis' leg, the extent of his collateral damage, and let Mike contort his way out of his clothes without wiping further sick up his nostrils or into his hair. It seems I may have passed my bug to Ellis. Whoops.

With fresh clothes and a full washing machine, normality is restored to the household and Mike plays with Ellis on the jungle play mat. Despite having recently re-enacted a modern interpretation of the famous scene from the Exorcist, Ellis is looking remarkably chipper, with lots of smiles and giggles. Mind you, he is probably recalling daddy's face at the moment of sick-tsunami impact. And then suddenly, a small fountain of brown sick shoots from his mouth, ricochets off monkey's bottom and splatters onto the mat beside him. So perhaps lying Ellis down after the first vomiting episode was probably not the wisest move. Let's chalk it up (and wipe it down) to being novice parents.

Ellis is fine within himself despite being sick again. It is curious how happy he seems, regardless of the intermittent emptying of his stomach. He is no more perturbed than if he had simply burped. We, however, are a little more circumspect now. Every time he burps, Mike and I scramble for cover, but no repeat performance is forthcoming. We get to bath time and beyond with not even a hint of having to change our clothes, which leaves a knotty dilemma: to milk or not to milk?

"D'you think we should give him some milk before bed?"

"God knows."

"It might make him sick again though."

"But it might not."

"No, good point."

"He hasn't been sick for a few hours."

"True...but he hasn't eaten anything either."

"I don't want him to be hungry in the night though, bless him."

"No."

"Maybe just give him a little bit, to try."

"Yeah, we could do. A half bottle."

"Mmm, might be worth it."

"...."

"So. What do you reckon?"

"I have no idea."

"No. Me neither."

Like all conversations involving Ellis-shaped decisions, it meanders around, gets lost, loses the will to live and ends up back where it started. Eventually, one of us gets bored with such flagrant indecision and decides to get Ellis some milk. He takes it enthusiastically, which I take as a sign that we have, finally, made the right choice in the whole milk / no milk debate.

I sit with Ellis on my lap after he has finished, winding him diligently - I don't want an errant burp to cause any unnecessary throwing up. Finally, I lay him gently in his cot and stroke his hair. He gazes up, contentedly, then lets out a tiny burp. I watch as his mouth fills up with sick and a dribble of white vomit starts to leak from the side of his mouth. Quickly, I pick him up and hold him to me, at which point I realise that the mouthful of sick was simply the warm-up act, and he projectile vomits every single drop of milk he has imbibed (plus another gallon or so he was storing in his thighs) directly at me. I look down. There is actually a deep triangular puddle of sick in my cleavage, lapping at the shore of my breasts, held in place by the manmade dam that is my bra. As I have long-since discarded my under-wired bras, I wear the quite unattractive feeding bras, which create a cavernous space between my breasts. It is this that has filled with vomit and it is quite vile. The meniscus of the sick is actually about to break over the top of the bra so I try to lean back to avoid dripping on the carpet. Both Ellis and I are staring at this vomit-breast pool. I have never seen anything quite like it and am not sure I am that fussed about seeing it ever again. I gingerly shout for Mike to come and help and to his credit, he does manage not to collapse in fits of hilarity but takes Ellis so that I can shuffle slowly toward the bathroom, slightly inclined backward like a really crap limbo dancer. Over the bath, I lean forward to empty my bra of sick. This was never in the fucking parenting guides.

TEETHING

Oh, this is terrible. One moment Ellis is his usual, happy, smiling self and the next his cheeks go bright red and hot enough to fry an egg on (well, at least warm up a bowl of butternut squash and prune) and he becomes a screaming banshee.

Now is the time for the Strawberry Saviour, that elixir of pain relief: Calpol. However, there is still at least half an hour before the strawberry loveliness takes effect, during which time Ellis is pretty much inconsolable. I dance, I sing, I put on silly voices for Mr Bunny, I do aeroplanes, I tap dance, I clap loudly, I do monkey impressions. Each activity distracts Ellis from his pain for about three seconds, before he ignores me and returns to his wailing. I am absolutely exhausted by the time the Calpol starts to take effect. I lever Ellis' mouth open with my little finger and peer in. Surely, after all that screaming, I should be able to see at least the tip of a tooth appearing. Not a thing.

I dig out a teething toy that I have, ripping it out of its packaging and giving it a cursory waggle in a mug of boiled water in a pathetic attempt to sterilise it. I give it to Ellis. He takes it in his hand, but has no idea what to do next. I try and offer it up to his mouth but he is not interested. Everything else he has ever touched, he has tried to cram into his gob, from socks to table corners, but the one thing I want him to chew on stays resolutely at arm's length.

We check the baby books that evening. Apparently, teething pain can occur around two months before the tooth actually puts in an appearance. Two months of this? Bloody hell. Do they do Calpol for adults?

SANITY TIME

Another NCT meeting. I don't think I have missed one yet, as they are little lifelines thrown into the sea of chaos and uncertainty that is motherhood. God, how our conversations must seem utterly inane to any eavesdroppers, but to me they are a source of comfort, information and hilarity. Sometimes when I have been on my own all day with Ellis, and he is having what I shall euphemistically describe as an 'off day' (i.e. he has been Beezlebub incarnate with attitude) it is difficult to keep on seeing the funny side when he vomits down my top (again) and won't let go of the spoon which is replete with sweet potato mush. But amongst the other seven mums, there is little that hasn't been seen, heard, dealt with or worried about and recounting the horror of my day makes it seem a lot funnier than I perhaps gave it credit for.

The talk turns to colic and to our collective diagnosis that all of our babies had severe colic, causing them to cry too much. We all pause, pondering this for a second, then laugh. Colic my arse. We had young babies. Who cry too much. In reality, we would have been lucky to muster one case of colic between us.

THE DUFFLE COAT OF RESPONSIBILITY

Having a child brings with it (and I hereby accept my award for Stating the Sodding Obvious) responsibility the likes of which I have never experienced. In the first days of having Ellis, this duffle coat of responsibility hung large and heavy from my shoulders, weighing me down and making me feel more than a little swamped. But as we approach that magical six-month mark, I feel the coat has become a lot more comfortable and is a much better fit. I move with ease around Ellis, not hindered by the weight of it any longer. As if I have almost grown into it. On occasions, some bastard flips the hood up, leaving me disorientated and in the dark, but on the whole, I am kind of liking my duffle coat. I may even get some elbow patches.

MUSIC TIME (24 WEEKS OLD)

A friend and I decide to take our babies to 'music time'. It has some ridiculous name – Bo Jangles, Mini Music, or some such rubbish. 'How a fool and her maternity leave pay are soon parted (let your middle class guilt about your child's development make you behave like a twat)' would have been more accurate, though. They would, however, struggle to fit that on the poster.

Eight mums with their offspring sit on the floor in the local community centre. I am already depressed, just by being in the room. Who the fuck decorates these places?

"So, what I have decided to do for the room is what I call 'taupe community chic'. The floor is a delightful linoleum tile in mushroom, with a subtle fleck of burnt umber..."

"Errr... isn't that beige?"

"No sweetie, it's mushroom. Anyway, to really set off the floor I have chosen a breathtaking fawn paint... but wait, that's not all... to appeal to the kids, I have pre-scuffed the walls with trainer marks. Totally cool."

"Are you actually a designer..?"

"Ahem. As I was saying. To really complement the walls we have this amazing, gritty, urban-yet-suburban detailing here."

"It's an empty picture hook."

"Sweetie, sweetie. It might look like an empty brass picture hook, but it is a witty post-ironic statement."

"The painter left it in the wall, didn't he?"

"To create the right ambience, I have painted shut all the windows and glued the radiator thermostats to ten, an inspired move that simply makes this room hot, hot, hot, sweetie. And to finish the scheme, I have gone for these one hundred percent nylon, totally flammable curtains with a pink and green floral pattern. The natural print theme brings the outside in, but the heavy lining blocks out most the light. Am I not a genius? And you'll notice that the curtains stop two inches above the bottom of the window for a really bang-up-to-date take on window coverings."

"You really are a fucking idiot, aren't you?"

So we settle down on the floor in a circle, corralled by an overly-cheery woman with a hideous tee shirt sporting the character that accompanies their brand. It is a pig-ugly doll with bright orange hair, an expression that says both 'too happy for my own good' and 'I may come alive in the dead of night and stab you through the heart with a rusty knife' and a pair of spotty dungarees that need to be burned as a matter of urgency. With the doll still in them.

We soon launch into the first song, carrying the babies in our arms as we march in a circle, round and round the lino, mumbling about the wheels on the bus. The leader produces a three dimensional version of the orange-haired doll which is even more horrendous in the polyester flesh and shows us what we should be doing with our children in terms of movement and action. It's alright for her, her bloody doll has no endoskeleton. Trying to get Ellis to wave his arms and touch his head is like having a fight with a bag of sodding tent poles.

On one circuit of the room, as I gingerly swing Ellis around whilst trying not to provoke him into regurgitating his mashed banana breakfast, I notice that the baby boy in front of me has his hair gelled up in some kind of spiky, David –Beckhamesque fashion circa 2002. I think I might regurgitate my breakfast on sight of this. Gelling babies hair? No. Just don't do it. It is pointless, vain and fucking ridiculous. And makes both baby and mother look like morons.

Never mind, I sigh, as we turn round and march back the other way, Ellis is probably enjoying it. I look at him and see a gooey trail of banana sick down his front. Oh good.

Finally, we get to sit back down and the woman hands out some instruments. Now this is what I have been waiting for. I can sing to Ellis any time I like, but I thought he would really enjoy discovering how to make musical sounds. He grasps a set of jingling bells and immediately puts them in his mouth. Not a jingle to be heard, just the faint rasping of tongue against metal. We then get a wooden clapper, which goes straight in the mouth too. I try not to think about all the other babies' mouths that have slobbered over it before Ellis and try to prise it way from his gums to show him what sounds it makes. Ellis has suddenly developed a vice-like jaw grip and I give in. This is not quite what I had envisaged for my son's first music lessons. A maraca comes our way and I have high hopes for it. Ellis takes it in his fist and repeatedly thwacks himself over the head with it. It certainly makes a sound, but wood on skull is not exactly what I thought I would be hearing.

To end the session, we lay the babies together on the floor for some 'interaction time'. The interactions consist of fists accidentally flailing into others' mouths, legs kicking torsos and wobbly heads bashing together as they lay or crawl on the floor. My friend's daughter, much more mobile than Ellis, rolls herself on top of him and stays there. I have a sneaking suspicion that this is Ellis' favourite part of the whole thing.

"And now it's bubble time."

Oh great. At the sight of those little orbs of evil, Ellis immediately starts to cry and I whisk him out of danger before more half-digested banana joins the happy throng.

Christ, I've got another five weeks of this bloody music torture.

ONEUPMUMSHIP

There is nothing quite so competitive as parenthood; it is an inevitable part of bringing up a child. In its most benign form, the competition is just about wanting reassurance that your child is roughly on a par developmentally with its peers. But let's not kid ourselves, mostly it is just oneupmumship.

I promise myself I will not be sucked into it. One of the NCT girls mentions that her baby has started to crawl, the first of the group. All the other mothers look at their offspring with barely concealed disappointment. I consider laying a trail of milky crumbs across the lounge floor to encourage Ellis to get a shift on but I fear he may take after his mother on the athleticism front.

I talk to friends about how Ellis is doing. "He's eating quite a range of mush now, he seems to quite enjoy his food." "Oh yes, well when my little one was his age he just couldn't get enough quinoa with blueberries. They're both super foods, you know." Really? How fucking super for you.

In a cafe I meet a friend with a little girl almost the same age as Ellis. I wedge Ellis on my lap to feed him. "My little button is sitting in a high chair now," she announces and plops the aforementioned pink bundle into a wooden high chair. The baby slowly slides forward and simultaneously slouches backwards, meaning mummy has to hook the baby's arms over the front bar to try and keep some semblance of balance. Oh yes, she's really got that one mastered, your genius daughter. I consider offering the services of a stapler to help proceedings, but think better of it.

The trouble is, talking to other mums means oneupmumship is inevitable. I chat with them, and mention as a relevant point that Ellis made a noise that accidentally sounded hilariously like a proper word. Oh god, I cringe, it sounds like I am boasting. Then someone else chips in with the fact that their little girl said 'mama' that morning. At six months old? Someone needs a hearing test. I breathe a sigh of relief: I have been oneupmummed and now do not look like the biggest knob in the room. Just the second biggest.

I share tales of Ellis' sleep patterns – or lack of them - dreaming of that utopian dream of 'sleeping through the night'. Does it actually exist? Will it ever happen? Or is it just a rumour put about by the medical profession to stop you throwing your baby out of the window in despair? "Oh," says a mum I meet, "when my little boy was Ellis' age, he was sleeping through." I don't know whether to punch her in the face for being such a show off, or cry.

"Really?" I ask, slightly incredulous. "Yes. Well, I had to get up four or five times a night to put his dummy back in as he was crying for it, and he woke up at about 5am every morning, but other than that he slept right through." Now this is taking oneupmumship to a whole new level. If I realised that barefaced lying was allowed, I could have trumped everyone I met. "Walking, you say? Well, it was funny this morning. Ellis back-flipped out of his cot and nearly landed on my toe! Oh, we did laugh."

OH, SO THAT'S HOW IT IS

As Ellis' food solids – well, mush actually, but technically I think they are referred to as solids – grow in size, we consult the child care books to find out what we should be doing with the milk. Do we carry on with it? Do we decrease the amount? Change the times we give it to him? Add some strawberry Nesquik and really give him a gastronomic feast? We decide the aim is to drop the lunchtime feed. Right, decision made. But hang on. This only throws up another barrage of questions. A gradual phase out or send him cold turkey? Do it now, or wait a while? Mike and I discuss it at length, pondering the options, weighing up the pros and cons, calculating the possible revised milk intake. There are a significant number of 'ummms...', 'errrrrs...' and 'not sures' that pepper our pontifications and by the time we have lost interest in the whole thing, we have come to precisely no answers at all. Eventually, we make some half-arsed declaration in the face of total ignorance that we will drop his lunchtime milk in a week. Or so. Possibly.

The next lunchtime, Ellis tucks into a bowl of mashed veg, followed by some fruit and yoghurt, before we sit down with his bottle of milk as usual. He takes the teat but after a few minutes it becomes very apparent to me that he is not drinking. I persevere for a while, pulling the teat out, nuzzling it back into his mouth, but Ellis gets irritated by this and his little lips clamp firmly shut against the teat-shaped mouth invader. He has decided: time to give up the lunchtime milk.

And at this moment, I have a slightly startling thought. This whole lunchtime milk scenario, innocuous as it may be, is exactly what being a parent seems to be about. You have the illusion of being in control, you go through all the decision making with earnestness and application, trying to source opinions and information to help, chewing metaphorical fingernails (I don't actually chew my nails, just in case there is a little bit of Ellis' poo hiding in there) with the angst of making the right decision. It feels very du jour, this approach. I can't imagine my parents' generation, or even less so their parents' generation, having such knotty dilemmas clog up their synapses and keep them awake at night. Crikey, it is not uncommon to hear tales of babies being left in their prams at the bottom of the garden when they insisted on crying in 'those days'. Can I imagine us, or any of our peers, doing that now?

"That's it, I have had enough. Arabella will not stop crying. I have put her at the bottom of the garden."

"Really?"

"Yes. She has to learn, and I have things to do."

"So you left her in the garden?"

"Yes. Well, in the shed. With the heater on. And I have set up the monitor, I'm playing her some Bach, there is a multi-sensory toy in her pram and I have rigged up the BabyCam, so I am watching her every twitch on my iPad."

I started this journey as a woman without a clue, then quickly evolved into a womb with a view. And now I am a mummy with a view. And perhaps half a clue. But as Ellis reaches the ripe old age of six months, I wouldn't go so far as to say I am in control. I have a sneaking suspicion that there is only one person around here who is truly in control. And it's not fucking me.

POST SCRIPT

Ellis is now four. The intervening time has been the proverbial roller coaster. Sometimes piss-your-pants funny, sometimes piss-your-pants terrifying. In fact, I have seemingly spent a large proportion of the time with a damp gusset, which just goes to prove: pelvic floor exercises – just sodding do some.

There have certainly been some fist-clenching moments, mainly around protracted negotiations regarding the use or otherwise of a hand as a suitable implement for eating Rice Krispies and the refusal to say 'please' unprompted, despite being more than liberal with spontaneous usage of 'more cheese', 'garden' and 'television'. And there have been a few white knuckle moments, particularly a head-first dive off a sea defence wall into the icy depths below (narrowly averted by SuperHero Dad catching Ellis by the ankle, for which he will forever be able to wear his pants outside his trousers without fear of ridicule from me).

Plus, we now have a baby. As if writing this book was not a salutary enough lesson that kids fuck up your life, we have gone and done it again. So for another nine months, I became once more a womb with a view. But that is another story.

And to really beat this analogy to within an inch of its sorry little life, when the roller coaster of parenthood is on its nine hundred and thirteenth circuit of the track, executing the same loop-the-loops over and over, I can't tell if I am grinning or grimacing or crying or laughing. But then the ride will take a new and unexpected turn and I forget all about trying to decide, as I am too busy clinging on for dear life in this unfamiliar, fantastic and crazy territory.

So would I get off this ride, even on the promise of getting my money back and a complimentary stick of candyfloss? Of course I wouldn't. Not even if they threw in a goldfish in a plastic bag as well. Although it might be nice to stop temporarily after the next circuit and get off for a little while. Just for a bloody good lie down.